GOING BACK TO T-TOWN

KARLOS K. HILL

General Editor

GOING BACK TO T-TOWN

THE ERNIE FIELDS TERRITORY BIG BAND

CARMEN FIELDS

UNIVERSITY OF OKLAHOMA PRESS : NORMAN

This book is published with the generous assistance of the Wallace C. Thompson Endowment Fund, University of Oklahoma Foundation.

LIBRARY OF CONGRESS CATALOGING-IN-PUBLICATION DATA

Names: Fields, Carmen, author.

Title: Going back to T-town : the Ernie Fields territory big band / Carmen Fields.

Description: [First.] | Norman : University of Oklahoma Press, 2023. | Series: Greenwood Cultural Center series in African diaspora history and culture; 2 | Includes bibliographical references and index. | Summary: "The life and career of Black jazz musician and big band leader Ernie Fields of Tulsa as told by and to his journalist daughter, who drew on interviews and tapes he made of himself recalling his band's days on the road touring Oklahoma, the American South, and elsewhere in the United States"—Provided by publisher.

Identifiers: LCCN 2022036513 | ISBN 978-0-8061-9184-3 (hardcover)

Subjects: LCSH: Fields, Ernie. | Ernie Fields Orchestra. | Band directors—Oklahoma—Tulsa—Biography. | Jazz musicians—Oklahoma—Tulsa—Biography. | Big bands—Oklahoma—Tulsa. | African American band directors—Oklahoma—Tulsa—Biography. | African American jazz musicians—Oklahoma—Tulsa—Biography. | Big band music—Oklahoma—Tulsa—History and criticism.

Classification: LCC ML422.F535 F54 2023 | DDC 781.65092 [B]—dc23/eng/20220809

LC record available at https://lccn.loc.gov/2022036513

Going Back to T-Town: The Ernie Fields Territory Big Band is Volume 2 in the Greenwood Cultural Center Series in African Diaspora History and Culture.

The paper in this book meets the guidelines for permanence and durability of the Committee on Production Guidelines for Book Longevity of the Council on Library Resources, Inc. ∞

*This book is dedicated to the memory of my father,
the late Ernie Fields, and my brother, Ernie Fields Jr., who followed
in Dad's career footsteps and became a legend in his own right.
This book is also dedicated to journeyman musicians and vocalists,
famous and unknown, who walk to the beat of their own drummer.*

Didn't We?

This time we almost made the pieces fit
Didn't we?
This time we almost made some sense of it
Didn't we?
This time I had the answer, right here in my hand
Then I touched it and it had turned to sand. . . .
This time we almost made our poem rhyme
This time we almost made that long hard climb
Didn't we almost make it?
Didn't we almost make it?
Didn't we almost make it this time?

—Songwriter: Jimmy L. Webb
Didn't We? lyrics © Sony / ATV Music Publishing LLC
Jama Music ASCAP

CONTENTS

ACKNOWLEDGMENTS

I set out to secure my father's place in music history, however small it may be. This labor of love would not have been possible without the cooperation of my father, Ernie Fields, who was always a great storyteller. We started talking about a book sometime in the mid-1980s and began labeling photos, tape recording his memories, making notes—many of which I was still finding as I was writing the last pages. They were invaluable. I have tried to keep Daddy's voice, retelling the stories as he told them to me and many others. I was encouraged by too many people to mention, but a few were particularly consistent: Boston historian Robert Hayden; longtime friends Alonzo Batson Jr., Rita Duncan, Rose Parkman, and Dr. Sandra Rouce; former coworker journalist Christopher Lydon; advocate Larry O'Dell of the Oklahoma Historical Society; my favorite biographer, Wil Haygood; and music enthusiast Dan Kochakian. Kochakian turned out to be a sleuth extraordinaire, finding all manner of info about Dad and members of his organization and passing it along to me. And, of course, my beloved husband, Lorenz Finison, PhD, whose contributions are extraordinary. He helped me nail down factoids, dates, newspaper stories about long-lost Ernie Fields alums, promoters, venues, and the like. He was my chief researcher, willingly diving down many an informational rabbit hole. I could not have made it without him.

My big brother, Ernie Fields Jr., provided an important link, given my obvious gap in experience and memories of the band, as he is fourteen years my senior and worked closely with Dad as he established his own music career. The two were very close, and much of Jr.'s business conduct is informed by the imprint of our father—namely, kindness and integrity.

The music industry is very different today from when Ernie Fields began his career adventure in the 1920s. The chitlin circuit has morphed into large performance arenas with big screens, strobe lights, and breakneck-paced choreography; recording studios have turned into garage band setups, with synthesizers and other high-tech machinery often overtaking the artistry of individual instruments. What appears to remain is the camaraderie and friendship among musicians. They are indeed a very special breed.

PROLOGUE

It's both an unlikely and a universal Horatio Alger story. We often hear tales of success from the backstreets of our nation's large and small towns alike. The subjects are sometimes fatherless or motherless kids who come from either the wrong or the right side of the tracks. They may be adults who forgo the family business or ignore older and likely wiser kin full of advice, based on their limited learned lessons, to pursue what seems, at least to some, an improbable way to make a living, never mind making a name for oneself and gaining success.

This is such a story. And Ernie Fields loved to tell the stories.

As a child, I heard them over and over in my dad's booming baritone voice, coupled with his hearty laughter. He'd tell them when his musician friends found their way back to Tulsa and to our home on North Peoria. They'd talk for hours, calling the roll, updating each other on the accomplishments and tragedies of their colleagues. Sometimes they would gather around the piano in our living room with their instruments and jam. They'd recall the where and when of each number and who had made a memorable arrangement of a tune. And then they'd laugh (and drink) some more.

The times they recalled were "the best of times, the worst of times," to use Charles Dickens's wording. It was the time from 1927 or so—less than a decade after the infamous Tulsa Race Massacre—to and through the turbulent 1960s. It was the time of our nation's Jim Crow or legalized apartheid—a time of rigid, unyielding segregation. It was dangerous just being Black, a time when smiling too much or not enough might make the difference in life or death. Traveling could be particularly dangerous. One never knew

1

when some unspoken custom or rule of law might be infringed upon—usually innocently, unknowingly. It was a time when getting food, using the restroom, finding overnight accommodations, and being paid fairly or paid at all was not always certain.

Ernie's was one of the numerous midwestern "territory bands" that sprang up during the 1920s and 1930s and generally performed in a specific geographic area, Kansas City being the hub. Among them were bands belonging to Jay McShann, Walter Page, Bennie Moten, and Clarence Love. That era also ushered in a transformation of jazz style that had been established and imprinted by New Orleans musicians. The changes would be in the instrumentation—the guitar would replace the banjo, the string bass would overtake the tuba, the size of groups would expand from combos to big bands, and blues was added to the "easygoing and swinging Kansas City style . . . which, while pleasing dancers, also encouraged virtuoso soloing."[1]

The stories Ernie Fields told of those days were without rancor or bitterness—only, from time to time, an occasional touch of annoyance at the inconveniences. Mostly he remembered a magical music time when jazz and swing were in their infancy, on their way to becoming America's unique gift to the world. He bridged the uncertain days between when jazz ruled and the new kid that became known as rock 'n' roll would emerge and soon take its place in music history.

Ernie would weave together vignettes of a lad from one of the almost unknown all-Black townships that dot the South and Southwest. Taft, Oklahoma, located in what was known once simply as Indian Territory long after the 1907 statehood, was his first remembrance of "home." He described himself as a "poor widow's boy" who was a trained electrician, graduating at twenty-one from Booker T. Washington's revered Tuskegee Institute, the bastion of trade schools. He would go far.

In the late 1920s, Ernie first started "gigging" in and around Tulsa, shortly after graduating in 1924 from the Mechanical Industries department of Tuskegee Institute in Applied Electricity. That extended until the mid-1960s, when at last came the national televised appearances and a gold record, signifying one million record sales. His sense of place extended beyond his Oklahoma base and encompassed places all over the United States—East, West, Midwest, and South—and even the Dakotas, Wyoming, and parts of Canada.

Sometime in the 1980s I began to record conversations with my father, prodding him for more details of the who, when, and where of his stories. I was also able to teach him how to record memories himself as they occurred at times when I was not with him in Tulsa. Interviewing members of his organization became urgent for me in the ensuing years. I hunted down saxophonist Hal "Cornbread" Singer at his home in Nanterre, France; featured vocalist Melvin Moore in New York City; trumpet player Jeff Carrington in Detroit; and tenor sax giant Teddy Edwards in Los Angeles, among others.

Unless noted otherwise, all quotations are from three self-recorded tapes by my father of his recollections about his "sidemen," his thoughts about race relations, and his investment strategies. I also drew quotations from several notes and letters he wrote over the years. Most quotes are from transcripts of long interviews at the Rutgers University Institute of Jazz Studies and the Indiana State University Center for Afro-American Studies—which were invaluable in my attempts to preserve Ernie Fields's voice.

Blessedly, I was able to persuade Dad to list names of those pictured in the mountain of photographs in his possession—many of which now reside at the Smithsonian's National Museum of African American History and Culture and anchor the new Oklahoma Museum of Popular Culture (OKPOP) in Tulsa.

While there are scattered mentions of Ernie Fields in some publications about the swing/jazz era, this memoir is the first and most definitive story of his contributions and accomplishments. How far did he go? Perhaps not quite as far as other trailblazers outside of music, like scientist George Washington Carver or athlete Jackie Robinson, or even his contemporaries in music, like Bessie Smith, Duke Ellington, Ella Fitzgerald, or Count Basie.

He went far enough, Fields would muse in his later years. Far enough.

What follows are selected stories he shared about Ernie Fields and his world-famous orchestra.

ERNIE FIELDS and his ORCHESTRA

EXCLUSIVE MANAGEMENT
FREDERICK BROTHERS AGENCY, INC.
New York   Hollywood   Chicago

Ernie Fields, 1940s. Author collection.

❦ 1 ❧

THE DISCOVERY,
A FIVE-DOLLAR TIP, AND
A CHANCE AT THE BIG TIME

John Hammond was *the* name back then. He had discovered Count Basie, who went on to great fame as a band leader, and he carried Harlan Leonard, a band out of Kansas City, to New York City. As he traveled across the country scouting, mostly in the Midwest and Southwest, Hammond first heard Basie on the radio. He went and found him. He found the guitarist Charlie Christian in a small honky-tonk outside Oklahoma City. He also brought the bands of his brother-in-law Benny Goodman, Basie, soprano saxophonist Sidney Bechet, and others to Carnegie Hall in 1938 for the legendary From Spirituals to Swing concert.

Much later, Hammond would have a hand in the discovery of Bruce Springsteen and Janis Joplin. But back in the 1930s he was the Man, the talent scout par excellence, the one for whom the title "jazz impresario" was made. He was always on the prowl for talent. In the late '30s, Hammond was still scouting, looking for someone he could maybe turn national, Ernie would recall often, and so Hammond's travels brought him back to Kansas City.

"He looked and hadn't run into anything and asked some questions," Ernie remembered.

Somebody asked him if he'd ever heard of Ernie Fields's band. The impresario got to talking around, and as Ernie tells it, of course Charlie "Yardbird" Parker, the saxophonist and composer, and all the guys in jazz knew about the Ernie Fields Band because "I had outstanding men, Luther West and all.

5

They hung out together and all," Ernie said. "They told him that Ernie Fields is in Tulsa, Oklahoma." So Hammond went to Tulsa.

Hammond went to the Club Lido, located at Eleventh Street and Elgin (now the site of a Home Depot box store). Back then, it was an art deco building, converted from a farm market built in 1929 to a dance hall that hosted many popular big bands of the day. Hammond started a conversation with one of the waiters, asking if he knew Ernie Fields. The Black waiter told him, "Yes."

Hammond asked, "How could I get a hold of him?" The waiter told him Fields had a telephone. So, Hammond asked if he'd mind calling Ernie, and the waiter made the call.[1]

"I wasn't in," Ernie recalled. "I was out on a gig that night. I remember that week and I was in a little hick town around."

The waiter came back and told Hammond that Ernie wasn't in, and "that I was playing that night. So Hammond told him again, go call and give him my room number, I'm in the Mayo Hotel and tell him to call me when he gets up tomorrow morning." The waiter called again and gave Ernie's wife, Bernice, the number at the hotel "and told her to tell me to call him." She agreed. The name John Hammond didn't mean any more to her than it meant to the Club Lido waiter. Hammond thanked the waiter and gave him a five-dollar bill. The waiter told him he didn't have change, but Hammond told the waiter, "That's yours." The waiter went back to the telephone a third time to call Bernice and said, "Mrs. Fields. I hate to keep bothering you. I don't know who that is, but you tell Ernie to be sure and contact that man. It must be something awfully important. He apparently is somebody big. He just gave me a five-dollar tip for a nickel telephone call!"

The next morning, "When I noticed the note, I asked my wife, 'What is this?'" Ernie said.

She explained, and Ernie recalled, "I don't know if I slept any more that morning; John Hammond wanted to talk to me." Of course, Ernie knew who John Hammond was. "So, about ten o'clock I called him."

"You up already?" Hammond asked. "I thought you worked last night."

"I'm up," Ernie said. "You said you wanted to talk to me."

Hammond had thought Fields would be getting some rest and would call around noon or one o'clock. "I've heard some nice reports on you up in

Kansas City," he explained, and said he wanted to catch the group. Could that be arranged?

Ernie said, "Sure."

"I called the boys and everything and they hadn't gotten up. I was glad I started early. . . . So, I told them and they were all enthused and we went to the Crystal Palace." By night a popular dance hall in Tulsa, the Crystal Palace was used for rehearsals in the daytime. (Ernie's former boss, Walter Tate from the Spotts and Tate Electric Shop, was a Palace co-owner.)

Ernie asked Tate if he could use the venue, and he said, "You know very well you can, and he laughed." The Crystal Palace Ballroom was just off Archer Street near Greenwood Avenue, now known as Black Wall Street because of the proliferation of Black businesses in that day. The ballroom was upstairs, over the Dixie Theatre.[2]

Ernie remembered, "We were all on time, whatever time he said, three or four o'clock, and Hammond came down." It was summertime, and Hammond was in his shirtsleeves. "We set up and played several numbers, and just from the first number you could just see he was all smiles. Then he would say, 'Play me a different type' and we would play that; and he was just all smiles." Hammond called the band terrific and he said, "I'm not a musician, but I do know what's good and what I like."

As a record company executive, Hammond was also responsible for helping desegregate the music industry. He was great-grandson of the self-made tycoon Cornelius Vanderbilt, who made his fortune in shipping and the rapidly growing railroad industry of the nineteenth century. Hammond was described as a "tall skinny white kid" with little physical coordination, who was born with several silver spoons in his mouth. (Another famous relative was Henry Sloan Coffin, noted pastor of the Madison Avenue Presbyterian Church in New York City.)[3]

Hammond talked that day about Willard Alexander, who he said headed the band department of the William Morris Agency. Hammond said, "If he thinks half as much of you as I do, he'll take us to New York on a tour and I'll get him to sign you up."

Hammond wanted to know when Alexander could come and hear the band. Ernie told him, "Well, I'll check my itinerary." He knew right then several things: He didn't want Alexander to come to some little hick town like where he'd played the night before. He tried to think of a town where he might have a decent crowd. In about two weeks, he had a date coming up in Wichita, Kansas. Hammond contacted Alexander and then promised Ernie, "We'll be there."

In April 1939, it was "important news in the band booking business" when the announcement came that Alexander had been signed to head the William Morris Agency's orchestra division. It was a significant step, one published report noted, because it marked "another step in the fight for superiority between [the] William Morris Agency and the Music Corporation of America (MCA) in the band field." Alexander had been band manager for MCA and was credited with the success of many bands, including Benny Goodman's. MCA had a stranglehold with little competition for years, until Alexander's industry-shaking switch.[4] The development made Ernie all the more excited about a possible meeting.

Hammond's pronouncement was followed by silence.

"I don't know if I even heard from" Hammond again before the Wichita date, Ernie recalled. His bandmates wondered if the talent scout was really Hammond. Nobody wondered more than vocalist Melvin Moore. Hammond had been particularly enthused about him.

Moore finally asked Ernie, "Do you think that was Hammond?" He didn't believe it. "John Hammond is a millionaire," Moore noted. Ernie knew that Hammond "practically made Benny Goodman . . . spent that money on him."

"But did you see how he looked?" Moore asked. Moore had observed a hole in Hammond's pants. According to him, "His ass was nearly hanging out." Ernie said he hadn't noticed. Moore insisted that it wasn't John Hammond.

Ernie said, "We all hoped it was."

In his autobiography, Hammond said he was "sufficiently impressed" to wire Willard Alexander to meet him in Wichita to hear the band.[5] Alexander came with Hammond to the gig in Wichita, which Ernie described as "a pretty nice dance. Some of the dances wouldn't be good."[6] Before they saw Hammond, Melvin Moore kept asking, "Where's your buddy John

Hammond?" as he never believed Hammond had scouted them out in the first place. Moore was convinced it was "some honky fooling me, trying to have some fun," a cruel joke played by an impersonator.

In those days, dance halls didn't have tables—people came to dance. It was a ballroom, not a nightclub. No tables, just some chairs along the wall, where folks sat during intermission. On a typical four-hour gig, the single half-hour intermission came after about the third hour. It was then that Ernie saw Hammond walking toward them, with a man he was sure must be Alexander. He was glad it was a decent crowd. He was glad he had started the dance on time. But most of all he was glad that it was really Hammond and really Alexander.

Hammond, according to Ernie, was "just tickled." An older, more subdued Alexander said he really liked what he saw. They were there almost from the beginning and had seated themselves unobtrusively in the back of the hall and listened. Alexander said he wanted to see how Ernie was going to arrange his program. They talked a little more, and then Alexander asked what Ernie thought was an odd question.

"Is there anybody in the band who can't be fired?"

When Ernie asked why the question, Alexander said that a lot of bands were doing all right but could always use improvement. He said he didn't want Ernie to get into a situation where he'd say, "This man stuck with me when I wasn't doing anything and I can't feel that I should let him go."

Ernie asked Alexander if he thought somebody should be changed, and he answered, "No."

Alexander promoted Basie's band. He was disappointed when another drummer, believed to be named Joe Keyes, was not with Count. When Alexander inquired, Count told him the man was a drinker and unreliable on the bandstand. Alexander told a story of Count's decision to keep an average trumpet player rather than good one, because he was reliable and "you could count on what he gave." Alexander added that nobody was indispensable.

Clarence Lee "Dick" Dixon was Ernie's drummer at the time. But he wasn't like "Papa" Joe Jones, the longtime drumming mainstay with Count Basie.[7] Count's drummer, Alexander said, had him spoiled. "Your drummer seems to be a little light, but he fits your music," Alexander said.

Next, Alexander said he didn't understand how a band like this wasn't signed with anybody yet, and said he wanted to sign it. He gave Ernie a contract. When Ernie started to read it over, Alexander told him to take his time. "Read over it by yourself and with your men and if you want to, sign it, keep a copy and send me the other two." He said one would be deposited with the union and the third was for Alexander's file. Ernie broached the subject of getting Negro bands into hotel ballrooms, many of which were segregated. They talked about a possibility in Philadelphia, where Count Basie had been. Then, Alexander said the magic words.

"I'd like to bring you into New York. I think I can do something for you." Alexander said Hammond was over at Columbia Records, and explained, "If he doesn't record you, I'd like to record you on a subsidiary."

In the 1930s, performing in New York City was the coveted goal of nearly every musician. Some might say it still is. Jazz impresario, critic, and record producer John Hammond discovered the talent, and then turned it over to Willard Alexander to arrange performances and recording opportunities—maybe even radio broadcasts. A radio broadcast from a popular ballroom would be the icing on the cake. With the nod from Hammond, Willard Alexander and the William Morris Agency took over. According to his autobiography, Hammond was particularly impressed with "two magnificent players: Hobart Banks, a pianist, and Amos Woodruff, a trumpet."[8]

The decision to actually go to New York City, it turns out, was another, more difficult matter. Ernie would say years later, "If there is ONE thing I still love your mother for is that she encouraged me to go without reservation. She said, 'You had that horn when I met you. You will never have to say that I told you to put it down. I'm wishing you luck.'" She told him to go—and to stay as long as he had to.

It was another story with the band members.

When he talked it over with the guys, all were, in Ernie's words, "tickled to death." All, that is, except his prized piano player, Hobart Banks. Apparently, Alexander said something about them being in New York for five years, and Banks said, "I don't think I can be gone from my old lady for five years."

It was a five-year contract, Ernie explained. "We're not going to be working every day. You can come home or your wife can come to visit you."

They had another few gigs, and when Ernie raised the subject again with Banks he said, "No, Fish"—the band members called Ernie "Kingfish," after the popular character from the radio show *Amos 'n' Andy*—"I'm not going." He talked about his little boy, and said he'd hate to leave the boy and his old lady and all. Ernie tried again to explain that the five-year contract with the booking agency didn't mean he was going to be gone from home for five solid years.

Ernie told him, "Well, I'm going."

Banks said, "I don't blame you." He promised to stay with the group until his replacement was on board.

So Ernie called the union in Kansas City and asked for a recommendation. They suggested Rozelle Claxton, who was originally from Memphis. Ernie wanted someone who could read music and was told Claxton could play anything Ernie wanted and was a nice arranger to boot. He called Claxton, who, of course, asked about the pay. Ernie told him he didn't work for anything below union scale, but to be frank, he didn't know what kind of gigs would be lined up. He told him to ask anybody about his reputation and "you'll get the benefit of the doubt if we get into the money." Claxton said, "just so I'm getting out of this area," he would go.

Ernie told him, "Come right on."

Ernie told Claxton to wait until he had an exact date when they were going to New York, as he wanted to keep Hobart working "because he's been very fair with me." Ernie promised to give Claxton a couple of weeks' notice and "get you in time." Claxton, he said, turned out to be everything that he'd heard. A fine pianist, as well as arranger.

Claxton happened to be friendly with the increasingly popular sax player Charlie Parker and later, in Kansas City, "introduced him to his fellow members of the touring Ernie Fields band." Parker then would bum a place to sleep "on the floor, on a couch, or in a chair," according to Claxton—an arrangement known as "carrying the stick." He would later recall and laugh remembering how people were awed by Parker's playing. "One time," he told biographer Stanley Crouch, Parker asked "one of Ernie Fields's alto men to let him play his horn . . . so the guy [likely Luther West] let him play his horn, and he was shocked because Parker played so much stuff!"[9]

Ernie started watching the trade magazines of the day and saw he was being promoted as a cross between the Duke and the Count—and as Hammond's discovery in Oklahoma! Excitement was building. The guys, Ernie said, were "smiling."[10]

Another matter, however, was the trumpet player Amos Woodruff, whom Ernie "loved as a musician," but who "read very slow." He did not sight-read the music very quickly, learned new pieces slowly, and would make mistakes. Ernie described him as "a terrific soloist" with a beautiful, sweet tone. If you knew anything about Harold "Shorty" Baker (described in some sources as "commandingly lyrical") of the Duke Ellington Orchestra or Louie Armstrong, that's the kind of style that Ernie said Woodruff had. Woodruff was a slow reader, but, Ernie said, nobody could "play it any prettier when Amos learn[ed] it."

On first trumpet was Jeff Carrington out of San Antonio, Texas, formerly with Terrence "Tee" Holder's band. He was with the Ernie Fields Orchestra from about 1937 to 1945. Amos was second or third trumpet after Jeff and Edwin Middleton. The guys started bugging Ernie about taking Amos—with the perspective that he might "embarrass us," Ernie observed. "He could catch on, but he was slow." The man who got Count Basie to New York was now giving Ernie a break, the others argued. "Amos will mess us all up," they said.

So, Ernie started reflecting on Alexander's words: "Is there anybody you can't fire?"

Then Ernie talked to René Hall, who was his principal arranger. Ernie could be critical of René for writing "so many notes that don't mean anything." René said—and it would be the only disagreement the two men ever had in their long friendship—"Keep Amos."

René counseled, "I don't think any of your arrangers arrange as hard as me, but Amos finally gets it, and when he gets it he's got it, you know, and I think you shouldn't worry about that."

The fellows also harbored some jealousy toward Amos. According to Ernie, in an Indiana State University interview, part of it stemmed from Amos being favored for solo work. Also, Ernie observed, many of the guys lived at home with their mothers—just as he had until just a few months before—but Amos lived in a hotel. In spite of being a slow reader, Ernie said,

"If we got those saddened weeks, he might say, 'Loan me five dollars a day or two.'" Before you knew it, he was handing it back.

"Never no trouble," Ernie said.

Amos was always sharp, too, he said, shoes shined and everything. What it was, Ernie suspected, was that Amos's old lady lived on Skid Row downtown. "You couldn't hardly tell her from white," he said. Apparently, she frequented downtown hotels "working." Some of the boys knew what was going on, Ernie said. Ernie "really didn't know what was going on," but he knew the guys were jealous. "They were just jealous as they could be."

Of course, Ernie said, "I had a little ego myself, and figured I better let them know real quick who is boss."[11]

Despite René's advice, Ernie decided to make an offer to someone suggested by Harry Garnett, the tenor sax man out of Chicago, and gave Amos his notice. Years later, he didn't remember the newly hired musician's name. He remembered that Amos took it hard. "He was going around like he lost his mother or something," Ernie recalled.

The band had a date in Tyler, Texas, and when not performing, they spent every waking hour drilling, rehearsing, getting ready for the Big Apple. Meanwhile, Ernie hadn't heard from Alexander recently and decided to give him a call from Tyler.

"When do you think you're going to get us going?" he asked.

He was told that the Apollo Theater opening week was set, but after that Alexander was trying to set up dates in Boston and Philadelphia and other venues on the East Coast. Then Ernie proudly told Alexander he had made a change in the organization, in the trumpet section. Alexander asked which one—as he had a clear picture of the group in his mind. Amos, he told him, was the heavy-set, dark trumpet player who sat in the middle. Alexander was not pleased. "The man almost jumped through the telephone," Ernie recalled.

"Fields," Alexander said, "you let me down, you let me down."

Then Ernie explained about the slow reading, and how hard they were working to improve and tighten every section. Alexander said he and Hammond marveled that a "kid" (Ernie was thirty-four) like him ("I don't mean that you are not twenty-one") had developed a band like that of a forty-year-old man. "Nothing no better hardly." He then asked, "Do you think I flew down to Wichita to see somebody that could read? I think I could have gone down in Harlem or up on Broadway and got musicians that knew more music than all of you put together. But Amos," he continued, "is better than all of them. Haven't you paid attention to the soul that man has when he plays?"

It seems they could get "readers" anywhere—what impressed Alexander was the feel of the group—the gutsy, Southwest flavor. "I'm not trying to run it, but I think you are starting off wrong," Alexander said.

Ernie thanked him and "just like that" called Amos back. He paid his replacement's fare back to Chicago. Amos made the trip and joined the recording sessions, doing all the solo work on the recordings, Ernie boasted, most notably solo work on the modest hit "T-Town Blues."

That was not all. Hammond noticed another change. He missed Hobart Banks. It turned out Hammond had plans for Banks, plans to send him to Benny Goodman's band. At first, Ernie resented the idea. "Are you trying to break up my band?" he asked.

Hammond's reply: "You're going to learn as a band leader you can always use money." Hammond explained it this way. He would buy Banks's services from Ernie—for $5,000. He wanted Banks to take Teddy Wilson's place. Hammond explained that Claxton was fine, but if Ernie had sold Banks, he would have found a new piano man—since Hammond knew folks in the area and Ernie Fields was new.[12] Banks, Ernie said, was as good as Teddy Wilson—and Hammond obviously agreed. Too bad Hobart would not come with them. Ernie wished he was there.

Later, Hammond brought Banks to the Café Society in New York City for two weeks. It didn't work out, partly because he was expected to play *and* sing. That wasn't Banks. He left after one week, but Hammond paid him for two weeks and sent him back home to Tulsa.

Meanwhile, Claxton was building a bit of a reputation for himself. In the January 1939 *DownBeat* reader's poll, he was ranked among the leading pianists and arrangers. Yes, he was ranked near the bottom rung—but all the same, the mention bolstered his reputation.[13]

On August 1 and 2 of 1939, the group went into the studio of Vocalion Records, arranged by Hammond. They recorded nine numbers, including the tune Ernie had penned, "T-Town Blues."

Label for "T-Town Blues," Vocalion Records. Author collection.

I'm going back to T-Town, to get my women in line
I'm going back to T-Town, got to get my women in line,
One, two, three,
Four, five, six, seven, eight, nine.

The Vocalion label, established in 1916 by a piano company along with a retail line of phonographs, first introduced single-sided, then double-sided disc recordings in 1920. During the 1920s the label began a "race series," records recorded by and marketed to African Americans. Around 1935, Vocalion's popularity was growing as it signed Billie Holiday, Mildred Bailey, and Hezekiah Leroy Gordon "Stuff" Smith, among others, not to mention Fletcher Henderson and Earl "Fatha" Hines.

For the Ernie Fields recordings, Melvin Moore did the vocals, with trumpet solo by Amos Woodruff. Slow-reading Woodruff was "always clean, and smiling," Moore recalled.

A few weeks after the session, Moore said, he was walking from the Woodside Hotel (located then on Seventh Avenue at 142nd Street in Harlem), where the band resided, to another hotel when he heard strains of his own voice singing "I'm going back to T-Town."

Someone was playing "T-Town Blues" and the sound was drifting out into the street. He didn't know where it came from.

"Oh, God, I'm a star here!" he said to himself, and years later he burst out laughing at the memory. "That was beautiful."[14]

Fields and Moore became lifelong friends. Moore joined Dizzy Gillespie's Big Band when he left the Fields organization. Ernie would muse in later years that Moore's loyalty perhaps stymied the singer's career. That he stayed too long.

Music scholar Gunther Schuller would make note of Ernie's 1939-era band in which Moore provided vocals—describing the recording session in his book *The Swing Era*. "In terms of its medium-tempo relaxed swing and, in general, a wonderful sense of rhythmic well-being, the band was hard to match, let alone beat," he wrote.[15]

Others on the trip and recording were the trumpet player Jeff Carrington and the Middleton brothers, identical twins—Edwin on trumpet and Edward on trombone. They "kept to themselves," Moore observed of the twins. They didn't play cards or gamble, like some of the band members did. They saved their money. They were really very money conscious. "Sent that money home to their wives" said Moore with a laugh. "They would take their money and go straight to the post office."[16]

Besides the recording breakthrough, Hammond opened Ernie's eyes to publishing his music—getting credit (and subsequent royalties) for his writing.

Another Vocalion recording session, on September 15, 1939, featured vocals by Moore ("Bless Your Heart" and "Just Let Me Alone"), the instrumental "High Jivin'," and "Blues at Midnight" featuring vocalist Leora Davis. This session had slightly different personnel, namely Vernon "Geechie" Smith on trumpet, Hunter Gray on alto sax, and Roy Douglas on tenor. Even with the recording successes, the time in the Big Apple was not all fun and easy sledding.

For example, before he went to New York City, Ernie bought "two sets of practically brand-new uniforms," for the seventeen-piece orchestra. He said he himself had four or five suits. They were going down to the Apollo Theater a day or two before their performance to have the uniforms and Ernie's suits pressed and installed in the dressing rooms. The valet and bus driver

Thomas Hamilton Zackery (whose sister, Laura Ann, was married to drummer Clarence Dixon) and an assistant got out of the bus. The bus was pulled into the alley by the theater while the rest of the band was getting settled at the Woodside Hotel, and the men went into the Apollo. In what Ernie said was no more than five minutes, they came back to find "the bus was cleaned out." Blessedly, no instruments were missing. However, to their horror, cases containing the band's uniforms were gone. Ernie's suits were gone too.

Describing the incident later, Ernie said, "That was really a blow."

Willard Alexander came to the rescue, putting to work on the emergency a tailor who provided uniforms for other big bands. By the time of the opening about a day and a half later, all the musicians in the band had one suit— and Ernie had two. The shows were successful. Ernie's former music teacher Eva Jessye, by now a famed choir director, saw one. "She was saying how nice it was, but why wasn't I singing something?" She had always encouraged him to sing, but he rarely did until later years.[17]

After triumphant appearances at the Apollo Theater and several ballrooms in and around New York City and upstate, things began to slow. It was, after all, the height of the Great Depression. They also faced growing competition from other orchestras. "We were catching as catch can and playing a date now and then," Ernie said. Alexander was encouraging, but some of the guys began to get antsy.

Ernie was a little antsy too.

This is the group that talent scout John Hammond and agent Willard Alexander heard, photographed circa 1940. In 1939 all of those pictured went to New York City, with two exceptions, trombonist Russell Moore, who joined them in New York, and pianist Hobart Banks. *Front row, from left*, Melvin Moore, Ernie Fields; *middle row, from left*, Hobart Banks, Buck Douglas, Hunter Gray, Luther "Spurgeon" West, Harry Garnett, René Hall, Russell "Big Chief" Moore, Edward Middleton; *back row, from left*, Robert Lewis, Jeff Carrington, Amos Woodruff, Dick Dixon, Edwin Middleton. Author collection.

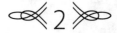

TO GO OR TO STAY?

He knew what his wife said about staying, but still, Ernie began to wonder, "Is this all there is?" The trombone player, Russell "Big Chief" Moore, a Pima "who weighed 350 pounds or more," had joined the band after the recording sessions and wanted to get out of New York City, get back out West. But times were proving to be tough—even as the worldwide Great Depression was drawing to a close. This period, roughly 1929 to 1941, would be one of the most influential times for American jazz. Jazz—the new music, with its syncopation and improvisation—would change America's musical land-scape and that of the music world forever. Of course, Ernie had no crystal ball and no sense that he might be on the cutting edge of something histori-cally important. He knew none of this, only that he wanted, needed to work and keep the orchestra working.

Ernie sought the counsel of his friend Count Basie.

Basie and Fields bonded early in their careers, when Basie often per-formed in Tulsa and Oklahoma City. Basie was exactly a week older than Ernie, and in those early days the two men often compared notes on sidemen, music venues, and the like. After a few months in New York, Ernie told Basie, "They don't have any work for me, so I think I'll head back to Oklahoma." Basie told him Alexander thought a lot of the band. "I wouldn't go back if I were you," Basie counseled. "Alexander is going to look out for you."

Basie told the following story. "Do you see that luggage with 'Count Basie' on it down in the basement [of the Woodside Hotel] where you all rehearse?" Ernie said yeah. Basie said, "I had to leave them there six months, a year ago," to settle a debt to Alexander. Basie was behind financially then,

Men listening to "Thursday Evening Blues," featuring vocalist Melvin Moore, are (*from left*) Max Silverman ("Maxie Waxie"), Herb Abramson, Melvin Moore (*seated*), Ernie Fields, Stan Kenton, Art Ford, and Ahmet Ertegun. Author collection.

but he stayed and "Willard knew that he was responsible for me. If you go back to Oklahoma, he's not going to be responsible." Ernie pointed out that he already owed Alexander about four hundred dollars for the uniforms. Count said, "Has he asked you for it?" Ernie said, "No." Basie pointed out that "Alexander knows you're not working." He advised, "You start worrying when he starts worrying; if he's not worrying, don't worry."[1]

Claxton said he would stay if the band stayed in New York. "But if you're going back to Oklahoma, I'm going on and hustle me another job, because I gotta go where the money is," he said.

Eddie South, a bandleader and violinist, had been begging Claxton to join him. He could offer $150 a week and lodging, for doing nothing but playing the white hotels. "I told him no, I'm with Ernie Fields," Claxton said, "but if you're all going back, I'm going to tell him I'll accept it." Claxton promised not to let Ernie down if he got other dates, "but when you head back," he said, "I'm going on with South."

Ernie was already playing some of Claxton's arrangements and had some more in the book. He recorded one number he had arranged, "Just Let Me Alone," with Melvin Moore on vocals. Alexander helped secure engagements in Philadelphia and the surrounding area and Chicago. Claxton went to Philly with the group, but "after that he told us he'd bid us goodbye," Ernie said. Claxton remembers staying through to Chicago, where they played the Savoy Ballroom. He then met South in Milwaukee, he told an interviewer in the Jazz Institute of Chicago Oral Histories.[2]

Ernie says he "thought and thought" about whether to go or stay. Ultimately, the decision was made to head home to Oklahoma. Some of the guys rationalized, "You're going back home with more than you came here with. We're with you. Let's go on back."

Heading back home, Ernie cobbled together a patchwork of dates, reaching out to popular country and western musician Bob Wills. He had helped the orchestra integrate many of his reliable venues that were formerly segregated. One was in the western Oklahoma town of Longdale, a small settlement on the other side of Enid. Ernie said it was "nothing but a room, but in that big barn, those country bums would come from everywhere."[3] When he booked there, he told Hobart Banks to meet him at Longdale, a mere stop in the road. Banks, who had been playing with the jazz violinist "Stuff" Smith, said, "I'll be waiting on you, Fish."

"I don't know how he got there—on the bus or what," Ernie recalled. The boys in the band teased Ernie about the country locale for a long time. Knowing Ernie was a big sportsman, with a weakness for fishing and hunting, René would ask if he had his shotgun along this time—because he should shoot Hobart. He was out on the road like he was hitchhiking, Ernie said. "If I had your shotgun or some birdshot," René surmised, "I'd shoot him—a man who couldn't go to New York City with us and meets us out here ain't got no brain. What kind of brain does that man have?" After that, Hobart Banks was an Ernie Fields piano mainstay, "almost," Ernie said, "to the day he died" in 1957.

Ernie had but one regret. Alexander had all but promised a radio broadcast from Harlem's Savoy Ballroom, to be carried nationally, which could really put Ernie on the map. It seemed to be all systems go from the hotel ballroom, with the broadcast to be carried on the CBS/NBC radio network. But then the noted drummer William Henry "Chick" Webb, the Savoy headliner, died in June 1939. The death hit the jazz world hard. Ella Fitzgerald became the Chick Webb band's leader—a position she held until 1942 when she left to focus on her solo career. The radio broadcast Ernie had been counting on disappeared, because Alexander thought it would be a better opportunity to introduce Ella as the new leader of the headline band. Ernie would get a chance later.

"Later" never came.

Postscript from an April 4, 1971, letter to me.

Hi Sweet: . . . Enjoyed the article on John Hammond. He is the one that considered me one of his discoveries in 1939. If I had not run back to Tulsa because things were not going just as I wished. I expected miracles to happen in three or four months. It didn't so I ran back home to your momma and bro. Couldn't stand to be away from them (smiles). The check is to wish and help you have a happy Easter. Love Dad.

$$\ll\!\!\!\langle 3 \rangle\!\!\!\gg$$

PREQUEL—FIRST APPLE BITE
AND BECOMING A UNION MAN

The 1939 run in New York City and environs was not the first time the Ernie Fields Orchestra traveled east. Ernie had taken his first big trip east with the orchestra (albeit with no bookings in New York City) in 1934 and again in 1935. He was traveling cross-country two years before the now-famous "Green Book" was published. The book was a primitive, Michelin-like forerunner that was touted as "The Negro Traveler's Guide to Jim Crow America." The book, which listed addresses of various establishments hospitable to Black people, began in 1936 as a way of reducing the chance of humiliation—and more importantly, the chance of racial violence. Ernie and his colleagues were on their own on the road, heeding the call of their ambition and whatever melodies swirled in their heads.

On that first big trip east, Ernie was in Albany, New York, when his son, Ernie Orlando Fields, was born on July 29, 1934, at the home of the elder Ernie's mother—530 East Marshall Place in Tulsa. It was a shotgun house just off Tulsa's famed Greenwood Avenue. Dr. Roscoe Bryant Sr. attended the home birth, even though the newly established Black hospital, Moton Memorial, was nearby, on the corner of Greenwood Avenue and Pine Street. The hospital, established in 1932, was named for Robert Russa Moton, president of Tuskegee Institute from 1890 to 1915, who had succeeded Booker T. Washington in that position. Ernie and Bernice would live with "Mother Fields" until they bought their first home in 1939, for five thousand dollars, a two-bedroom brick bungalow at 1852 North Peoria Avenue in Tulsa. Relatives insisted the price was too high. As one put it, "Your grandchildren will be paying for it."

Soon after their son's birth, Bernice sent a short note to her husband. It read:

Dearest Sweetheart

Baby and I are fine. He weighed 8–1/4 lbs is big healthy baby. I sat up some this morning. Have good appetite am not losing any weight. Will be up and about in a few days. Little Ernie is cute. He really reminds me of you.

Mrs. Ernie Fields

While my mother was one of few words in her letters, my father was much different. While on the road, he wrote long missives regularly to his bride (they had married on February 25, 1933), vividly describing his experiences. My mother kept many of the letters, wrapped in a plastic bag at the bottom of a bedroom drawer. One day in the 1980s, she quite unexpectedly shared them with me.

One such letter was postmarked June 29, 1934, sent special delivery (the old-time version of Express Mail.) Special delivery meant that the letter would travel by airmail, not by train, and upon arrival would be brought to the designated address by the postman straight away. The cost then of that special service was eighteen cents; it required one ten-cent special delivery stamp and one eight-cent regular postage stamp. This letter was particularly descriptive.

The return address was 11 Hazelwood Terrace, Pittsfield, Massachusetts, the address of promoter Earl L. Roberts, who helped secure bookings in the region for the fledgling organization. Pianist Leslie Sheffield knew Roberts, as he previously had been east with the Al Trent Orchestra, and made the introduction. Alphonso Trent's group, regarded as one of the first big bands to hail from the Southwest, was, according to Ernie, "the caliber and had the personnel to have been [as] worldwide known as Cab Calloway or Duke Ellington, but seemingly just did not get the breaks and was not at the right place at the right time. Trent was ten or twelve years before there was a Count Basie band."[1]

Sheffield was with Ernie's organization in '33 and '34. He continued through '35, when his arrangements were cited in a November 5, 1935, article about the Fields Orchestra in the *Times-Advocate* of Escondido, California, saying, "Leslie Sheffield, pianist and one of the band's four arrangers, will give you a treat that your feet can't resist." Also on that first big 1934 trip east was drummer Dick Dixon, who joined Ernie in 1931. Dixon would go on to anchor the orchestra for nearly two decades.

Written in longhand, Ernie's letter was four pages.

Burlington, VT
Thursday Morning

My darling Wife,

Well I am back in the wide open country again some what. And the Mt. and Lake air really feels wonderful. And you may notice that we have also added another state to our list, "Burlington, Vt." Will be here two days.

Well about N.Y.C. arrived there mon. morning about 12:30 a.m. Put up at 145 st. and <u>Lenox Ave</u> in the heart of Harlem. Will try and remember that address and maybe you and I may come back there some day.

That night at the Savoy Ballroom met Claude Jones[2] a baby boy who is with Fletcher Henderson's Orchestra. Of course, he has been around the city for about 14 yrs. Also Lester Young who I knew real well in Okla. Formerly with King Oliver's orchestra. Flood trumpet player from Tuskegee playing with Teddy Hill's[3] orchestra. One of the well-known bands in the city. Hadn't heard of them before because they haven't been on any of the chain station hookups. Heard them they are good and on a good job in the city. . . .

. . . Those that I knew before and those that I met all tried to treat me very nice it seems. Just a little nicer than the people usually are in these parts. They maybe speak and that's all. Spent about two hrs at Fletcher Henderson's apt. He was real nice. Got me in line with several people that may be a big help to me. Also met his wife.[4]

If you remember the first letters that you forwarded to me after I left. One was addressed Sonny Boy. You changed it. Well it was from Miss Eva Jessye[5] a former Taft teacher. I had her address so I went by. And I really had a hard time getting away from her. She has a real nice studio. Was glad to talk to her because she can be a great deal of help to me in the game. She entends [*sic*] to make a tour with her choir in those parts this fall. Gave me a picture of herself and autographed it. Will send it home because its large and I know I would bend it all up. Haven't had any pictures made but when they once meet you so many want pictures I should have some cheap ones that I could give away. And in the dance halls so many fans come with cards and their books for you to autograph.

Was thrilled several times driving in the N.Y.C. The only law seems to be watch the lights and every man for himself. Go as fast as you can, turn around in the middle of the street. Just try to keep out of the other fellows way. The only trouble I had was going in the one way streets the wrong direction. They have so many of them.

Got good before I left. Went up town Broadway by myself. Rode the sub-way. What do you think about riding about 8 miles under-ground. And under the city all the while. Well its like that. . . . Went to the Capitol Theatre. Enjoyed the picture two orchestras and the theatre a palace. But I have been trying to figure out was it worth .85 that what it cost to enter.

N.Y. City is really the place. Every thing you ever heard of or think you want or want to see is here. But unless I could get in the right click and get in big, I would much rather be in Okla. When it comes to living. Because if I couldn't live in the big way I wouldn't want to be there. All of those that I know say I am crazy to go back to Okla. They are all talking about Jimmie Lunceford's orchestra. They said he was around New York about a year before he got his big time break. There is also a Tuskegee boy in his band.

Bought me a summer robe in the city (I think its pretty)

Sweetheart if letters seem to come a little slow some time please don't get the blues. I stay busy and then get lazy too so that's why. But I will try and write letters instead of cards. But so often I think of you and can write card real quick.

I got tickle when I read your last letter. Saying that people say I am big and famous. Don't let them go to far tell them they are wrong. It looks mighty little to me. Have to be all these many miles away trying to make a nickle or so. And then on top of that away from you. . . .

Glad you are playing bridge and trying to enjoy your spare time. I guess you have the souvenir that I sent you from Albany to keep your cards in.

You said or asked have I played any more big dances like the one I spoke of yes. On the 4th of July played to about 2000 and two police men had to work during the dance to keep the people away from the pit. And I couldn't hardly play that night for autographing.

Well will sign off until next time.

Love to all.

I wrote Clarence a card also Lydia[6]

Your Ernest

Cards and letters to his wife during that time, addressed to Mrs. E. L. Fields, bore postmarks from many New England towns, large and small.

June 18, 1934, Bridgeport, CT

My darling Bernice,

Getting ready to go to work. Spent a real pleasant day. Went sightseeing this a.m. Went to the beach that is out front. "Long Island." Was on Atlantic last night on our way there. The ballroom where I play tonight is on waterfront is a real beautiful resort. Cab is playing about seven miles from here at one of the beaches. Went to show. Saw "Sisters Under the Skin" and "Murder at the Vanities." Extra Good. [Ernie drew an arrow pointing to the word "Murder."]

During that time, Oklahoma native Roy Milton, who had started with Ernie's organization at its earliest, in the late '20s and early '30s, was with the orchestra as drummer and vocalist. Later, in the early '40s, Milton settled in Los Angeles, organized his combo, His Solid Senders, and became a nightclub and recording star. With Camille Howard on piano, his recording "R. M. Blues" rose to No. 2 on the *Billboard* R&B chart in 1945 and No. 20 on the pop chart. Later, he traveled throughout Europe. But he always remembered that he got his start in Tulsa.

⊶◇⊷

Ernie had started "gigging" in the late '20s. Holding down a job as an electrician, he was putting to use his Tuskegee Institute education that stressed learning a trade. It was while at Tuskegee that Ernie's interest in music was ignited. He bought his first horn, a secondhand trombone, for six dollars. At first, he thought of himself as an athlete, playing football or baseball, but eventually he soured on both.

Employed fresh from Tuskegee Institute at Spotts and Tate Electric Shop at 128 North Greenwood Avenue, Ernie was sent one afternoon on a call to the Elks Apartments, housing that was next to the Royal Annex Hall. It was a dance hall on East Archer. He heard some fellows rehearsing there. After listening from outside for a few minutes, he said in an undated letter, "I went in and listened a few more minutes. I couldn't listen long because I was on Spotts and Tate's time."

He introduced himself to the young men and said, "You guys sound fine."

One of the musicians, Roy Randall, told him he was not hearing the entire group—that they would play a high school dance on Friday night—and invited him to come and hear the entire group. Ernie did, and he heard the other members, including Eddie Madison Sr. on trumpet, Luther West on sax, and Milton on vocals and drums. "They really sounded good to me," he said in the letter recounting the beginnings of his own group. The group invited him to bring his trombone and sit in sometime. Ernie took them up on the invitation and began playing with them. Besides the pleasure of being able to play "my bone," he said, "the extra nickels were a big, big help." He was not getting a regular salary at the electric shop, "only $1.00 an hour and some days only three hours that day." The money from gigging, Ernie recalled, sometimes augmented his electrician wages by fifty dollars a week.

A group called the Royal Entertainers was formed, and the guys, many of whom, like Ernie, held down other regular jobs, asked him to be their leader. That original group, some of them "high school boys," included Roy Randall on piano, Eddie Madison Sr. on trumpet, Lawrence Heatley Sr. on banjo and vocals, Arnold Booker on sax, Oscar "Haircut" Warner on drums, O. Z. Burley on fiddle, and Roy Milton on drums and vocals. Ernie felt it was fortunate, almost from the beginning, that he developed the idea of not "playing all the time of what I wanted to play. I played what the people wanted me to play." He credited that flexibility for giving him "a lot of white work also."[7]

At some point the guys said, "You seem to know a little bit more about music and how things should be than us," Ernie remembered. Maybe it was because he was a little older than some of the guys, or perhaps because he had college training. Whatever the reason, the men suggested Ernie make the band his own. It was called the Royal Entertainers because of the Royal Annex, where he'd found them. But even then, Ernie wanted it to be E. L. Fields and the Royal Entertainers. Later, he shortened his given name, Ernest Lawrence, to Ernie. He said it was partly the suggestion of a promoter named Mr. Furr, who booked them into the Rainbow Ballroom in Denver, who suggested the initials weren't suitable and his full name was too long.

Thus he decided the name should be the Ernie Fields Orchestra, named after him since he was indeed the leader. Ernie also said he needed to have a bass man, and brought in Theodore Shirley from Sand Springs, who had played in Ernie's brother Clarence's high school band. They were on their way!

It became clear to Ernie early on that being a member of the American Federation of Musicians union could be an advantage. For one thing, many of the more desirable establishments, particularly white ballrooms, required union affiliation. Ernie explained in a 1979 interview, "So they couldn't say that I don't like your music, but they would ask, are you, you know, you belong to the union? You tell them no, well then I'm sorry, I can't play anything but union in here."[8]

Another advantage was that the union provided a life insurance benefit. Never mind that the policy paid less for Black musicians (five hundred dollars) than what was said to be the payout for dead white union musicians (a thousand dollars). "At the time I first began playing, there was a lot of places that you couldn't play if you weren't in the union," he told the interviewer. He also wondered sometimes if that was an excuse not to hire a Black band. "And I frankly think that is, for one reason, believe it or not, that some of those knew that [some] maybe the Blacks didn't belong to it."[9] That, he said, was bouncing in his face a lot.

Just like the insurance policies, the union locals were segregated. The closest Black local to Tulsa was in Dallas, No. 186. He and his band members joined that one, as it was affiliated with the national "and everything," Ernie said. It was Dallas or nothing.

The first union local for Black musicians was chartered in Chicago in 1902, shortly after the Supreme Court ruling that said "separate but equal" facilities on racial grounds were acceptable. Of the original fifty Black American musician union locals, the majority were in the South, but there were northern cities with segregated locals too, including Boston; New Haven and Bridgeport, Connecticut; and Atlantic City, New Jersey.

Before integration, there was some wage protection for Black union musicians, according to James Petrillo, American Federation of Musicians (AF of M) president, in a 1971 speech at the annual convention. When Black musicians performed in a white club, he said, the Black local had to enforce the wage and working conditions of the white local. Also, if someone was denied admission in a white local, he or she could join the nearest local that would accept them and receive "all the privileges of membership of that local."[10]

Joining the Dallas local provided some comfort but didn't solve all Ernie's union problems. It was not quite as simple as that. There was a tax imposed if a union member played out of his "jurisdiction." Ernie explained, "So then, I was still union, but when I came into Tulsa [his home], it's going to cost me. Usually it doesn't mean much, but every little bit counts." It would cost him five or six dollars to play in Tulsa, because he didn't belong to the Tulsa [white] local. He got to talking to the folk in Dallas and was told, "As large a group as you have, get your charter."[11]

That's exactly what Ernie did. He chartered a union local with his orchestra.

The white local in Tulsa, No. 94, had been established in 1906, and there was another white local, No. 316, which was chartered in 1911 in nearby Bartlesville. Both were "closed," meaning Black musicians were not allowed to become members. According to one reference, Local 808 was the only "Negro musicians union in Oklahoma, founded by Ernie Fields, February 20, 1939." Another reference indicated that July 24, 1944, was the date that Local 808 received a charter to operate in Tulsa. Whatever the date and the minimum number needed for a local—Ernie thought it was twenty—he enlisted all the musicians in his organization, along with a music teacher or two: teacher and guitarist A. G. Rogers (1896–1956), who became the local's first president and secretary, and J. William Baul (1880–1961), who was the first convention delegate. Baul lived a few doors from the Fields family, at 505 E. Marshall Place. Other members of Ernie's band who were charter members were René Hall, Robert Graham, Edward Middleton, Hunter Gray, Clarence Dixon, Leomine Lewis, and Harry Talley, according to a Tulsa newspaper supplement called *Applause.*

"It went on like that for years and years," strictly for the Black musicians. Local 808 was segregated and small, with no rehearsal hall, as the larger Local 94 had.[12] Years later Tulsa's Black local would have its own rehearsal hall on North Lansing Street, off Pine Street.

Meanwhile in Chicago, the Black local was almost as big as the white local "money-wise," Ernie said. When they integrated, they listed both local numbers, No. 5 and No. 208, in the newly merged organization. "Same thing in Kansas City," Ernie recalled, but in Tulsa, when the Black musicians merged with the white Local 94, No. 808 disappeared.[13]

Ernie Fields Band Christmas card, early 1930s. *Left to right,* Leslie Sheffield, piano/arranger; Hubert Scott, trumpet; Eddie Nicholson, drums; Pee Wee Wiley, vocalist; Jeff Carrington, trumpet; Salva Sanders, piano; Ted Shirley, bass; Joe Walker, sax; Leon Dillard, trumpet, O. Z. Burley, guitar/fiddle; John Clarke, sax; Leroy "Pete" Bailey, sax. Author collection.

Much later, a former vocalist in the Ernie Fields Orchestra, Estelle Edson Banks, would become involved with the Black Los Angeles local, No. 767. She had begun work on a master's degree at UCLA, and as part of her thesis research on Hollywood studios, she organized a panel discussion with key musicians of Local 767 and the then all-white Local 47. Edson believes the discussion led to the merger of the two unions in the early 1950s—the first locals of the American Federation of Musicians to do so. She enlisted pianist Marl Young (1917–2009) for advice when she was writing her thesis "The Negro in Radio." Why, she asked him, were there no Blacks working in the industry—particularly on the networks, ABC, CBS, and NBC? Was it because the musicians' union was segregated, and all the Los Angeles contracts were negotiated by the white local? At that time, it was a rare instance for a Black musician to get a studio call, even though the Black local adopted pay scales negotiated by white Local 47. The panel, according to one article, was the first public discussion of the issue; before that it was only talked about in meetings in private homes. Both locals eventually approved the proposal, and segregation officially ended in the Los Angeles musicians' unions June 23, 1953—*before* the Supreme Court's historic *Brown v. Board of Education of Topeka, Kansas* decision in 1954.[14]

Edson remembered that René Hall, often sparse with words, gave her the biggest compliment: "At the end of the merger vote, when it was clear the two unions would be one, he said, 'Estelle Edson, girl, you've scored a big one. You started something that should have been done a long time ago.'" Such praise from her "first teacher out in the world" was a big moment for her, she said.[15] Long before the union activism, "She was some kind of singer!" recalled her former bandstand mate Melvin Moore.[16]

Drummer Al Duncan, a Fields alum, remembered that his uncle Ben Johnson, who played cornet for minstrel shows, was secretary-treasurer of (Black) Local 627 in Kansas City in the 1940s. Duncan went to Kansas City every summer and lived with his uncle. "He made me learn all the rules and regulations" he said.[17]

Long after Ernie left life on the road, he remained an ardent trade unionist. He turned his interest to promotion and became a licensed booking agent. His business card read: "Ernie Fields Artist, Inc.; AFofM License No. 9488—representing orchestras, combos, vocalists and dancers." He liked being around young musicians, he said, and of course, he liked "the nickel or two that I may pick up sometimes." He bemoaned the fact that young Black musicians were slow to become union members, or, if they were members, to participate in union business meetings. "You may be able to get twenty new white youngsters a year [joining the union] and maybe one Black or none." Instead of complaining about rules and regulations, come in and work to change it, he said. The young white musicians "are full of ideas—especially since the music industry and music is changing."[18]

But integration also brought about some unintended consequences, including a dilution of Black representation as delegates and voters at national conventions. As Black locals were swallowed by the mergers, delegate strength went from a high of seventy-three when locals were segregated to a low of ten Black delegates in 1974.

In part because of Ernie's union advocacy, the Fields family became a part of the trade unions for their professions. My mother was a member of the Tulsa Classroom Teachers Association and for a while was an officer of the Tulsa Negro Teachers Credit Union. Ernie Jr. remains active with the American Federation of Musicians, and his knowledge has proved an asset in preparing contract estimates and payroll for the numerous productions for which he is engaged as the music contractor. I entered the union world as a broadcast journalist, joining the American Federation of Television and Radio Artists (AFTRA). It is now merged with the Screen Actors Guild (SAG), forming SAG-AFTRA, where I proudly maintain membership to this day.

Ernie Fields would marvel at his professional good fortune whenever he considered his rise to stardom from his humble beginnings as a self-described "poor widow's boy."

FROM NACOGDOCHES TO TAFT TO TUSKEGEE

The Fields family came from East Texas around 1905 or 1906 to Oklahoma—the place where, according to the Rodgers and Hammerstein song, "the wind comes sweepin' down the plain." The place where I don't ever recall seeing wheat wave or it smelling sweet, as the song that was adopted as the state's anthem suggests.

Oklahoma did not become a state until 1907. Before statehood, it was known as Indian Territory. (With *Okla* meaning "red," and *homa*, "home of," the Choctaw-derived name loosely translates as "home of the red man.") It was the final stopping-off place for the so-called Five Civilized Tribes (Cherokee, Choctaw, Chickasaw, Creek, and Seminole) and their slaves and some free Blacks. Forcibly removed, they would end up in Oklahoma after a long, arduous journey, having been driven from Florida and Georgia and other southern enclaves along the infamous Trail of Tears of the 1830s and 1840s.[1]

While Native Americans set up their designated "nations" in Oklahoma, Blacks established their own self-protected towns. There were some two dozen of the small, mostly agrarian municipalities. They had names like Bailey, Canadian Colored, Ferguson, and Liberty. In twenty-first-century Oklahoma, only about a dozen remain: Redbird, Rentiesville, Boley (believed to be the oldest incorporated Black township in the United States), Langston, Tullahassee, and a place called Taft. Taft is about nine miles from Oklahoma's eleventh largest city, Muskogee.

The Fields family arrived in Taft with five of six children aboard a wagon, fleeing Nacogdoches, Texas, in the dangerous East Texas area, 335 miles along Highway 271. Driving time by car would have been at least five and half hours. By wagon and along unpaved roads, who knows how long the journey took? The 1910 census has the Taft population at 352. Taft would become home for the state's Black orphanage—called D.B.O. for Deaf, Blind, and Orphaned—and the state's Black mental institution.

By 1920 the town's population blossomed to 553, and included another East Texas family, the Copelands, who came from Saint Augustine, Texas. The largest population was in 1940—a whopping 772. It's been a steady decline ever since, with the 2015 estimate being 245 residents, a decline from the 250 recorded in the 2010 census.

Taft is where the family of former slave Thomas Jefferson Fields and his wife and mother-in-law settled. Thomas is believed to have been born in 1848 in Tennessee and lived until 1906. His wife, Mary Jane (Garrett), was born January 15, 1865, and died October 23, 1963. Her mother, Amelia Garrett, also a former slave, was born August 10, 1858, and died September 15, 1939. Records show Thomas and Mary were married in 1885 in Texas. Their children were Thomas Jefferson Fields Jr., Willie Fields, Joe Ella (Fields) Copeland, Clarence Fields, Evelyn (Fields) Bates, and Sonny Boy, a toddler when they reached Taft, who would grow up to become Ernie Fields.

There are two stories about how and why the Fields family fled to Oklahoma. Each tale was remembered and recounted to me differently by different relatives. The oral history was told to children and grandchildren, only half of whom—in the time before the television series *Roots* was popularized—listened to it or remembered it, and fewer than half of whom cared about it. Until now.

The first story has the bold, elder Tom Fields deciding to run for some local political office or commission in Nacogdoches. We are told he ignored admonishments and efforts to discourage his intent. He ran as a Republican, and apparently he split the vote, causing local horror over a Republican loss. That led to threats, forcing the family to hurriedly sell everything they could and leave. The only comfort was that eldest son Tom Jr. was already in Taft.

The other tale passed down is that the younger Tom had made the mistake of threatening a white man with a baseball bat or some similar implement—another no-no of the time, forcing him to flee. Now, with more threats and anticipated danger, the rest of family left East Texas for the promised land of Oklahoma and the safety of the all-Black municipality of Taft.

Ernie's mother, Mary Jane, brought her mother, Amelia, with them to the "new land." In the 1920 census, Amelia, then seventy-five, was listed as born in Texas, and her father and mother were listed as natives of Texas too. Amelia's occupation was listed as "general, farmer."

The youngest on the trip was Tom and Mary Jane's son, born in 1904 in Nacogdoches. He was called Sonny Boy and later named himself Ernest Lawrence Fields. Why he had to name himself is unknown—but he says he was known as Sonny Boy Fields well into fourth or fifth grade. The nickname brought teasing from classmates and charges that his folk didn't think enough of him to give him a name. Ernie would retort that they wanted to make sure he had a name that he was satisfied with. According to Fields, he picked out his own name—never recalling any particular reason why—but it was the name he chose and maintained until much, much later. He admitted in a Rutgers University interview that the teasing and wondering about his parents' motives did hurt his feelings.[2] He claimed a Muskogee newspaper noted his naming with an article proclaiming "No more Sonny Boy Fields, it's now Ernest Lawrence Fields."

As his next oldest siblings were nine years older (Evelyn) and twelve years older (Clarence), he remembers being doted upon—not "spoiled," he said—but "looked out after." He wondered how the family made it, as he didn't remember ever going hungry. He was not allowed to drop out of school but was permitted to accept jobs or paid errands during out-of-school time. "They wouldn't take me out of school to do any kind of work," he said. "Whatever I did, had to be after school."

As he got older, he wondered "how in the world my mother ever managed to get along with what little we did, trying to farm around," he said.

Much earlier, Ernie's father, when a recently freed slave, had managed to make his way to Nashville, Tennessee, to enroll in Roger Williams College, a school that was known primarily for Bible study. The historically Black college, founded in 1866 by the American Baptist denomination, occupied twenty-eight acres on a knoll near Hillsboro Pike. Tom Fields's Bible, which survives, is inscribed in pen with a graceful signature and the date 1877. He became a Baptist minister, and the "sheepskin" earned from his college study was a source of family pride. How and why he then made his way to East Texas is unknown. Nor is it known what prompted his flirtation with politics. In Taft, he met an untimely death in 1906. He was walking near two men who were arguing and was reportedly felled by a stray bullet.

From all accounts, the family was what in hindsight was considered "poor." However, they were musically inclined and performed as a group (all except Sonny Boy), singing and playing instruments around the region. I imagine they may have accompanied their minister father on his dates preaching at various churches in the many surrounding all-Black enclaves. Brother Clarence remembers the family hosting the famed choral director and music teacher Eva Jessye in their home whenever she was in the area.[3] Ernie remembers her teaching music in Taft and said she "seemed like saw talent in me, some kind of way." Jessye was the first to teach him piano, and suggested he should sing, too. Ernie would visit with her in her New York City home when his orchestra first traveled east in the early 1930s. Ernie's two sisters both played piano (Joe Ella, the eldest girl, also gave Ernie lessons), and the boys "had a little singing trio and they would sing around." He said he got a "kick out of it, but never, never dreamed that would be my livelihood." But he loved music and would walk for miles to "little country picnics" where there always would be music, "maybe a horn or guitar or piano up on a wooden platform." He enjoyed listening but said, "Looked like no bug was on me to really learn how to play anything."

While the family was in Taft, Mary Jane Fields was sufficiently friendly with the Copeland family from Texas that in 1909, when the second of the Copelands' seven children—a girl named Myrtle Bernice—was born, Mary Jane went to visit, taking five-year-old Sonny Boy along with her. After the visit and on the way home, it is said that Sonny Boy told his mother, "Mrs. Copeland sure has a pretty baby girl!"

The family story that was most often repeated, with little variation, was the survival story. Mary Fields, after her husband died, was perplexed as to how to make a crop and feed the family—and perhaps make some payment toward a mortgage. All this, without the benefit of a mule that was either dead or just gone. Her mother reportedly told her, "When I was a slave, the

Garrett-Fields family, photographed between 1898 and early 1900s. *Seated, from left,* Evelyn Fields, Amelia Garrett, Joe Ella Fields, Thomas Jefferson Fields; *standing, from left,* Clarence Fields, Willie Fields, Thomas Fields Jr., and Mary (Garrett) Fields, wife of Thomas Jefferson Fields. Author collection.

master used to hitch us to the plow." It is said the two women took turns pushing and pulling the plow. The crops were planted and raised, the family fed, the farm redeemed. And the rest, as they say, is history.

Ernie always knew he wanted to, really had to, go to college. He also knew he and his family didn't have college money. While still in high school, he started figuring how to make money during the summer and save for college. The first job was water boy on a section crew that worked laying railroad track. The section hand foreman told him that between toting water he also had to cut weeds. He gave him a blade. "When I started to cut weeds, they'd say, 'water boy,' so I'd get the water and go around to them and everything." He didn't feel he was able to save enough, fast enough. So his mother suggested he go live with his sister Joe Ella, who was by this time married and living in Muskogee, nine miles from Taft, and try his hand at shining shoes, "if nothing else."

While working in a shine parlor in Muskogee, he learned an important lesson and made a valuable friend. He thought "there were but three kinds of shoes, that is, white shoes, black shoes and tan shoes." One day, he was shining a man's shoes. He had tan shoes, "and I was just shining the heels. I was going to make them shine like the toe." As Ernie told the story, all the other boys were laughing and "would say little words, this and that, and I didn't know what they were talking about." When he finished, the man handed him a nickel, and everybody fell out laughing. All the boys laughed except one boy named Walter Thomas.

Thomas told Ernie he was lucky to get the nickel. He wasted all that time on a man who usually didn't tip well, if at all. Walter then took him aside and "told me all the old names, what they mean." "Cush" meant to expect a quarter tip. There was a slang term for nearly everything, which meant Ernie had lots to learn. "The guys had been working there, they knew how to work for a nickel, a dime, and you're never going to get a quarter in those days," he said. Ernie and Walter became what Ernie called "buddy-buddy." When the weekend came, Walter would invite his new pal to "do this and that and I'd say, no, I'm saving my money." What are you so tight for, Walter nudged? "I'd say I'm trying to save money to go to Tuskegee." His friend said he was working for school too, the Kansas Vocational School in Topeka. His friend Walter would save his hide again later, interceding with a shoe when Ernie got ready to put polish on a customer's suede shoes (having never seen such a shoe as that before).

Ernie followed in his older brother and trumpet player Clarence's footsteps in going to Tuskegee Institute to study and learn a trade. He first considered auto mechanics, then studied to be an electrician and graduated in 1924. But it was not all wires and currents. Deciding that his five foot, ten stature was not sufficient to pursue football or his beloved sport of baseball, he noticed the band seemed to attract the attention of campus coeds.

But he didn't have a horn.

He promised the bandmaster, Capt. Frank L. Drye, who wondered how his brother Clarence would let him come without a horn, that he would come up with one.[4] The Tuskegee University Marching Crimson Piper Band had a reputation of excellence, boasting a well-organized band of forty-five pieces and an eighteen-piece orchestra as early as 1906. The title of captain was applied to the directors because, at the time, the band was under the school's Military Department.[5]

"I sure wish I could be in that band," Ernie confided to a classmate who was a trumpet player. The classmate found someone at the school who wanted to sell a trombone. Ernie excitedly arranged to purchase the horn for six dollars, making a down payment with the only money he had, three dollars. When he took the horn to the director, Captain Drye said, "You have a horn but you can't use this." All was not lost. Captain Drye sent the badly marred instrument out to be repaired and when it was returned, Ernie said, "I thanked him" and started from the beginning, taking lessons in the second band. That was the middle of the school year.

During the summer Ernie made a pact with a fellow student, clarinet player William Moore (who also was an applied electrician major). They would both work the summer at the campus power plant, and Moore would show Ernie music drills—a few hours every morning and before going to bed. When school started in the fall, "I was in the band—they put me in the band," Ernie said. Captain Drye had another surprise for Ernie when he summoned him to his office in the middle of the school term—a brand new Conn trombone. And he moved him up to second chair.

Part of the fun of band was the ability to travel with the football team. Ernie recalled a trip to Montgomery when they played Alabama State. Erskine Hawkins, who was playing with that band, was originally from Birmingham. The Bama State Collegians would be one of the few southeast college bands to gain national acclaim. After moving to New York City, the Collegians, directed by Hawkins, became the Erskine Hawkins Orchestra and produced a string of national hit records.

After Tuskegee, fate and opportunity would intersect by way of Walter Thomas, Ernie's friend from his shoe-shining days. Thomas's sister, Cleora Butler, would later live in Tulsa and build a popular catering and cooking business that served many of the wealthy oil families. When Thomas got his first big break in music, the opportunity to join the Missourians, he alerted Ernie and said he thought they could use him. The group was led by a singer named Cab Calloway, who would later take over the orchestra and give it his own name. Calloway and his orchestra would appear in Tulsa annually, playing first at the old Orpheum Theatre for Tulsa's whites and then for the Black community at the Crystal Palace Ballroom—where the likes of Duke Ellington, Count Basie, and Jimmie Lunceford would play. While in town, Cab and Thomas would stay with Thomas's mom, Maggie, who also had a reputation for cooking. In fact, they were in town in June 1937 during the highly anticipated boxing match between Joe Louis and Max Schmeling. A picnic in the Thomases' yard was planned, but the fight was over before most could finish loading their plates with fried chicken and picnic trimmings that included homemade ice cream.[6]

Thomas gave Ernie a chance. After college, Thomas had emerged as a carpenter, who, like Ernie, took music gigs on the side. He told his pal this time when he was on a gig in Tulsa, that he thought he might be able to get Ernie on, too.

Ernie Fields, mid-1930s.
Courtesy of the Henry Jacob
Amundsen (Bestepappa)
Family.

Thomas said, "I'll tell them the kind of fellow you are, and I think I can get you in," Ernie recalled.

Thomas went on to dates in Missouri or Kansas but soon called back and told Ernie, "Come on!" The promised wage was fifty dollars a week. Ernie considered the offer. In his regular job with his music on the side, sometimes he made more than fifty dollars in a week. That was because he had a boss who was lenient and would let him off so he could travel from time to time. So, he turned Thomas down.

"I told Walter that I believe I'll stay on where I am," Ernie said.

Later, when the name was changed from the Missourians to the Cab Calloway Orchestra, "They contacted me again," Ernie said. Thomas said, "It's going to be sensational, you better come on now." The group was heading on a tour in the East, so Thomas warned Ernie, "They won't be trying to get anybody from back this way after then, and you'll be right in on the ground floor." Ernie told him no. "I believe I'll stick with my little job and these boys [the musicians] for a while yet. Thomas said OK and went on," Ernie said.[7] Thomas, who became known as "Foots," went on to enjoy an outstanding career as a saxophonist, flutist, and arranger. Among his arrangements was Calloway's signature 1931 hit, "Minnie the Moocher."

Ernie "went on" too.

⚜ 5 ⚜

ON THE ROAD, FOR
BETTER OR WORSE

The 1920s through the 1950s was the period known as the Negro Holocaust—a brutal chapter of American history when lynching and other forms of inhumane violence against Blacks, if not commonplace, were a regular occurrence. It was mostly in the South. The threat of violence was ever present.[1] It was a time of particular fragility for Black men—a time when smiling too much or not enough could be a life-or-death decision. In spite of the real or perceived dangers, Ernie Fields decided he and his fledgling group would hit the road.

In the very early days—the late '20s and early '30s—the musicians traveled in two cars, with the instruments stored on top of the cars. Some states required purchasing a commercial license for the vehicles—but Ernie ended up getting a permit (which was cheaper) or sometimes, if stopped by the highway patrol, talked his way out of paying for either one. Band members at this time included Wellington "Frenchie" Hughes, a sax player and Tuskegee classmate, and Salva Sanders, the piano player whose style Count Basie fell in love with when he was barnstorming around Oklahoma.[2]

At first, the band performed mostly in nearby venues, in Oklahoma and Texas, Arkansas, and Missouri. Ernie was also getting access to some what he called "quality" venues in Tulsa—like the exclusive Tulsa Club. His was the first "colored" band to perform there.

"They weren't saying 'Black' then," Ernie pointed out.

The Tulsa Club engaged him for a week. Later, he played for the debutante "coming out" party held at the club for Joan Skelly (around 1928). She was daughter of the millionaire founder-owner of Skelly Oil Company, William Skelly. (The company later became Getty Oil.) The band's engagement was a first that helped put Ernie on the map. An article in the *Evening News* of faraway Wilkes-Barre, Pennsylvania, dated Tuesday, July 3, 1934, noted, "Ernie and his musicians played a whole season at the famous Tulsa Club, the first race band to play there and the only race band to play at the famous Club Boga in Oklahoma City."

One of the earliest introductions of the musicians to unpredictable white racist rage came in the late '20s on one of the band's first out-of-town trips. With the promise of ten dollars per man, they headed out to play in Gladewater and Longview, Texas—about 275 miles away. Those were big oil boomtowns then. Ernie borrowed money for gas and expenses from his brother Clarence, at the time a Sand Springs high school music teacher, and Peter Bailey, the tenor sax player, borrowed his father's brand-new Studebaker to make the trip.

The constant rain created a lot of mud, so it was nearly impossible for patrons to attend. The white promoter at first welched on the pay. To boot, Ernie got what he called "my first taste of really the South." Something had happened at the hotel where they were staying, and Peter walked in as Texas Rangers were questioning people there. Before he knew it, a ranger slapped Peter and "practically knocked him down," Ernie recalled. "Nigger, don't interrupt," the ranger reportedly said. "Don't be coming in here when you see that I'm busy." Ernie felt awful, as Peter had made the trip as a favor to him. Peter's dad had warned, "I don't know about that car down there, something might happen." The incident, coupled with being stiffed on pay, left the band members bewildered.

Peter said, "We ain't got no money, let's go back."

Ernie sought out the promoter, who insisted he would make good, and reminded him that another Black act he booked, the popular Sugar Lou and Eddie (an orchestra out of Tyler, Texas)[3] was paid. "I don't work no bands and don't pay them," he said. According to Ernie, he made good on his promise, and the band headed back home to Tulsa—at least with their pay.

However, after the Tulsa Club engagment, business really picked up. More dates here and there emboldened Ernie to say to his boss that he might not return to his job at the electric shop. His boss, Walter Tate, had been generous about Ernie's absences, and even with the semi-resignation, Ernie said, "He smiled and said, 'Well, it's up to you.'" Tate told him "if I didn't make it, I could have my job back." So he told the guys they would try it.

He would be booked again in Longview, Texas, where a December 15, 1931, story in the *Longview News-Journal* promoted an upcoming "Collegiate Nite" at the Winter Garden dance hall, where the Ernie Fields "Tulsa Club uniformed orchestra" was described as "one of the best ever to play in East Texas."

An area booker/promoter came through and said he wanted to carry the group on tour up through Kansas, Nebraska, "and so on and so forth," Ernie said. "I didn't know what to think, but the guys said, 'Man, let's go. Let's try it. Let's try it.'" By this time the band had changed a bit, with vocalist Roy Milton (billed as an "entertainer") as a mainstay—no longer playing drums. Ernie consented.

Soon, Omaha-based promoter Phil Dorsey approached Ernie about participating in a Battle of the Bands. This one was proposed for Denver, Colorado—Ernie Fields versus Smiling Billy Stewart. Stewart, known as a showman, had a fairly well-known band at the time, based in Florida. It was the official band of Bethune-Cookman College and was said to empha-size brass and section work. Stewart found moderate success but never recorded. (It was common for college bands to become pro. For example, Jimmie Lunceford's band was formed with several of his Fisk University and high school classmates.) The Depression was forcing groups to seek bet-ter pay away from their neighborhoods.[4] Ernie seemed to be having some decent luck as a result.

For the Denver trip, Ernie recalled luring trumpet player and Trenton, New Jersey, native Herbert Scott away from Bessie Smith's vaudeville show. There was Hobart Banks on piano, Roy Milton as singer, Luther "Spurgeon" West on alto sax, and Eddie Nicholson on drums. Ernie recalled he "had one or two little gigs, but the main one was to play at the Battle of the Bands." It was billed as a "winner takes all" event, but Dorsey told him, "Don't worry, you'll get your price and [Stewart] will get his." For the battle, Ernie was instructed to set up at one end of the hall (at the Rossonian, located in Denver's Five Points), and the competing band was at the other end. "You'd play a number, and if you got a hand, the people would crowd around you." Then the other band would play and most would go to the other end of the hall. It went back and forth like that. "And so it seemed like it was even all along," Ernie said.[5]

Milton remembered them starting with "Under Your Window Tonight." Instead of a microphone, "We had to sing through a megaphone," he recalled in a 1980 conversation with Ernie.[6]

"I had some little sparklers up in my megaphone," he added. The men laughed at the memory, with Ernie saying, "I'll never forget when you were fixing it."

The group gave their best tunes, "our best shots," said Milton. A foxtrot version of "I'll Always Be in Love With You" is what they did next. Usually, it was performed as a waltz. "Nobody could sing it better than Roy," Ernie said. Then the trumpet player Scott told Ernie, "Miff, call it." (They sometimes referred to Ernie as Miff Mole, after Irving Milfred Mole, the white jazz trombonist credited with creating the first distinctive jazz style.) Ernie recalled, "I knew when Roy sang that tune, that would settle it," he said. "I called it and we swung that down and Roy got out there and the people got to whistling and howling and carrying on and Billy Stewart" looked angry.

Stewart's group next swung into "Ring Dem Bells" from the popular 1930 comedy film, *Check and Double Check*, which featured Duke Ellington. Milton said, "That band showered down on us like showers of rain."[7] After that, fans never returned to the other end of the dance hall. "Scotty looked around and said, 'I believe they got us,'" Ernie recalled. Roy Milton called the event "the most embarrassing thing I experienced in my whole career!" They thought, according to Milton, "that we were hot stuff." But it boiled down to "six against fourteen," Ernie recalled—"Six little green musicians" against Stewart's group, about which Ernie explained, "You couldn't see the men for the instruments hardly."

But there was a takeaway for Ernie. First of all, he did get paid. He also met another Denver promoter named Jones who promised, and delivered on, more dates for the band. Jones told him, "Smiling Billy is a long way from

Florida. He comes once a year, but I'll have you in here a lot of times." Also, Ernie had been advised often to get a "big band." He had taken a little six-piece band to the Denver competition. "We did all right, but Smiling Billy Stewart had about a ten or twelve, no I think it was twelve or fourteen, he had a big band, it was a good band." He'd never heard of them before—they were Smiling Billy Stewart and the Sarasota Serenaders.

MANY LESSONS LEARNED

After the Battle of the Bands, Ernie went back to Tulsa, with building a larger organization front of mind. Soon after, sax player Spurgeon returned to Xavier University in New Orleans. "I never would encourage him to stop school," Ernie recalled, so he used a local kid named Earl Bostic when Spurgeon was unavailable. He liked Spurgeon better as a bandman than a lead sax, "but boy, I tell you, Earl Bostic blowed more horn. He was just a genius," he said.

Bostic was a Tulsa kid whose father was a junk peddler. Bostic was being groomed by William Jett, the Hampton Institute–trained band director at Tulsa's Booker T. Washington High School. Tuskegee and Hampton, according to Ernie, were closely related, and Ernie and Jett were "buddy-buddy and ran around together." Jett would often tell Ernie, "I'm going to have a good man for you," talking about Bostic's progress in the high school band. Jett sent Bostic home to practice with the school's clarinet, and one day his father heard the boy practicing and picked up the instrument and broke it in two.

He didn't want his son "blowing that thing around here," Ernie recalled. The boy's mother cried and called Ernie, saying, "You're a good friend of Mr. Jett. Call him and tell him what happened, but I'll pay him for it." Jett told Ernie not to worry, he would pay for the school's instrument. "She and everybody," Jett reportedly said, "are going to be proud of that boy. The old man just doesn't know." The father was clear, Ernie said, "He didn't want his son to be no musician." After high school, he did not join the Ernie Fields Band. Instead, Bostic went on to graduate from Xavier University in New Orleans and is regarded as a major influence on John Coltrane. Coltrane at one point in his career toured with Bostic, whom he described as "a very gifted musician. He showed me a lot of things on my horn. He has fabulous technical facilities on his instrument and knows many a trick."[1]

At some point in the '30s, the Fields band purchased a used bus for travel. It had belonged to another music group, headed by a white man named Jack Crawford. (Crawford, a popular midwestern band leader, died in 1948.) It looked something like a stagecoach, "with a caboose on top," Ernie recalled. "It looked ridiculous but was better than piling into two cars." The bus, he said, was so cheap he paid cash for it. Crawford was getting a new bus, and someone from the Chevrolet dealership called Ernie about the old one and promised, "We'll make you a good deal on it."

The bus was emblazoned with the words "Ernie Fields and His Orchestra." (Later versions amended it to "His Nationally Famous Orchestra" and much later to "World Famous Orchestra.") Ernie also hired what he referred to as a valet—someone who would help with the luggage, set instruments up on the bandstand, and drive the bus. Most importantly, a qualification for the valet/driver was also "mechanic." Ernie would muse later in life, "We might have something today, if the bus didn't break down so much."

Two long and then two short horn blasts were the signal the driver gave to alert the musicians it was time to board the bus and depart. Usually the staging area was the Small Hotel, or whatever theater the group had been using for rehearsal. In Tulsa, the last stop was always Ernie's home on North Peoria. If I happened to be home at the pickup, I would put on a show—that is, screaming, crying, and begging my father not to leave.

Once, the bus had only gone less than a mile when Ernie remembered something left behind. They turned the bus around and returned, only to discover me cheerily playing on my swing, no sign of the distress witnessed less than fifteen minutes before. The guys never let Ernie forget that scene and dubbed the little girl "The Great Pretender."

The musicians had various names for the bus—sometimes "The Ark" and sometimes "The Stagecoach." That was because, as René Hall observed, the first bus—the used one—was oddly shaped. If you were sitting in the back of the bus, you couldn't see out the front because it was, in Hall's words, a "strange contraption. It was shaped like the old-time stagecoach." It was built, he said, like an opera house—in other words, the front seats were the

Believed to be the first bus purchased for the band. Photo courtesy of Claudette Black, whose father, Thomas "Zack" Zackery, was the driver.

only ones where you could see out of the windshield. By the time you got all the way in the back, all you could see was the dashboard.[2]

Whenever the bus pulled in front of the Small Hotel in Tulsa to pick up or drop off musicians, those in close proximity would joke, "The Stagecoach is coming. Let's rob it!"[3]

"That's how funny it looked," Ernie recalled.

It was not wanderlust that had the musicians on the road. Audiences in some cities began to request groups other than local talent—in part because of the miracle of radio, they heard the new and exciting embryonic sounds of swing and jazz music. Also, due in part to an improving highway system, long-distance travel was getting easier. One historian explained, "As the jumps between towns became longer, the musicians found themselves living totally on the road, eating and sleeping in their buses for weeks at a time. This was particularly true for black bands, who could never be sure when prejudice would deny them a place to eat or sleep in the North and who knew that Jim Crow would always severely limit their access to public accommodations in the South."[4]

At one point, a Mr. Johnson was the bus driver and mechanic. While the orchestra was on the bandstand playing, Mr. Johnson would tune up the bus and get it ready to take the group to the next job, Hall explained.[5] Russell "Big Chief" Moore was in the band then and on the bus. He used to complain that the heat pipe that ran the length of the bus would burn his shoes. Hall said Mr. Johnson was temperamental—and wasn't that good a driver. One rainy night they were headed from Silver City, New Mexico, to Albuquerque. The bus driver was tired and the road was "curvaceous and dangerous," as René

Hall told the story. Mr. Johnson, he said, was driving very erratically. That was when Jeff Carrington, the first trumpet player, started "hoorahing" Mr. Johnson about his driving, telling him, "I'll drive this motherfucker." Before you knew it, they nearly ran off the road. The guys scrambled out of the bus, fearing an explosion. The driver of an oil tanker passing by dumped some oil on an old spare tire so they could burn the oil to keep warm. When daylight came, they were shocked to find that the bus was jammed against a tree at the edge of a cliff with about a two-hundred-foot drop. They had thought the bus had come to rest against something solid.

Long story short, the bus was rescued, though it sustained some damage. When the crippled vehicle got back to Tulsa and rolled up in front of the Small Hotel, where many of band members rented rooms, someone asked, half joking, "What happened? Indians attack your stagecoach?"

The Small Hotel, named for owner Wellington H. Small,[6] was built in 1926 at 615 East Archer Street, right at the bottom of "deep Greenwood," often called "the stem." Next door was a café run by Small's wife, Eva, according to Small's niece Faye (Small) Fields. Small lived at the hotel but moved to a two-story brick home on North Peoria around 1960 when urban renewal and a highway, the Crosstown Expressway, destroyed the hotel and most of what remained in the storied Black Wall Street along and around Greenwood Avenue.

According to Small's niece, whom he raised, the money to build the hotel came from loans to Small from the Mayo family, who built Tulsa's most luxurious downtown hotel, the Mayo Hotel, and the Hanna family, who owned the local lumber company. And, she said firmly, "He paid them back."[7]

True to his word, Ernie built a larger organization than the motley band he featured in the Battle of the Bands. The band grew to twelve or more artists at times, building on his Tulsa Club triumph and budding reputation. A June 24, 1932, ad in the *Asbury Park Press* in New Jersey said the "Sea Grill Inn, now under new management and new ownership," would feature "Ernie Fields in Person and His Full Band, Two Shows Nightly." The performance in the Garden Grill Dining Room, including supper and dinner dances, cost $1.50 and $2.00, and the ad specified, "No other charges the entire evening."

The band's second bus was a school bus. It was "brand new," Ernie said, and he had it painted blue and white.[8] Melvin Moore remembered the vehicle not so much for being new as for being "nice and warm." By this time, Thomas "Zack" Zackery was the bus driver. In addition to being a "shade tree mechanic" who could keep the bus running, Ernie boasted, Zack was a "professional" bus driver—he had "taken the test and was licensed for it."

The bus carried forty gallons of gasoline on each side. "I would usually try and keep it pretty well full," Ernie said. "But any time you stopped at a service station, even if only I was going to put gas in one side, that was a pretty nice sale for the average station." Ernie would always ask if he and the other musicians could use the restroom before putting gas in. If they said no, "I would drive on."[9]

The days on the road were not without challenge, but Ernie Fields considered himself blessed, he said when he tape-recorded himself telling his memories. His days on the road, though sometimes stressful, were seldom violent. "I learned to pray early on. I also learned to watch as well as pray. I just guess the good Lord just made a way."

One close call came in a small town in Louisiana, where the band played a dance. When it came time for the dance to close, "I went into our theme song, and was doing a little talk, thanking the dancers and all and saying goodnight," Ernie said. Suddenly a white "feller" ran up to the bandstand and shouted, "Nigger, what do you figure you're going to close this dance and I just came in here?" Ernie apologized, and said it was time for the dance to end. Looking at his watch, he said, "It's a few minutes past my contract now." Then the man brandished a pearl-handled .38 or .45. "It looked big," Ernie said. "It looked like a cannon to me." Ernie repeated, "I've already stopped." A couple of people on the dance floor grabbed the rabblerouser and then the proprietor, who was white, came and told the man, "If you are arguing about the money, I told you when you came in, it was about time for the dance to close. You said that didn't matter, you wanted to pay and come in anyway. Seems you just want to start trouble." He gave the hothead his money back and ordered him out. Those are the kind of things, over the years, Ernie said, that "made me not get evil about the white man."

That was not the only time the band would depend on the kindness, or sometimes ignorance, of strangers. In an era of rigid segregation and significant racial hostility, it was a game of chance on what to expect when encountering certain whites. Sometimes dumb luck saved you from catastrophe, as was the case one late night in Henryetta, Oklahoma. Henryetta was known to be a very prejudiced town. Ernie said he never saw it but "they say" there was a sign that read, "Nigger, read and run. If you can't read, run anyway." No Black people lived in the town, but the band played in areas around Henryetta and on occasion passed through.

The bus driver apparently was tired, so he turned the wheel over to Ernie so he could rest up. René Hall warned that whenever Ernie was driving "you had to watch him like a hawk" because he often dozed at the wheel. Ernie did go to sleep this time, apparently, and before he knew it, the bus plowed into the rear of a stopped automobile. On impact, the males in the car scattered and disappeared. What also scattered on impact was several jugs of moonshine whiskey. (Oklahoma was a dry state until it repealed Prohibition in 1959.) The noise of the crash attracted the police.

Ernie told them the vehicle had been stopped in the middle of the street but he didn't see it. When the officers, who were white, saw the whiskey, they sided with Ernie, and declared that the people in the car must have either been parked in the street or driving drunk and backed into the bus. The police were apologetic, and said they had a good idea who the moonshiners were and promised, "We'll get 'em." Noting that the bus radiator appeared damaged, they even suggested repair options. Ernie and the band were relieved more than anything, having imagined outcomes that could have been much, much worse.

There were other unpleasant "trial and tribulations," Ernie's wife, Bernice, once recounted in an undated letter to me. The band was in Alabama one night and it was two degrees below zero. They couldn't get rooms anywhere. One of the guys suggested they "throw a brick through a window so they will put us in jail." Ernie wanted no part of Alabama law enforcement. Instead, someone suggested a nearby barracks of some sort. "There were only cots," Bernice said. "The only cover they had was their overcoats."

The letter also recounted an engagement somewhere in Mississippi where "they played Saturday and Sunday nights for whites and Monday night for Blacks." They returned the next weekend, Bernice wrote, saying René Hall had told her the story, and "the whites had broke up all the

Ad from the *Mississippi Enterprise* of Jackson, August 3, 1946. Courtesy of Dan Kochakian.

glasses in the dance hall" because they wouldn't drink out of glasses that "the niggers had drunk out of." Recalling the incident in a conversation at his office on June 23, 1987, Hall placed it in Bartlesville, Oklahoma.[10] Wherever it happened, the facts of the incident were the same. "Some bunch of white guys came up and went behind the bar and broke all the glasses. That's a fact," said Hall.

Getting food while on the road could prove challenging. When sax player Leon Wright was in the organization, way before men's fashion caught up to him, he wore an earring in one ear. One night after a late performance, the group could find only one restaurant open—and it was white. Wright decided to add a beret to his "costume" and speak French to the proprietor. They were allowed to eat because the owner thought they were foreigners.[11]

Ernie recalled another visit in Mississippi, sometime in the '40s, when the band pulled up to a small convenience store. He and the fellas walked around and picked up the items they wanted and made their way to the cash register to pay. While they were shopping, two or three young "colored lads" came in, picked up a few items and made their way to the cash register, too. The cashier told the youths, "They are not from here," nodding toward the musicians. "You have to tell me what you want and I'll get it for you. You do like you always do the next time you come in." When Ernie got back outside, he said he would never forget what happened next.

The front of his bus, where the destination appears on commercial buses, had his name, Ernie Fields. One of the kids looked at that and said he had never heard of that town and wondered where it might be. The other kid replied, "It must be from up north somewhere."

Ernie said he never made enough so that the band could fly from gig to gig, but on occasion they would travel by train. During the war, gas was rationed, so he decided train travel would be a way to "build up" their ration of gas stamps. He agreed to leave the bus in Pensacola, Florida, travel by train to the other gigs, and make their way back to pick the bus up again in Pensacola. At a Jacksonville, Florida, depot, all the fellas were clustered together gabbing and laughing as they waited for the train. All except for a young tenor sax player named Julius Muse out of Seattle.

"Being raised in a different area," Ernie reasoned, "he didn't look for a gang of Negroes. . . . He'd be off by hisself."

Ernie noticed a policeman say something to Muse, who then pulled out his billfold, and the two of them left. Muse returned and said, "Pardon me, Ernie, that officer acted like he was crazy. Wanted to see my ID, where am I working and all that stuff." When Muse asked why, the officer reportedly told him he better have a job "or I'll bag you." Muse told the officer, "I'm working every night. Waiting now to catch a train to go on the next job." Proclaiming that "ain't no job for a nigger," the officer promised if he was still there when he returned, "I'm going to bag every one of you niggers."[12]

A perplexed Ernie found the station manager, who herded the men inside a gate that he said was not city property. "I'll guarantee he can't touch you on railroad property," the manager told them. About five minutes later, the officer returned with several more policemen and shook his finger and said, "You niggers better be glad you where I can't get you." About a month later, after they had returned, it was "all over the *Chicago Defender, Pittsburgh Courier* [Black newspapers] that another musician, Jay McShann, had been bagged in Jacksonville and charged $25 in court." Yeah, Ernie said, "they got him." When Ernie saw the fellow Oklahoman later, he said the police made him lose a date. McShann had the money to pay them off, but they insisted he wait and pay when the court opened. "Kept them there all night and charged them $25 apiece."[13] Everybody, Ernie bemoaned, "don't know what the Black has gone through."

Throughout the late '30s and the '40s, as was the case earlier, there were usually advertisements of Ernie's upcoming appearances in local Black and sometimes white publications. There were also almost always posters produced for display in local business establishments. One undated ad from what is believed to be an Oklahoma City publication promoted a dance, "Ernie Fields and His Premiere Colored Band and 14 Artists, Saturday Night 9 until Morning (no dance Sunday Night)." It boasted "Direct from Los Angeles where they played a Thanksgiving Dance, featuring 'Pee-Wee' the bouncing, singing syncopator. $1.00 inc. tax for evening or a dime a dance at McQuin's Pavilion." The *Detroit Free Press* on March 4, 1943, announced an upcoming Ernie Fields and Orchestra stage show featuring blues singer Ada Brown and comedian Pigmeat Markham, set to run for a week, starting March 5. It was slated for the 2,500-seat Paradise Theater on Woodward Avenue at Parsons Street in Detroit. Attractions to follow were Cab Calloway, March 12; Count Basie, March 19; Erskine Hawkins, March 26; Jimmie Lunceford, April 2; Fletcher Henderson, April 16; and Louis Jordan, April 30. A promotional flyer offered a bargain: Come before 5:00 P.M. and save twenty-five cents.

An item in a society column of the *Cleveland Gazette* dated December 9, 1944, boasted that Ernie Fields opened at the New Club Alabam on Central Avenue at Forty-First Street in Los Angeles, on Friday, November 17. It said it was the orchestra's first engagement on the Pacific coast. Vocalist Melvin Moore, the item continued, "has already sent out a challenge to anyone who thinks they can beat him singing the blues." In its heyday, the Club Alabam was at the center of a "jazz corridor" along Central Avenue that included the Dunbar Hotel next door, which was considered the crown jewel of the area. Among other performers there were Lena Horne, Count Basie, Billie Holiday, and Louis Armstrong, who it is said stayed at the Dunbar Hotel and played at the Club Alabam. The club attracted interracial crowds. Movie star James Cagney attended a fundraising event there to benefit the Scottsboro Defense Fund for the nine young Black men falsely accused of raping two white women in Alabama in 1931. The restored structures now house low-income apartments.[14]

During that era, taxi dances or so-called jitneys were popular in many dance halls across the country. "Ten cents a dance," Ernie recalled. "We got to play a few of those and it caught on." As he explained it, "You would go into a place, and the guy says you've got to do so many dances an hour, to figure out the money he's going to make. If I remember it, I believe no dance could be over three minutes." The proprietor would sell tickets to men, and there was some arrangement to pay the young women who attended. The band, he said, was paid a percentage.[15] At their peak between the two world wars, taxi dances were at one point the centerpiece of many dance halls. The dances were described as well chaperoned with careful attention to the single women in the hall's employ and the long line of young male dancing partners.[16] While Ernie took every opportunity to work and keep the band working, theater engagements, not taxi dances, became his bread and butter.

In another undated letter, Ernie said, "For a long time I was known to have the fever that I could never pass up a talented musician whether I really need him or not and if they wanted to join my band." That was the case with jazz trombonist Benny Powell, whom he met in the '40s while touring in the New Orleans area." Powell (who had joined his band in 1948),[17] Ernie said, "left my group and went to Lionel Hampton and from Hamp to Basie."

Ernie was a regular at Baltimore's Royal Theatre. There were frequent ads in the *Baltimore Afro-American* mentioning him, including one on September 15, 1945, heralding "One week beginning 9/14, America's Sweetest Swing Band, Ernie Fields and His Sensational Orchestra featuring Jackie (Moms) Mabley, Mel Moore, Hop, Skip & Jump, Ballard & Ray." This ad announced "a week starting February 8, 1946" and noted "On screen, Richard Dix in *The Voice of the Whistler*." Then on December 28, 1946, another ad announced Ernie Fields was with Eddie Heywood Jr. for a "Big Holiday Stage Show."

Whenever the younger Heywood (1915–89) and Ernie's paths crossed, an embarrassing story came to Ernie's mind. He loved to tell the story of his audition for the band of Heywood's father, Eddie Heywood Sr. (1901–42), very early in his career. Heywood happened to be in Tulsa, working a circuit known as the Theatre Owners Booking Association (TOBA) that had shows in Black theaters from town to town.[18] The headliner was the comedy act Butterbeans and Susie. Heywood wanted to augment his group with a sax or perhaps a trombone player, or both, and "inquired around about musicians," stressing that potential candidates "must be able to read." He was playing at the Dixie Theatre, which was "three or four doors from the electric shop" where Ernie worked, and Heywood left word there for Ernie to come by and see him.[19]

"So, I went, and he told me he would open in a day or two and I would be able to work with him a couple of weeks," Ernie recalled.

Ernie, who prided himself on his ability to read music, went to the rehearsal, and "the first number we did, everybody was smiling," he recalled. In fact, Ernie said, they seemed surprised. Next they "threw out the finale and everybody was grinning" about his performance. However, the trumpet player sitting next to him "saw I was reading it to a T, but he says, 'Let's jam a little.'" Eddie bristled at the suggestion, noting, "You're the very one who didn't want to rehearse, and the man [Ernie] came here and played the hardest stuff we have in the book." The trumpet player gave a wink to the drummer, and when they started playing, Ernie said, "I will never forget it." It was the introduction to a number they had played. All joined in, each taking solos, and "of course I caught on," and someone said to Ernie, "You take one." Ernie did.

After the extemporaneous solo, he said, Heywood turned around in dismay "and he stuttered, you know, real bad, and goes ba-ba-ba-ba, I never seen nobody play that much music and can't play a damn thing." Reading music was no problem for Ernie. But improvising? That was a problem. Ernie admitted, "I never did amount to anything as far as jamming."

Years later he would repeat the story to Eddie Heywood Jr., who he encountered on the road after he had his own big band. "He told me his dad had told him about me."[20] Heywood Jr. would be one of the features at the Apollo Theater in Harlem and the Royal Theater in Baltimore. A jazz pianist like his father, he wrote the jazz standard "Canadian Sunset."

The *Chicago Defender*'s March 10, 1945, edition featured an ad for the Regal Theater on Forty-Seventh and South Parkway for "One Week with Dorothy Donegan, Ernie Fields and his Amazing, Razzle-Dazzle and Torrid Band plus Melvin Moore, Estelle Edson, the Four Elgins, Howell & Bowser," adding, "On Screen, Dark Waters." (Bert Howell and Buddy Bowser were a comedy team, sometimes featured with Duke Ellington's show in the late '40s.)

Ernie crisscrossed the country, across the chitlin circuit of the South, the theaters and ballrooms of the East and Midwest, the barns and arenas of the Southwest and West, as well as military bases all over the country.

Vocalist Jo Evans, who was with the orchestra in the late '40s for four years, remembered the military "had a certain amount of money they could use to hire entertainment for the bases." She recalled a base in Raleigh, North Carolina, "where snow was up to our waists," then another in Florida, "where it was hot."[21]

A *Pittsburgh Courier* review of a Memphis engagement said Evans "came on with blues which is always big in Memphis." It also cited the band's introduction of "a fine modern arrangement of 'Memphis Blues,'" noting that the house rocked with a fast-moving show from then on.[22] Evans said that during that time, they played a lot of country clubs, "very classy show places," and they paid well. "Even though it was very prejudiced then, they hired our band and we were very entertaining," she said. She performed the popular songs of the day as well as her modest hit "Goody, Goody Baby." She was also called upon to perform blues numbers, which "kind of upset the house." She said Fields insisted that she dress fine. "I had a good pair of legs and I showed them." Summing up her years, she said, "That was a good gig with Ernie Fields. I enjoyed it."[23]

7

MUSICIANS COME, MUSICIANS GO

In a lot of ways, the orchestra was like a family, with stern but tender-hearted Ernie Fields as the father. There were rules and regulations. Being tardy for a rehearsal or arriving late on the bandstand or to the gig was not tolerated. On the other hand, Ernie was not a drill sergeant. There was drinking and gambling on the bus during the long hours on the road going from gig to gig. Some got along well with the "family," others not so much.

There were lots of reasons a musician would leave the organization. Most often, they or their spouse tired of the life on the road. Some wanted to pursue solo careers or to settle into careers outside the music industry. Musicians left to go to more famous groups sometimes, other times to less-famous ones. There were instances of alums forming their own groups that stayed in one city or town, even at one venue. Some would become world-famous in their own right. Or they became teachers, postal workers, janitors, ministers—it ran the gamut. Some disappeared, never to be heard of or from again. Some died.

Probably the most heartbreaking death in Ernie's mind was that of pianist Salva Sanders, who was with his group in its earliest days, in the 1930s. Ernie would tell Salva's story over and over again. The Oklahoma native came to Ernie from the Southern Serenaders, a group that Salva led in the '20s and that Ernie would ultimately take over. (The group is not to be

ESTELL EDSON
Featured Vocalist With
Ernie Fields and his Orchestra

EXCLUSIVE MANAGEMENT
FREDERICK BROTHERS MUSIC CORPORATION
New York   Hollywood   Chicago

Estelle Edson, vocalist,
mid-1940s. Collection
of the Smithsonian
National Museum of
African American
History and Culture,
Gift of Ernie Fields Jr.
and Carmen Fields;
Ernie Fields Sr. Estate.

confused with the Southern Serenaders that some sources say was a pseud-
onym for Fletcher Henderson's Orchestra.)[1]

Sanders was described as a pianist in the Earl Hines style.[2] He was on the
first trip Ernie made to the East, in 1934, and the earlier dates in Washington
State and Oregon. "You talk about playing blues, he could play you the blues,"
Ernie said. Whenever Count Basie was in Tulsa or Ernie was in Kansas City,
or wherever the two schedules intersected on the road, like a time in Chicago,
the pals touched base. Count caught a matinee show then, and he reportedly
told Ernie, as he had many times before, "I wish I could play like Salva."[3]

It turns out, Basie may have borrowed from Sanders what became one of
his signature piano traits. "That little finger thing," Ernie called it, "where at
the end of a tune he added three notes." The figure is in the treble, at a song's
end, three staccato high octave notes—the first one an eighth note on the
second beat, followed by an eighth rest and two more eighth notes. It became

known as "Count's licks." Ernie and a few other alums from that era swear the figure came from Sanders—but they used a harsher characterization of the gesture than "borrow" when they recounted the story. Count idolized Salva, according to Ernie. "Salva had that little fingering that Count finally perfected," Ernie said, and added, "I'm telling you the truth."[4]

While Salva was good at the card games and gambling among the band members, he had a conservative streak and would give Ernie money to hold for him. The guys, he said, would kid Salva, accuse him of starving himself, because it looked like he wasn't eating very much. In fact, Salva was losing weight. He would say he wasn't hungry. After they got back from a trip in the Northwest, frugal Salva had enough money to buy a car.

Melvin Moore described Sanders as a slightly built man, maybe five foot, six inches and "very, very thin. I guess he might've weighed 110 pounds." He only knew him for about a year but said, "I liked him a lot." Moore respected him, too, as he was older, and in that day people "respected your elders," Moore said. Most of all he respected that fact that Salva sometimes chased him away from card games. "He made me stop playing, 'cause he was takin' my money, you know."[5]

At some point, it became obvious that Sanders was ill. At first, they thought maybe it was a bad cold or tuberculosis, or perhaps something more serious. People didn't know as much about cancer back then, but that is what, in hindsight, the band members think it must have been. Ernie remembers that Salva smoked a lot. Whatever it was, Ernie wanted to get his favored piano man the best of care. He offered to send him to Rochester, Minnesota, where the Mayo Clinic was located.

The clinic, founded by Dr. William Worrell Mayo, an immigrant from England, by this time was being run by his two sons, Charles Horace and William James Mayo. Go there, Ernie urged Sanders, and promised to pay his way. About this time, Charles Mayo died of pneumonia on May 26, 1939, while on a trip to Chicago to get some new suits fitted. That knocked the wind out of Salva's sails. "Why should I go there," he reasoned, "if the guy can't even cure his own brother." Barely two months later, on July 28, the other Mayo brother, William James, died of stomach cancer. He had been too weak to attend his beloved brother's funeral.

Sanders died in 1939 too. He wasn't even forty years old.

Another favorite musician was Roy Milton, who said he left Tulsa in 1935 to strike out on his own. He was friendly with a drummer, Samson Pratt (not a Fields alum), who played around Tulsa and said, "Let's go to California." So Roy told Ernie that he and Pratt were going to California. Roy Walker (who had played with Louis Armstrong) followed suit, saying he was going to try California for a while. Walker had a car. He had married a girl in Tulsa who had what Ernie called "an average job and was doing pretty good." Walker, according to Milton, told the boys they could share gas costs for the trip to California, saying, "I believe we'll do better than we're doing now." So, the three of them, Milton, Walker, and Pratt, left for the West Coast. When Milton left, Ernie had to hustle to find a vocalist and that's when he got Earl "Pee Wee" Wiley, who was with a group called the Texas Rangers. Once in California, Milton formed his own group, called His Solid Senders.

Milton performed at local clubs and recorded occasionally. He had a breakthrough hit in 1945 when his "R. M. Blues," on the Jukebox label, reached No. 2 on the *Billboard* R&B chart and No. 20 on the pop chart. His popularity continued into the early '50s with several hit recordings and personal performances. He and Ernie stayed in touch, and Ernie recorded reminiscences with his former star colleague in Ernie's Tulsa home in September 1980.

Calling Fields "Daddy," Milton said, "We had some lovely times." He noted, "I was just getting my feet wet, so to speak." The two recalled Milton's football exploits at Tulsa's Booker T. Washington High School under legendary coach Seymour Williams. Milton's grandmother made his football uniform. He was captain of the team in 1928 and was known as a triple threat. He could throw. He could run. And he could punt. He proved to his grandmother, who did not want to go to the trouble of making the uniform unless he was "sincere" about football, "I wasn't joking."

Earning a scholarship, Milton first went to Sam Houston College in Austin, Texas, and then to Langston University in Oklahoma. He joined Ernie's band from Langston. In 1931, Ernie "offered me more money than I ever made in my life," Milton said. In those days, he said, "A dollar was a dollar." And he'd been in the business ever since. Milton recalled, "When I was in your band, I didn't have dreams of going far. I was just enthused over what I was doing at the moment."

Milton's father had been a gospel singer and "brought me up in the church doing gospel singing," Milton said. Ernie said Milton had left Tulsa when things were "dull"—up and down. But times were lean in Los Angeles at first, too. Milton played what he called a series of "little gigs that would tide us over." Places in San Pedro, Wilmington, and other little suburban towns around Los Angeles, "until things got better." He had formed a quartet that included "Little Joe" Walker, Freddy Mason, and Betty Jones. Milton and his quartet finally landed at Louie's Café on Pico Boulevard in Los Angeles, and played there for four years. "For so long they called me Pico Roy," he said, as he played up and down Pico. "And that's where I started."[6]

In 1946 Milton started working at a club on First Street in San Pedro, in what was called the Cobra Room—and worked there all during the war. Meanwhile, Ernie recalled, if his band had to ride overnight to make it to the next gig, somebody invariably would say, "That's some Roy Milton stuff." Both men laughed. They recalled how Milton would play Tulsa every Thanksgiving. Ernie said it was "double Thanksgiving or Christmas or whatever you called it then," when Roy Milton came to town.

Ernie expressed admiration for the fact that Milton was able to make trips overseas, and Milton told Ernie that people outside the U.S. "know more about you [Ernie] than you know about yourself." Although Milton turned down opportunities to go overseas during World War II, he did a long stint at the Club Alabam in Los Angeles that was broadcast and released for the servicemen in Europe. Of going overseas, Ernie said, "That's the one thing that I missed out on."[7]

Milton was a featured performer in the Los Angeles Cavalcade of Jazz at Wrigley Field in 1950 along with Lionel Hampton and his orchestra, Dinah Washington, and other artists. Some sixteen thousand were reported to be in attendance. Milton continued to record and perform into the 1970s and appeared as a member of the Johnny Otis Band in the Monterey Jazz Festival in 1970. Roy Milton died in Los Angeles on September 18, 1983.

The '40s were probably the heyday for the Ernie Fields Orchestra, if you measure it by the caliber of musicians who spent some time in the group. One particular member who went on to fame was Yusef Lateef, whose given name was Bill Evans. In his autobiography *The Gentle Giant*, Lateef recalled joining the group. He'd been playing occasional jobs with the likes of Oran "Hot Lips" Page at the Apollo, and Roy Eldridge. His ability to join many different groups, he believed, was in large part because of his ability to read music well. He said, "When the opportunity came for longer employment with a territory band out of Tulsa, I took it."[8]

Lateef recalled that Ernie's group had been taken over from pianist Salva Sanders. By the time Lateef arrived, Melvin Moore was the only one left from the group that made the 1939 recordings at John Hammond's behest. During that tenure, Lateef recalled, members of the orchestra included Amos Woodruff (trumpet), Hunter (Harry) Garnett (alto sax) and Buck Douglas (tenor sax), who Lateef said "was the main soloist." In a *Cadence* magazine interview, Lateef said he recorded with Ernie Fields in 1946 or 1947, although he is not credited. "I don't know if he released 'em or what but I certainly recorded with Ernie Fields." He didn't remember any song titles.[9] Later, in his book, Lateef mused, "It would be nice to hear it"—"if it exists."[10]

Moore said he and Lateef were roommates on the road. "We smoked all the time," he recalled in an interview. "We'd get into town, get us some marijuana. That's the first thing we did."[11]

Saxophonist Jimmy Heath remembered meeting Lateef when the Fields band was passing through Wilmington, North Carolina, in 1945. At the time, Heath was with the Calvin Todd / Mel Melvin Band, and Lateef still went by his original name, Bill Evans. "We knew that this was a very good band," Heath wrote in his memoir, *I Walked with Giants: The Autobiography of Jimmy Heath*. "It wasn't quite a big band, but they had excellent arrangements" by Charles Sherrill. It was "a hell of a band" as far as Heath was concerned, much better than his group, and "a little older." Another thing Heath noted was that the band had "a very good singer, Melvin Moore."

Heath enjoyed going to the Fields group's rehearsals, mostly to hear the arrangements, which "made their sound more intricate." Of Lateef, he said he didn't notice any "overwhelming ability" on the tenor sax. "He just had a good sound."[12]

Lateef was studying Islam. He was "Muslim-minded then, and he was very sincere," Ernie remembered. At five in the morning, he would "turn to the sun and pray." He would ask Ernie "if it would be all right for the bus to stop and he would face the sun."

Lateef was "quite a showman," Ernie said. His duets with fellow tenor sax man Leon Wright would "steal the show." "Yusef was a great big guy and he would be blowing and would spread his legs out wide and Leon would get off when he started blowing and just go through his legs, and when he would do that the house would go loud."[13]

Lateef remembered Fields, he told an interviewer in 1989, as "an astute businessman."

Lateef stayed for several months "before deciding to try my luck in Chicago." He studied Islam for several years before he converted and around 1950 formally changed his name from Bill Evans to Yusef Abdul Lateef. "I took Yusef after the prophet Joseph, and Lateef meant gentle, amiable and incomprehensible."[14]

Melvin Moore was singing in Oklahoma City in the late 1930s, mostly with the Don Albert Orchestra, a well-regarded group out of New Orleans that finally came to Tulsa. "I had been going wild over Roy [Milton] and Pee Wee [Wiley], but [upon hearing Moore] this is it," Ernie said. When offered a job, Moore said he had promised his dad he would finish high school. He had another year. But he could still make a few gigs in the '30s, since Tulsa and Oklahoma City were close. Ernie thought it seemed Moore was "thinking right," plus Ernie didn't feel his band was as good as Don Albert's anyway. So, Ernie picked up somebody else, but if he had a "real good gig, I would get Melvin to come over from Oklahoma City."

Unbeknownst to Ernie, Moore, in his own words around 1936, "ran away to San Antone, Texas, to continue work with Don Albert." He left behind a fifteen-minute radio show that had made him well known to many in Oklahoma City—where he was considered, in his words, "a top singer." He said of joining Albert, "I couldn't wait to do that!" But when Moore's father learned his son was dropping out, he "like to died about that: 'three credits and don't want to finish high school, blah, blah, blah.'" During the time with Albert, travels took him to New York. When Ernie learned that he had dropped out of school, Moore said, Ernie "cussed me out." He said, "Man, you're not going back to finish?" Moore did return to high school and finished "in '38—or probably it was '37," he recounted. Near the Christmas holidays he got an invitation to go to Tulsa and work with the Fields organization. He did, and shortly thereafter he joined full time, for, he said, either three or five dollars a night, just in time for a tour in the West. "I wanted to travel some," he said. "I'd never gone west."

"I was supposed to go to Langston University, but I told my dad, 'Man, I've been out, I've seen what life's about, and you'd only be throwing your money away.'"[15]

Moore would join card games with the guys and acknowledged that Salva Sanders was "a big hustler and most of the time he'd win." The games were mostly poker or blackjack, and Moore said that whatever they played, Salva "would always win." They'd play on the bus, mostly, and sometimes after dances ended, back in the hotel or rooming house. But cards were not Moore's only weakness. He admitted with a laugh that every now and then, "I'd get drunk and want to fight everybody."[16]

Much later, the two musicians would laugh and kid each other, each blaming himself for Moore staying with the band so long and perhaps missing opportunities for success as a single act. "As I said, we were just too loyal to each other," said Ernie. He believed a bandstand accident might have had something to do with it. While the band was down south somewhere, Moore was hanging up a speaker. "We didn't have all these extra roadies that we call them now," so Ernie said he paid Moore a little extra for putting up the speaker. He slipped off a ladder and hurt his head, badly enough to be hospitalized for at least two weeks. The band left him behind "for a while" to recuperate.[17]

During Moore's hospitalization, Ernie continued to pay his salary. Ernie regretted that decision later, because "after then Melvin just knew that he shouldn't leave me." Dubbed the bronze Perry Como, Moore finally left

Fields to go with Dizzy Gillespie's Big Band around 1949 or 1950. He later spent time with the popular Lucky Millinder Orchestra. Rumor had it that Moore "had part ownership in your [Ernie's] band, making him loyal for so long," mused Preston Love, who was in Millinder's orchestra with Moore.[18] Millinder (1910–66), who reportedly could neither read nor write music, play an instrument, or sing, had a highly regarded orchestra.

Moore next briefly joined the New York City–based orchestra as a featured vocalist led by pianist Elliott Lawrence, who was white. Lawrence had booked a tour down south and sent promotional photos of Moore to the booking agency. The agency suggested Lawrence leave Moore behind. In a handwritten note, Ernie said that Lawrence canceled the southern tour when the promoter saw Moore's picture and asked Lawrence to slight Moore. "He wouldn't go," Ernie said. (Lawrence would go on to be conductor and musical director for every Tony Awards telecast from 1965 to 2011, among many other major musical broadcasts. Born February 14, 1925, in Philadelphia, Lawrence died July 2, 2021, in New York City.)

Moore looked at his long Ernie Fields tenure this way: "If I had to do it [again], I'd probably do it the same way. . . . Ernie has always been all right with me, all the way down through the years, you know." He added, "I mean, I've never wanted to be a star. I just like to sing."[19]

During the relationship, which extended throughout the rest of their lives, Ernie and Moore each maintained an unshakeable admiration and respect for the other. Ernie thought there was no other vocalist who matched Moore's talent. Ernie overlooked Moore's affinity for games of chance with cards—and what others in the band considered his way with women.

Moore's flirtations led to the birth of his daughter, Melba, on September 29, 1939. Melba's mother, Catherine Davidson, "presented" the child to a surprised Moore during one of the band's many Dallas stopovers, Moore recalled. Melba would grow up to be a singer in her own right, using the professional name Melba Joyce. She described her absent father, who did not marry her mother, as devoted and watchful. "I knew he loved me deeply, even though he was not home a lot," she said in a telephone interview in 2019 from her New York City home. Her father was "warm, lovely, wanted to teach me and [for me] to know stuff." Telephone calls came from around the world during his travels not only with Ernie Fields, but later with Dizzy

Gillespie, Lucky Millinder, and the Ink Spots. Melba said her father spoiled her with "so many dolls, and beautiful clothes." He also gifted her a type-writer, because, as he told her, he "thought you had something to say."[20]

Fields felt Moore's artistry was unmatched, believing he was even better than the great Ella Fitzgerald and "should have been as big as Billy Eckstine. He could scat like Ella and do jazz and turn right around and sing you the blues and then sing you any sweet number," he said.[21]

Moore had a sense of pride about his craft, and coupled it with a wicked sense of humor. He would often proclaim, "I'm a vocalist—not an auto mechanic, travel agent, red cap" or anything else. "I'm a vocalist."

Ernie explained, "If one of the drivers or valets asked Melvin for a wrench or something, he'd say, 'What do you think we're paying you for? I'm a vocalist, don't ask me for nothing.'" He was entitled to the bragging rights; one report noted that famed critic Leonard Feather placed Moore at the top of his 1946 rankings of swing singers.[22]

Ernie Fields (*left*) with his favorite vocalist, Melvin Moore, at the Rose Room in Dallas, early 1940s. Author collection.

Ernie from time to time rattled off the list of musicians he'd worked with, famous and not so famous, and would make this observation: Even if he got out of the band and didn't get big, he undoubtedly was worth something, "else I wouldn't have had him in the band." To Ernie, "A man that perhaps never takes a solo is just as important in the part that he's playing as that soloist, because most likely, he is setting a riff to help send that soloist." Please, he implored me often, "mention as many names at least that I give you, and I still would be leaving out some, I'm quite sure."

Probably the most famous musician to "get away" was a young trumpet player named Miles Davis. "I could have had him in my band once," Ernie said.[23]

"In fact," Moore claimed, "I found Miles!" Moore insisted he was the first to meet and advocate for Davis. As Moore told the story, the orchestra had some dates in the Saint Louis–East Saint Louis area. He said that Ernie's trumpet player had gone to Boston to bury his dad, so "we were missing a trumpet player." He boasted he heard the five-piece band that Davis was performing with at an East Saint Louis club. And "this little cat was playing funny, you know. He had a different style, but it was real, real soft." Ernie said it seemed like "every time I look up, there would be Miles." Moore finally asked Davis if he was ready to do a little traveling and the answer was, "Maybe so, man." Since Ernie's group was in Saint Louis for a week, Moore said, he talked Davis into going with them. "We went to a place called Mounds, Illinois, right out of East St. Louis." After the week, Ernie said something like, "The little cat plays nice, but you can't find him, can't hear him back there."[24]

Ernie described it this way: "Who the hell knows what he's playing?" Apparently, he played very softly. So, said Moore, "We had to send him home."[25] Years later, Ernie, a little sheepishly, would say, "Miles! I could have had him in my band."[26] René Hall would continue to tell the story about Davis with a laugh. "Ernie wouldn't fool with him!"[27]

SOMETHING A
LITTLE DIFFERENT

Some may call it a gimmick. For Ernie Fields, creative entertainment was how he kept going, sold his organization to patrons and reinvented himself to distinguish himself from his peers. In some forty years leading the organization, he would try many different "tricks" to keep his audience entertained—whether musically on the theater bandstand or with a dance hall floor show. At first, he used stock arrangements of the popular tunes of the day, but he was always on the lookout for something new, different, and unique. White arranger Dave Duncan from Ponca City, Oklahoma, formerly with Jack Teagarden's group, did arrangements for the Fields organization in the 1930s. Then there were René Hall, Charles Sherrill, and Jack "Earlie" Scott. Ernie tried for "a long time," he said, without success, to attract pianist and arranger Tadd Dameron (born February 21, 1917; died March 8, 1965), who would become known as the most influential arranger in the bebop era. "I'd say to René, you see how those arrangements are? They are good and it's not a lot of notes," Ernie said. Basie's band, Ernie maintained, was known for its "economy of notes." Ernie wanted his sound not to be ordinary, to be special so as to appeal to what in modern times became known as a "crossover" audience. Hall was a gifted "triple threat" who played trombone and guitar and arranged, but some of the musicians complained that his pieces were often intricate, with "too many notes." Pianist Rozelle Claxton, who was enlisted for the trip to New York City in 1939 at John Hammond's

THOS HODGE, Latin one Leg Dancer
Featured ERNIE FIELDS Orchestra

ERNIE FIELDS ARTISTS
1852 N. Peoria Ave
Tulsa 10, Okla.

Thomas Hodge, a one-legged dancer, late 1940s or early 1950s. Author collection.

inducement, also provided well-regarded arrangements. During the '50s, Scott did some arrangements, but was regarded more as a copyist, providing instrumentation for the arrangements as well as being a versatile musician on guitar, electric bass, and keyboard. Trombone player Parker Berry was also one of Ernie's favorite arrangers.

But it wasn't only about music. It was about a show! For that, Ernie counted on a variety of featured singers, from Melvin Moore and Leora Davis in the '30s to Ann Walls and "Little" Clifford Watson in the '50s and '60s. There also was a collection of dancers—the exotic Clarise Ford (referred to by vocalist Jo Evans as a "shake dancer" and in at least one newspaper mentioned as "Rose Ford, Exotic Dancer De Luxe"[1]) and a series of one-legged dancers that included Thomas Hodge and Frank James. Yes, one-legged dancers. Hall once said that between "Mr. Upside Down" and the one-legged dancers, Fields had quite a combination. "You could have opened up your own Barnum Bailey," Hall teased, referring to the famous circus master P. T. Barnum and the Barnum & Bailey Circus. "Barnum Fields," he said.

Tulsa native Frank
James dancing on
one leg, late 1940s or
early 1950s. Author
collection.

The featured act—not "peg-leg," some of the promotions noted, but one-legged—would begin with Hodge on crutches and the exotic dancer on stage or the front part of the dance floor near the bandstand. The two would dance, dance, dance together. The exotic dancer would then take a solo, and Ernie would come out and kick one of the crutches away from Hodge. The music would continue. Then the one-legged dancer would begin his solo with fancy moves. At some point, the second crutch would be kicked away and solo would continue. Two men, Hodge and James, were featured this way during extended tenures with the orchestra.

Of the one-legged dancers Fields employed, Tulsa native James, who joined the band around 1947, would gain modest fame in his own right. As James told the story, he lost his leg in Tulsa in a 1947 accident when he was pinned between two cars. After three months in the hospital, he went out dancing after only a week back at home. "I watched for a while, then decided I could try it without crutches. An old friend danced with me. Pretty soon we were jitterbugging." He added, "Perhaps the couple of drinks I had earlier gave me the courage but I found I still had it." Ernie Fields's dance band was there that night, and shortly James had a place in the band." One newspaper review noted his dance moves "would defy the balance on many a two-footed person."[2] Another article in the December 22, 1951, edition of the *Oklahoma City Black Dispatch* said, when James dances, "the crowd is hushed and attentive with men and women alike shaking their heads in utter disbelief."[3]

James was not the only one-legged performer over the years. From time to time, a one-legged dancer would leave the organization. With what was considered some speed, Ernie had a replacement ready. It happened often enough that the joke among the band members was that the dancers were former musicians who had crossed Ernie, been hobbled, and were kept on his farm—to be brought up from the "reserves"—when needed.

There were other show aspects. Advertisements in the mid-1930s and early 1940s referenced the Four Happy Jacksons, or the Happy Jackson Quartet. For gigs in western Massachusetts in the summer of 1934, after the Jacksons had played with Cab Calloway in Albany, one newspaper ad referred to the Jackson Four as the "Mills Brothers of the South,"[4] and another called the quartet "the Mills Bros. of Savannah, Ga."[5] The Mills Brothers, a singing group from Ohio who used their voices, in four-part harmony, to imitate orchestra instruments, had become a nationwide sensation on radio and in films. Whatever became of the Four Happy Jacksons is anybody's guess. A Google search only comes up with the Jackson Five, featuring Michael Jackson, and then a reference to the jazz vibraphonist Milt Jackson's Quartet.

Jazz violins were sometimes featured with some big organizations, but not all the time. Of those featured, Claude "Fiddler" Williams (1908–2004) was among the most well-known. Williams had carved out a niche. Initially, the Muskogee, Oklahoma, native became known as the first guitarist to record with Count Basie. But after hearing a violin performance, he decided that instrument was for him and joined up with the Dark Clouds of Joy, led first by Terrence "Tee" Holder and later Andy Kirk (then renamed the Twelve Clouds of Joy). Soon Williams's swinging jazz-bluesy style had an admirer in a young Tulsa native, O. Z. Burley. Burley's jazz inclination was also infused with some of the popular country and western sounds of the region. Ernie, if anything, wanted to please an audience.

While Burley was still in high school, he caught Ernie's attention. He was short in stature, barely five feet tall, but was an intuitive, raw talent. Ernie said Burley, "a youngster going to school," quit high school and began playing with him (and others) and had a regular job. The kid had real talent. "Really, in age and experience, O. Z. wasn't as good. But as far as the average person that just didn't know, he could be considered very, very good," Ernie said. He felt the young man was "getting on the wrong track fast," and tried to encourage him to stay in school. He felt Burley could "give Fiddler a fit anytime" and was destined to be as good.

Fields loved to feature Burley, because when he ran across groups where Claude was featured, "I could feature a fiddle, too." Since he played to both white and Black audiences, "I could throw in one of those Bob Wills tunes, then have the fiddle working, and O. Z. was just a lifesaver to that."

There was also an unexpected specialty act—Gab Galloway. The moniker Gab, not Cab, Galloway was the creation of a promotion agency. McFadden was the name Ernie remembered, even though he didn't recall where he met the booking agent or his first name. But he vividly remembered what he thought was an unsavory trick. If nothing else, Ernie considered himself a man of integrity, a man of honor—and a man whose word was worth something. As he remembered it, McFadden heard the band and promised a tour and reliable bookings with ironclad contracts. "If I'm going to get it, I'm going to get it," he told Ernie. "But you'll have something to expect. A good percentage deal." Stuff like that.

Pee Wee Wiley was Ernie's star vocalist then, and he apparently bore an ever so slight resemblance to the popular "Hi-de-hi-de ho" band leader, Cab Calloway, and hence the Gab Galloway ruse. "He [McFadden] didn't tell me at first, before it ended up when he sent me the window cards," Ernie said. The band leader didn't like what he saw, but it was too late.

Cab Calloway was known for shaking his long, very straight hair when he sang. It became a trademark, a special affectation, and sometimes the butt of jokes. When Ernie was doing a show with Moms Mabley once, she turned her attention to Ernie's piano player, Charles Sherrill, also known as "Jazz Baby." In her joke, Cab Calloway was her man. She'd turn to Sherrill and say, "Boy, you can play that piano, but them knots in your hair, you just can't shake it and make your hair come down like Cab." The tricky promoter never made a reference to the Fields singer's appearance, only that his vocalist was "as good as Cab." He then had window cards made up featuring "Gab," G-A-B. "But everybody just looking at it thought it was Cab," Ernie fumed.

He started the tour.

Several dates in Kansas or Missouri were lined up. On the very first one, Ernie remembered, they had a decent-sized crowd. Everything was going "good," he said. The band was nice, other than that lie about Gab Galloway. Ernie said he called on Pee Wee to do a number. Next thing he knew—and he noted, "You know it takes a Negro"—some in the audience "went to hollering, 'When he gonna shake his head and make his hair come down?'" The house was in an uproar. Ernie saw McFadden was in the house, "just grinning and everything." A frantic Ernie found him and asked did he hear what folks were saying? "Ah, they'll stop. Not as good a job as he's doing." But Ernie wasn't so worried about the job Pee Wee was doing as about some who were talking about getting their money back. "Of course, him being a paddy," Ernie explained, "he and the proprietor came to the bandstand and said, 'You all are reading that wrong. That is Gab Galloway, not Calloway." Of course, with two white men saying it, the crowd got quiet and the show went on, Ernie recalled. "They were fixing to tear things up till they spoke up. Pee Wee did the rest of the program being Gab Galloway," Ernie said. "He tore it up. He was just terrific." They all laughed about it after. "All that paddy got to do is say something and it must be correct."

"Gab" went on to make three or four engagements after that, but Ernie said, "It begins to be too much of a headache." He told McFadden it was misrepresenting, and "I don't want to do that."

He said, "I'm trying to get on up there," and he didn't want a bad reputation. He told the promoter that anytime "we go anymore, it's going to be Ernie Fields Band, none of that Gab deal."

He and McFadden didn't "have any falling out or anything," Ernie said. "I just had them to understand it had to be my name." The band members backed him up, some saying, "Maybe you not big enough to be this and that but you big enough for us. And we got enough good a band, nobody don't have to call us anything else." All the guys, he said, were in his corner. No more Gab Galloway![6]

But there were other gimmicks. Long before Flip Wilson introduced "Geraldine" to the world on his television show—the character was played by Wilson decked out in a dress and wig—Ernie had tried something similar. It was with two tenor sax men, Leon Wright and Harold "Geezil" Minerve, who often had a duet together; Wright would wear a dress for this specialty act.

Listening to the opinions of the guys, and to his own powerful conscience, which dictated that he do the right thing, formed a hallmark trait for Ernie. Eugene White, known as Mr. Upside Down, was a Tulsa resident who had toured with the band on the West Coast. The act had Ernie standing, holding a microphone, and smiling, while White stood on his head singing. This captured the attention of a photographer. As Hall would tell the story, the photographer had been engaged to make promotional pictures of two singers with the band, White and Leora Davis. As fate would have it, the photo of Mr. Upside Down appeared soon after the session, in *Jet*, a popular Black weekly magazine, sister publication to the trailblazing monthly *Ebony*. Davis was incensed that White got the national spotlight. Some others in the band complained to Ernie that White needed better shoes, as often those he wore were scuffed and well worn. Others complained that White's legs were "ashy" and he should generally be better groomed, as was Ernie's expectation and demand of all others with the organization.

They need not fret for long. During a subsequent performance, White went into his upside-down act, and to everyone's dismay, a pistol fell out of his pocket as he was singing on his head. That was it.

Ernie fired him.

❦ 9 ❧

KEEPING HIS NAME
FRONT AND CENTER

After Ernie left New York around 1940, the challenge was to keep working and keep building on the New York success. René Hall had surmised the main reason for Ernie's group returning to Tulsa was that Hammond and Alexander's focus was mainly on Count Basie and assuring his success. Multimillionaire Hammond, Hall said, "had sunk so much money into Basic's Orchestra till he didn't want any band to eclipse them."[1] As promised, Alexander delivered on dates here and there, mostly on the East Coast. Meanwhile, Ernie reached out to other booking agents and agencies, such as H. E. Schoonover of Idaho and Reg Marshall out of Hollywood, California, which resulted in tours to the Northwest and the West Coast.

"We made that round again, which was not new to us at all," Ernie observed.

Always, always, the road led back to Tulsa. In the Portland, Oregon, area Ernie heard two men from Seattle, pianist Creon Thomas and sax man and arranger Kenny Pernell, who joined the group. Thomas "played a little fiddle," too, Ernie said. Important in the Oklahoma, Texas, and Kansas area, "I could throw in a little western, country-western touch at times, and besides that, he played very nice jazz fiddle." Ernie prided himself on having a variety "of whatever the paying customer asked for."

About that time, he had the opportunity to make a tour with Bill "Bojangles" Robinson (born May 25, 1878; died November 25, 1949), believed to be the highest-paid entertainer in America in the first half of the twentieth century. Robinson had distinguished himself not only as a tap dancer but also as a movie star, having taught child star Shirley Temple how to dance. Ernie said the tour was set up by an agency he had signed with that apparently had a relationship with Marty Forkins, Robinson's longtime agent. It was explained to Fields that Robinson wanted "everything to be perfect, and so on and so forth," which proved, he said, "to be exactly right." Ernie said Robinson was described as kind of hard to get along with, but good at heart.

A note in the *Dallas Morning News* made mention of the potential pairing: "Negotiations were brewing Monday for a New Year's Eve show and dance at Fair Park Roller Rink which may see the appearance here of Bill Robinson, the star Negro tap dancer." It continued, "If Robinson can be obtained the entertainment will be built around a colored revue with music by Ernie Fields' Swing Band."[2]

From the beginning Ernie insisted, "I had to be billed." It was understood that Bill Robinson was heading the show, but "I had to be billed as Ernie Fields Orchestra." In that way, Fields was able to get his name in major theaters, exposure that he otherwise might not have gained that soon, around '40 or '41. He had already done the average venues that Black bands performed. "A-class" venues were the Regal in Chicago, the Howard Theatre in Washington, D.C., the Royal in Baltimore, and the Apollo in New York City. And there were some small Black theaters in the South and Midwest. But this time, he was going through with Bill Robinson in some of the top houses in the country. After the tour was over, "I'd been in bigger and better theaters and it was nice publicity to say that I had worked there—and got a very fine review."

That was the case with the Oriental Theatre in Chicago, where he got an "extraordinary review." The theater, which had opened in 1926 as a first-run movie house, had over two thousand seats. Another Chicago show was front-page news, in the April 4, 1942, edition of the *Evansville Argus* newspaper, a small Black weekly in Indiana that published from 1938 through 1942. Sure enough, Robinson was the name in the headline (albeit misspelled): "Bill 'Bojanges' Robinson And Big Show at Coliseum Tonite."

But Ernie Fields was in the story too. "Ernie Fields, whose orchestra will augment the great acts," the paragraph began. After the Robinson stage show, which would start at 9:00 P.M. and cost sixty cents, "Fields will also play a dance, starting at 10:30 P.M." The article also noted the orchestra was "in third place in the 1941 *Chicago Defender* popularity band contest and high 'up in the money' in the *Pittsburgh Courier*'s. He has a swing band that is really mellow." It also noted that those who wanted to stay for the dance would have to pay an additional ninety-nine cents. The Coliseum was known then as the premier location for events.

For Ernie's Oriental Theatre appearance in Chicago, the services of tailor Harold C. Fox were enlisted. He made the uniforms for the group. In a handwritten letter to Ernie years later, Fox recalled that white promoter Erv Brabec (who would become president of MCI, one of the largest music corporations in the U.S. and Europe) approached him Wednesday at noon, got him the measurements on Friday morning, and "you opened in Fox Bros. swinging uniforms. Swinging Band. Swinging uniforms." He said Ernie Fields was "my first band that I dressed and then went on to fame as the tailor to the entertainment World. After you and the great recommendations from all your band members, twas a piece of cake, and I can honestly say I made costumes for about 98% of all show people." Fox's bragging was perhaps not an exaggeration, as a *New York Times* obituary on August 1, 1996, said he was the clothier of choice for big band musicians like Dizzy Gillespie, Woody Herman, Stan Kenton, Louis Armstrong, and others. Fox was also credited with inventing and naming the "Zoot suit." His letter to Ernie noted, "So, the big surprise!! I went to the Oriental to see my uniforms and take care of any complaints and I did get to see Bojangles and your great band, and what a show band. Wow." Fox further claimed that he was a musician before he inherited Fox Brothers Tailors, and "when I heard your great band, I was so inspired, I decided to put together a band in Chicago. It was the Jimmy Dale Band." He boasted it was a mixed band, "black and white musicians playing together in harmony and loving each other and fighting Jim Crow etc. on all fronts."

The association with Robinson allowed Fields to get some mileage out of his Vocalion recordings, some of which were unknown to those audiences. "The group stayed together quite a while following the Robinson tour," he said, and he considered it "one of my better groups." He recalled that the group included Paul Quinichette on tenor—similar in style to Lester Young and Luther West, top first alto man—and that doors to theaters like the

Oriental, previously out of reach, were open, thanks to the Bojangles name. Also helpful in the region was Chicago bandleader King Kolax, who helped secure one-nighters after that. Kolax was also an executive with the local Chicago musicians' union.

Dayton, Ohio–based journalist and music critic A. S. Kany, who also was a *Billboard* "stringer," reviewed the group's Colonial Theater appearance in Dayton for the *Journal Herald* newspaper. He heaped praise on Robinson's performance and his youthful appearance. "He informs the audience he is 63 years of age . . . and he's as lithe and limber as a youngster of 20." He also expressed admiration for the Fields group that accompanied Robinson: "furnishing a large part of the program . . . and put over some hot numbers [that] prove themselves great audience favorites."

Kany continued: "The band [opens with] a special arrangement of 'Good Enough to Keep,' presents 'Moonlight Cocktail' in a manner making it even more beautiful than ordinarily, with the electric guitar carrying the melody, and gets right into the groove with Ernie's own special arrangement of 'Swing Junior' in which the drummer goes places the average skin-beater wouldn't dare to tread." Kany deemed the two vocalists, Melvin Moore and Estelle Edson, "excellent," praising Edson for her version of "I Don't Want to Walk without You" with its "articulation as clear-cut as crystal" and for going "hi-de-ho with 'Swing Time in Harlem.'" He called Melvin Moore "outstanding with 'White Cliffs of Dover' and other numbers." The program was rounded out with Ross and McCain, who formed "a smart, sleek dance team, presenting fancy ballroom figures and then swing about with abandon, but not abandoning the utmost grace imaginable."[3]

Years later, in a joint interview with another territory bandleader, Clarence Love, Ernie said that insisting on keeping his name up front made a big difference for him. Love's group "was such a smooth band," Ernie said. "You talk about admiring a band, I did. But Clarence made his big mistake by not insisting on his name being used." Ernie claimed that decision "was his ruination."[4]

The Ernie Fields name was mentioned prominently in a short item in the October 1944 *Baltimore Afro-American* about a tour with singer-pianist Dorothy Donegan. It noted Fields's band would be "furnishing the musical background for the all-colored vaudeville unit" set to tour the nation's

Sidewalk sign for
Bill Robinson Revue,
early 1940s. Author
collection.

theaters. The first date, it read, "will be January 18, 1945 at Chicago's Regal
Theatre." Providing the "background" music was no problem for Ernie as
long as it was always clear that it was *his* band and musicians.

Helen Humes (June 23, 1913–September 9, 1981) had been with the Basie
band for several years before pursuing a solo career. She too, would credit
John Hammond's discovery with boosting her visibility. The talent scout–
producer heard her in New York, singing with Al Sears at the Renaissance
Club. Through Hammond, she recorded with the Harry James Orchestra
and joined the Basie organization. Hammond produced the second Carnegie
Hall extravaganza, From Spirituals to Swing, where Humes and pianist-
composer James P. Johnson were featured performers with Basie. The performance was on Christmas Eve 1939. During her solo career, Humes often
played New York's Café Society, accompanied often by Teddy Wilson and
Art Tatum, the Famous Door with Benny Carter and the Village Vanguard
with Eddie Heywood Sr.

During a solo venture, Humes's agent or promoter or "someone," according to Ernie, got in touch with him in Indianapolis. "I had begun to make some noise," he said. They wanted to make a tour and went to "laying down money," he recalled on a self-recorded tape. And they said, "We know the biggest amount it will cost your band, but now, we got to pay Helen so much 'cause we have advertising her name. We won't have to give her no more money. It will be Helen Humes's band." Ernie said, "Hell, no. Forget it." He told them it was going to be Ernie Fields featuring Helen Humes. "I got them jarred right quick on that," he said. They did make a "nice tour," believed to be in 1942, he said. He also noted Humes was a nice person to get along with. "No grumbling whatsoever." He said she got the money she was getting and was glad to work and have a good backup band."[5]

Ernie always saw that it was in "my name." "Whoever it was, I would feature them, and I'd feature them just as big as we could make it." But he always insisted it be the Ernie Fields Band. "I stood up for that."

He also stood for playing all the angles.

By the mid-1940s, without a recording contract, he started his own label, Frisco Records, based in Tulsa. Among its modest releases were "E. F. Boogie" (which Ernie wrote) and "Thursday Evening Blues," featuring Melvin

Label for "Thursday Evening Blues," Frisco records. Courtesy of Dan Kochakian.

Moore vocals, released in 1947. He also re-recorded "T-Town Blues" in 1949, with vocalist Teddy Cole instead of Melvin Moore, who was by that time with Dizzy Gillespie. Other recordings included "Big Lou" and "Christopher Goes Bebop," penned by Ernie and his pal René Hall, and "Traveling Blues" written by Fields and someone named Dortch.

"I wanted the idea to be national, and I had an artist draw out the Golden Gate Bridge and had the Frisco name and the picture of the bridge. I did several numbers on there and it did very well,"[6] Ernie recalled. He provided his own packaging and was his own distributor. He would send the records to promoters, booking agents, and others to assure them his organization was as active as his peers of the day—even though it wasn't. Tulsa businessman Edwin Elkins Conley (1915–89) was his partner. Conley, who had a pressing plant in Tulsa, was also a songwriter who also had established another record company. Ernie's only national hits came in 1939 and 1959, "but I recorded all in between there," he said.[7]

He insisted, however, "Frisco was my label and we only recorded my band, nobody else."[8]

Ernie also took advantage of every publicity opportunity, noting a reader poll published December 20, 1941, in the *Chicago Defender* newspaper that placed him eighth on a list of best bands, with 16,508 votes—right behind Louis Armstrong's 17,676 votes, and just ahead of Earl Hines, who got 14,150 votes. Count Basie topped the list with 30,100 votes. A similar 1949 poll in the *Pittsburgh Courier* was headlined "Top Ten Bands in Land Picked in Courier Poll." There was Ernie Fields, smiling in a photo with the March 26 report, along with Erskine Hawkins, Duke Ellington, Stan Kenton, and Woody Herman. The story said, in part, "Ernie has a band that can jump, switch to sweet numbers and mix 'em for any dance crowd. Fields has played for many big festivals and special events as well as doing a top job in night clubs and one-nighters. Style marks this organization."

❦ 10 ❧

OLD HABITS DIE HARD

The music landscape is littered with territory bands of the 1920s and 1930s who, for various reasons, did not make it past the 1940s or 1950s. Many traveled beyond their southern or midwestern home bases, going east to New York City, north into Canada, west to the Northwest, and most anywhere in between. These groups, like the Fields organization, were an invaluable training ground for countless great and not-so-great musicians who switched from band to band or established their own groups. That many of the highly regarded orchestras are not known is partly because they did not get the opportunity to record. Their skills and triumphs reside, for the most part, only in the minds of the people who witnessed their artistry up close.

That is the case with Terrence "Tee" Holder.

Holder (1895–1983) was much admired for at least two reasons. First of all, he purportedly had one of the sweetest sounds heard from a trumpet player. He was one of the "popular trumpet stars of the Southwest," preeminent in Dallas and its environs, according to composer-historian Gunther Schuller. Many concur with that talent assessment, but it cannot be confirmed because, as far as anyone knows, Holder never cut a record. Ernie said, "Look like he could just develop and make a band." In that day, in the late '20s and early '30s, the two big names in bands in the Southwest were Alphonso Trent (1902–59) and Holder.

Trent enjoyed impressive firsts, among them having the first Black ensemble to work all-white hotels in Texas. They played the Adolphus Hotel in Dallas for eighteen straight months, starting in 1925—a record never matched. During that stint, Trent's was the first Black group to broadcast

Members of the Ernie Fields Band pose on the A-24 "Dauntless" fuselage assembly line.

Ernie Fields stands in the cockpit of an A-24 Dauntless aircraft fuselage during an open house at the McDonnell Douglas plant no. 3 in Tulsa to show off its assembly line, circa 1942 or 1943. Courtesy of Tulsa Air and Space Museum.

from a major hotel outside New York City, on the 50,000-watt KFAA radio station in Dallas. Additionally, Trent's band is believed to be one of the first to use the string bass as well as a "band singer" in an orchestra in 1924, ahead of Bing Crosby. Trent alums include Harry "Sweets" Edison and Sy Oliver.[1]

Whenever the old-timers got together and called the roll, Holder's name would be in that number. Besides the sweet, soft yet full sound he could make without the benefit of a mute, Holder could also assemble some of the most talented musicians ever in his orchestras. Names like Budd Johnson, a reed man and arranger; Carl "Tatti" Smith, trumpet; Harry Lawson, trumpet; Lloyd Glenn, piano and arrangements; Buddy Tate and Earl Bostic (a Tulsa native), tenor saxes; Fats Wall, alto; Andy Kirk, tuba and bass saxophone, who in 1926 joined the Texas-based band and later ended up leading it; saxophonist John Williams and his wife, Mary Lou; and many, many others. Frequent road trips moved the group to clubs and ballrooms between Dallas, Fort Worth, Tulsa, Oklahoma City, Kansas City, Little

Rock, and back to Texas. Holder was known to go toe to toe to take on the Blue Devils, Bennie Moten, and other prestige bands of the area in popular musical "battles of bands."

Ernie considered the Muskogee resident Holder his friend. Trent and Holder were hot stuff of the region in those days, and as a fledgling musician and bandleader, Ernie was glad for their attention and guidance. Holder had come from pianist Al Trent's band—where he is believed to have been one of the originals—and formed his own group, the Dark Clouds of Joy. Trumpet player Holder, who moved his group to Tulsa around 1927, would hold what was called "closed rehearsals." Not just anybody could come sit in or even sit and listen. "You'd come to the door and they would say, Ernie Fields is here, he's got a little band, and he [Holder] would say, let him in. And then I'd go and rehearse, and I learned an awful lot from him," Ernie recounted.

On one such occasion Ernie heard Holder lecturing his guys, telling them, "I don't want to see what happened last night." Apparently, someone playing a solo made an error and the others on the bandstand started laughing. "Everybody went looking around at each other." The leader told them if they weren't playing their horn and setting the rhythm for the soloist, if he played anything wrong, "You better be grinning and clapping your hand like he played it right." He made it clear he didn't want to see that happen, and the guys, Ernie said, "took it in."[2]

The group reportedly played arrangements that they worked out by ear and remembered by rote. Holder was hard-driving and unrelenting about rehearsals. Holder and Ernie were pretty close, Ernie said, especially after Kirk went on to the "big time" with Holder's band.

But, alas, Holder's other claim to fame was that he was a schemer—using all manner of trickery to evade his many debts. Various reference sources refer euphemistically to Holder having an "unstable personality" or being prone to "domestic" and financial troubles. All considered him a brilliant trumpet soloist but a poor band manager. Ernie gave one example: Holder would pull into a service station and in addition to filling up his vehicle with gasoline, he would order anything from new tires to an oil change or a brake job. He would indicate to the attendant, sometimes right away, sometimes a little later, that he was at that moment short of cash but he was working in town that night. Chances are, Ernie said, there was a poster or placard

in the station window or nearby business promoting the dance that evening. "I guess you saw that sign," Holder would say. "Oh yeah, that's me."
The impressed but unwitting attendant would provide service, and then for
the oil change would ask what kind of oil he preferred. Holder's usual reply,
"Make it Quaker State." He liked the top of the line whenever possible. It
got to be an inside joke among Ernie's musicians whenever there was an
occasion for an oil change—somebody would invariably shout out, "Make
it Quaker State." Jeff Carrington recalled, "After we got through with work,
Tee would say, let's get packed up and get to the next tittie." When reminded
that he'd promised to go back and pay the filling station, Holder would say,
"Shit, that white man don't need that money. Let's go."[3]

But that was not the most galling of Holder's escapades. What got him in
trouble and led to him losing the confidence of his musicians, and ultimately
losing his band, was that he seldom paid them. Holder, described as "bald-
ing with a broad smashed nose and lantern jaw," had a gambling problem.[4]
Poker, craps, anything. "He would gamble with all the guys' money," Ernie
said. "I was right there." Ernie said, "He had about a ten- or twelve-piece
band, which was big, they were only getting about $700 a week, that's less
than a hundred dollars apiece." Holder was married to a woman in Dallas,
and when he got paid by promoter William P. Falkenberg, he would walk
out the door, get in his car, and head for Dallas. If he won, when he came
back, they would get their money and might get a tip. "But if he lost, I'll see
you next week."[5] Sometimes, Ernie said, he'd come back and "wouldn't have
a damn penny." It would pile up so that he was almost always owing the
guys. "He was a gambler from his heart," Ernie said.[6] Kirk would sometimes
come by the electric shop where Ernie worked to borrow a dollar here and
there—until "Tee came back or he could draw from Falkenberg," who was
running the Louvre Ballroom, where the group performed.

Most of the musicians were living at the Small Hotel, near what was
known as "deep" Greenwood Avenue, in the famed former Black Wall Street
district. That was the big Black hotel then, where traveling entertainers of
note stayed when in town. Owner Wellington Small was mad when the
band members couldn't pay, according to Falkenberg, but he didn't blame
the guys, because he knew what was happening.

"So, one-time Tee was just gone just one time too many," Ernie recounted.[7] Falkenberg, who was president of the Tulsa Amusement Company and manager of the popular music venue Crystal Park, said he told the guys, "You all are getting to be too much of a headache. Can anybody else run the band? I don't have anything against Tee, but I'm surprised you all are not tired of it. You begging me for money, after I already paid Tee. You owe your hotel bill, you got nothing to eat. You need somebody else to handle the money." Music historian Gunther Schuller said Holder "abandoned his orchestra."[8]

What happened, according to Ernie, is that Holder came back from Dallas, and the band members voted him out. They weren't going to put him out of the band, because they all liked him, Ernie said, but they wanted him to let somebody else handle the business side. They voted for Kirk to do that. Holder didn't want to stay on if he was not the boss—all the way. Holder reportedly "just smiled" and said, "Well that's what you guys think. No hard feelings."[9] In no time, Fields said, Holder had another band. Just as good.

Kirk, meanwhile, was making some leadership decisions. He renamed the group Twelve Clouds of Joy. Pianist Mary Lou Williams was filling in because Holder's regular piano man, Marion Jackson, took sick. Kirk confided that he decided to keep Williams so she could be with her husband, saxophonist John Overton Williams, and do arrangements. Then he asked Ernie if he could borrow a few dollars to get some manuscripts. Ernie loaned the new leader three dollars. He said, "Yeah, and he paid me back too."

After Kirk took over his band, the resilient Holder joined forces with Kansas City bandleader Jesse Stone, who came to Dallas to help Holder build a new band from scratch, using his arrangements—and young musicians whom the co-leaders drilled relentlessly. Holder was back in business again and again, one of the top territory attractions. "That second band had Earl Bostic. He had Buddy Tate, out of Sherman, Texas. Yeah, he had the best," Ernie recalled. One of the musicians who left when Kirk took over was trumpet player Jeff Carrington, who joined the Ernie Fields organization. "When he said he was with Tee Holder, I knew he could cut it," Ernie said. "I sent him a ticket [from Dallas to Tulsa] and he came on and joined the band."[10] Carrington had many tales to tell, some very good, most of them funny, about "the way Tee went about things," Ernie said. "He just messed with the guys' money," he said. "Other than that, you just couldn't beat Tee Holder."

Around 1932, many orchestras fell victim to the Depression. In fact, Ernie recalled, Holder often went to various colleges and universities in the territory to recruit new talent. "He could just develop and make a band," Ernie observed. But word was, he never lost the love of music or the love of gambling. There were reports of Holder sightings into the 1960s, still having the "sweet" trumpet sound. Other references suggest he abandoned music altogether, moving to Billings, Montana, to work in a copper mine. Chief among the lessons learned from Holder, Ernie said, was that the leader "turned me against gambling because that's the way he lost his band."[11]

In February 1983, Holder was in a nursing home in his native Muskogee. Having gathered in Tulsa to celebrate Ernie's fiftieth wedding anniversary, vocalist Moore of New York City, trumpet player Carrington, who lived in Detroit at the time, and Ernie went to visit the respected colleague, who by now "had a foot or something amputated." From their reports, it was a pleasant visit. They could see his trumpet case in the closet and asked, "Tee, are you still playing that pretty trumpet?" He replied, "Once in a while." Holder seemed to remember them and appeared clothed in his right mind, they reported. That is, until the trio prepared to end their visit.

That is when Holder remarked, in all seriousness, "I'm thinking of starting another band." As the men looked at one another, puzzled, Holder added, "I think I'll round up a few college kids to start out. Of course, I ain't gonna pay 'em nothing." They all laughed, and then Carrington looked at Ernie and winked.

The men chuckled as they shook their heads for most of the fifty-mile ride back to Tulsa. Ernie surmised, "Tee was just a guy that, as good as he was, just lie and just believed in beating and conning people."[12]

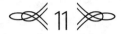

OFAY CATS

When it comes to integration and the music business, Benny Goodman gets credit for adding gifted vocalist Billie Holiday to his organization in 1933. Maybe so, as far as white bands with Black musicians. Ernie swears his was the first Black band to hire and travel with a white musician. His name was Dave Duncan (born 1905), a trombone-playing kid out of Ponca City, Oklahoma, who admired the band and who begged Ernie to let him do some new arrangements for him. It was around 1928, Ernie recalled.[1] It was unheard of. It was novel and probably dangerous. Even the most innocent "race mingling" could result in an arrest, as was the case with Louis Armstrong in 1931. He was arrested (but not charged) for sitting next to a white woman on a bus, even though she was his manager's wife.[2] When Ernie gave the youngster the nod, Ernie had to beg his own mother to allow Duncan to stay in their home so he wouldn't have to travel the nearly one hundred miles home after gigs. Mary Jane Fields had been concerned about what "they" would think (whoever "they" were), but Ernie pointed out she was sounding like "them" and not the good Christian woman he knew her to be. She grudgingly acquiesced, and, according to Ernie, "the guys in the band warmed up to Dave, too."[3] Realizing how revolutionary the gesture was in that day and time, Ernie said, he told Duncan, "You can say you're the manager or anything," and Dave said, "I understand." The Duncan arrangements, he said, "had us in good condition." Duncan also would occasionally sit in on piano.[4]

Then, in the early '30s there was a white sax player named Grant Williams who joined him from the band of tenor sax Alvin "Fats" Wall—not to be confused with the much more famous "Fats" Waller, who was Black.

But the most memorable, and the one whose story was repeated most often, was tenor sax man Harold Eiler (or Iller or Iler, depending on the source) who was with the orchestra about a month in the '40s for a swing through the South. There were apparently few incidents—until they got to Jacksonville, Florida.

Parker Berry had warned Ernie about hiring a white man and traveling in the South. Hadn't Ernie seen that, while touring in the South, when Nat King Cole had "sent his lobby picture down [to the promoters], they saw the white boys and told him he couldn't bring 'em?" Berry theorized that Cole could afford to cancel, "but I don't believe we working enough that we can afford to cancel," Berry told Ernie. Ernie told his trombone player he was wrong. "We won't run into anything, and the boy can cut the book."

The first challenge came after bringing Eiler from Minneapolis to Tulsa and checking him in to the Black-owned Small Hotel in Tulsa. Speaking of owner Wellington Small, Ernie claimed, "You couldn't hardly tell him from white." He looked at Eiler and sized him up to be transient, but asked him how long would he be staying. Eiler replied that he didn't know. "I'm with Ernie and he's going to stay around as long as he can until we go out for a gig—maybe four or five days." Small said he didn't know—that long? "I'm not supposed to rent to any whites." Eiler asked him, "Well, aren't you white?" Small said, no, he didn't claim to be. And they laughed. Small rented him a room and said that because he was in the band, if anything were said, Small "can get by that."[5]

Actually, Small's comment about his racial self-identification was not quite true, at least in one instance. His niece Faye said that during the infamous 1921 Tulsa Race Massacre, one of the marauders apparently approached Small and asked, "Are you a nigger or a white man?" Small said then, "I'm a white man," and the rioter left him alone. He claimed that was the only time and that he never attempted to "pass" or deny being Black again.[6]

Jim Crow laws were so strict, Blacks and whites were not only forbidden from playing music together but also couldn't play baseball on the same field or stay in the same hotels. To Eiler's utter frustration, a Black taxi driver could not drive him to the white hotel—nor could he stay at the Black hotel with the rest of the band.

Eiler's presence brought elevated blood pressure to Ernie and Eiler when they were in Jacksonville, or maybe it was Miami, for a date. When they arrived, Ernie automatically headed for a taxi with a Black driver to take him to the Black hotel. Eiler followed him, but the driver quickly informed him he couldn't carry him. Just as Ernie had instructed him to say, Eiler said, "I'm the band's manager." The driver replied, "I can't lose my license 'cause you the band manager. Get you a Yellow and go on up there and check 'em in." A red-faced Eiler made it to the hotel, "had to get in the Yellow by hisself," Ernie said. At the (Black) hotel, the clerk told Eiler, "You can't stay here." Ernie sent him to a white hotel and told him in which hall to meet the band later for the performance.[7]

They had a two-night stand at what Ernie called a "very elite Black dance." When Eiler arrived, Ernie could tell he was kind of "down and out." It turned out he was worried about how he would get back to his hotel later, because the white cab driver told him he wasn't allowed "over here after 12, and we don't get off until 1." Eiler just shook his head, saying, "I didn't know the South was another world. I've been to school, but I didn't know all this." All was well for much of the dance, but at one point Ernie noticed the white ballroom owner in the back with a policeman. "I'm looking and making out like I ain't looking, but I kicked the band off in a hurry," he said. The manager and officer stood looking right in front of the band, "just looking and looking."

During a break they made their way over to Ernie, and the manager made small talk, noting that the group had performed there before. He complimented the music that evening. There was a check of union cards, which blessedly only have the local number and make no reference to race. An ever-more nervous Ernie, noting the stony face of the white officer, added to the chitchat, mentioning that he had played there before. Finally, the manager introduced the policeman, who was wearing a big white Stetson hat, and they shook hands. (Ernie observed that the deputy didn't take the hat off "in the house, you know.") The manager noted, "I was just telling the officer that I'll be darned if that Creole doesn't look like a white man." Ernie agreed. "Damn if he doesn't," Ernie said. They all laughed and the officer left, apparently satisfied that no law was being broken. A relieved Berry said, "Ah, Jesus, we done made one more round." When the dance was over, the club owner agreed to give Eiler a ride back to the hotel. Eiler was glad to "find one decent white man down south." The club owner replied, "I'm not white, I'm a Jew."[8]

Then there was a kid named Eli Wolinsky, an alto sax player, out of Denver who joined the band around 1952. Ernie recalled playing at a university down south "somewhere"—and for a meal, promoters had set a special table for the band. The band started over to the table, including Wolinsky. Some white guy said, "You don't have to eat over there, that's just for the band." Wolinsky pointed out, "I'm in the band." The man said, "You white, you don't have to." Wolinsky replied, "That's what they say. 'Course my mama is white, my daddy is Black, but I took after her." The "paddy turned red," Ernie recalled. Berry later told the sax player, "If I hear you say that again, I'm going to kick your ass before they do." Wolinsky's retort, "The hell with them." Wolinsky was remembered as a "fine, fine alto man," by Ernie, "one where soul rubbed off from playing with Nat Towles and Preston Love."[9]

Ernie hired a teenager from California named David Sherr in 1960. Sherr details their meeting in his blog, *Bel Air Jazz*. Besides his musical attributes, Fields indicated, Sherr may have had another advantage. "I like to think I'm big enough to hire a man 'cause he can play," Sherr said Ernie told him when he was hired. "Not just colored, and besides, sometimes we can't get something to eat out there on the road and you can help with that, too."

While America was changing, Jim Crow was very much alive, especially in the South, and in the days before the public accommodations title was signed into law by President Lyndon Johnson as part of the Civil Rights Act of 1964, it remained iffy whether Blacks would be served in eateries along their travel routes. In addition to his horn playing, Sherr's white skin could be an additional asset for the band. However, that asset, he said, was never put to the test. "It never happened," he told me in a 2015 interview. "I'll tell you what did happen. We played in Buffalo, Oklahoma [a small panhandle town whose population peaked at 1,618 in 1960], and we had to stay eighty miles away in Baker, Oklahoma, because the empty, as I recall, hotel in Buffalo wouldn't rent to us."[10]

Sherr's brief tenure in Ernie's organization was in the waning days of big band and the transition to more blues and rock 'n' roll. He was also constantly reminded, he said, that he was only holding a spot for Ernie's son to graduate from college and join the band.

Sherr's blog is rich with many memories from his days on the road, first with the (white) Ronnie Bartley Band, then with Ernie Fields's band, and with stories about personalities of some of the other personnel. The musicians had assigned seats on the bus, and Sherr's was third from the rear on the right. He noted that the bus only had seats, no bunks, and that it was "neat and clean and the engine sounded powerful." Spurgeon West and his then-girlfriend (later his wife) Madeline were in the seats in front of his and often included him in their conversations. When he could, West tuned a portable radio to the Saint Louis Cardinals baseball games.

"They were the first people to talk to me," Sherr said. "I loved that cat." It turns out West heard Sherr practicing, and unbeknownst to him, mentioned his talent to Ernie, who told him later. Spurgeon, Sherr said, was "an interesting guy, a smart guy, nice guy. He drank way too much."

Lafayette Waters, "who is *very* quiet, sat on the last row" of the bus and usually wore an ascot tie, Sherr recalled. Vocalist Ann Walls often walked the aisle, shuffling a deck of cards, looking to enlist players. Harry Lewis and Wyatt Griffin said they were "in," but Sherr demurred. Since he'd earlier declined an offer of shared food, Walls said, "You don't eat, you don't gamble, what do you do?" Sherr replied, "I play the saxophone." Laughing, she pointed to the silent musician in the back of the bus, sometimes referred to as a mannequin. "That's Lafayette Waters," she said. "He plays the drums." During his time with the band, Sherr said, Waters never said "two words to me," but it was all right. He never spoke to anyone. The card games seem to never end, he observed, noting, "Ann Walls is usually ahead."

Sherr's first gig with the group was in Chicago, where starting Friday, May 13, 1960, they stayed at the Sutherland Hotel. He loved the shower there because it had "hot, cold, in between, on, off, fast, slow, the works." He noted that "our band had top billing" in a magazine on the nightstand advertising "The Al Benson Review—Rhythm and Blues Star Parade—Eleven Record Stars—Thirty Great Entertainers." Others mentioned included Irma

Thomas, Frankie Lymon, Major Lance, Redd Foxx, Bill Black's Combo (to everyone's surprise, a white group), "and our Ann Walls," among others.

Opened in 1919, the Sutherland was located at the northeast corner of Forty-Seventh Street and Drexel Boulevard in Chicago. Middle-class families, buoyed by the Supreme Court ruling that banned restrictive real estate covenants, began moving into the area. The hotel still refused to serve Black patrons until the 1950s, when new owners invested in it and integrated it, then hired a Black insurance executive as its manager. The manager, Earl Clark Ormes, promoted the hotel as "The Southside's Most Progressive Hotel." Along with other popular venues like the Savoy Ballroom, the Regal Theater, and the Palm Tavern, the Sutherland Lounge hosted many jazz performers. (Lou Donaldson was there while Ernie Fields was at the Regal.) The lounge closed in 1964, and after years of poor maintenance, the hotel closed in 1982. Developed and converted into affordable housing, it is one of few buildings remaining in the Kenwood section of Chicago that reflects a jazz heritage. In 2011, it was listed on the National Register of Historic Places.

The performance was slated for the Regal Theater, where they were set to rehearse in the afternoon. Four local musicians were hired to augment the Ernie Fields ensemble. Sherr said they were Bugs MacDonald, alto sax; John Avant, trombone; and Paul Serrano and King Kolax on trumpet. After a rocky rehearsal, with some of the performers arriving late or not having charts, a less-than-stellar show followed that evening. When it came time for Ernie's big hit, "In the Mood," Sherr had not had time to learn the choreography. He described what followed as a comedy of errors. Harry Lewis, West, and Fronzelle Littlefield were out front, but West turned the wrong way and Littlefield tried to dodge him. After that, Sherr wrote, Al Benson (who had organized the show) insisted "the saxophones . . . play 'In the Mood' without the choreography." Altogether they played three shows. Sherr said there was a crowd around the bus as "we prepared to leave for Muskegon, Michigan." In Muskegon, on May 20, 21, and 22, they backed up a relatively new talent named Marvin Gaye, doing his book as well as Ernie Fields's own material.[11]

Sherr's days with the band were numbered—not because of his pending replacement by Ernie Fields's son, but because he took sick in Denver a few weeks into the tour. He was left in the care of Ernie's wife's sister, Madestella

Ernie Fields and his saxophonists, mid- to late 1940s. *Left to right,* Warren Luckey, Harold Eiler, John White, Harold "Sy" Cannon, and unknown; Ernie Fields; and unknown trombone player (*seated*). Author collection.

(Copeland) Holcomb. All the guys were nice, he said, except the older, also mostly silent, Jack Scott. "It was hard to like him," he said, "I tried, you know. Maybe there was some reason for it. He was older than Ernie, Sherr thought, reasoning, "Probably Jack had been through a lot [of racial stuff]."[12]

The silent ones were never hostile to Sherr, or cranky with one another, considering the long stretches of time on the bus. It was, I surmise, for Sherr, Wolinsky, Eiler, and Duncan, just the way it was.

Bernice (Copeland) Fields, 1930s. Author collection.

BEHIND THAT PREPOSITION
(TRANSLATED: WHERE YOU COME FROM?)

Bernice (Copeland) Fields, Ernie's first and only wife, was a schoolteacher, the fact of which he was particularly proud. He deferred to her judgment on many things, including discipline of their children but, in particular, matters of spelling, grammar, sentence structure, and the like. If anyone uttered the phrase "Where you at?" or something similar, the quick reply from Bernice was always, "Behind that preposition." Some people got it. Some people didn't.

She was also responsible for managing money. What was not used for her husband's musical expenses or band salaries and keeping the bus or automobiles on the road, Ernie dutifully sent home. Bernice, just as dutifully, paid household bills—those that her teacher's salary did not cover—and saved the rest. That there was ever something to save was always a source of amazement to her husband. He would sometimes mock her thrift, urging me to ask her for money instead of him doing it. "Your mama," he'd claim, "has money left over from her first paycheck."

West Caroga Lake [New York]
July 17, 34
My darling bunch of sweetness,
    Slept under blanket, sheet, quilt, and it felt fine. I might could have used some more during parts of the night. They say it is usually cool nights but those that live here say it was extra cool last night.

Wired and wrote you a card last evening just before I went to work.

Glad you are keeping account and trying to save what can. I knew you would. I feel better or as good when you have it as I do when I have it. I hope I can send that much this month. May not be able to send quite that much this month because we have been lucky enough to work in one spot quite a bit this month and we don't make quite as much as we do when we do a lot of one-nighters. But I like the stands much better. Put what you can in the bank but don't want for a thing that what little money I send you will buy. In a hurry to go to Utica N.Y. on some business. May write you when I come back.

Your Ernest

The couple met (the introduction during her infancy notwithstanding) around 1929 at a Home Show in Tulsa. Bernice, who was teaching in Bixby, went there with a friend, Ella Latimer, who turned out to be a Tuskegee classmate of Ernie's. When he was introduced to Bernice, Ernie said, he was immediately impressed. Her hair was cut in a cute bob, he said, and she "looked just as pretty from behind as she did in front." He explained to me that he was referring to her haircut.

The Fields group was featured entertainment at the Home Show, and the young bandleader was sufficiently impressed to ask if he could drive Bernice home after the show ended. She agreed. Not being familiar with what is involved at the end of a performance, by the time the bandstand was broken down, the instruments loaded, musicians paid, and whatever wrap-up business was attended to, Bernice Copeland assumed she was being stood up.

"Ella, he's trying to dodge me," she said. "He was just being nice because you introduced me." She was getting ready to leave.

He caught her just in time.

Bernice taught in rural schools in Oklahoma, schools that were segregated, with those designated for "Negro" students being substandard. Having studied home economics at Tuskegee (arriving in 1925, the year after Ernie graduated), Bernice taught the practical skills to her charges. She lived (and had at one point worked) in Beggs, Oklahoma, a rural community about thirty miles south of Tulsa where the principal industry was hog farming.

She would also teach in a one-room schoolhouse in Watonga, Oklahoma, which was nearly 150 miles from Tulsa.

The first lesson in her class was often making a pillowcase. The next one, an apron. These lessons she carried into her personal life, having learned them and taught them at the height of the Depression and the subsequent years of struggle in the Black community. She herself dutifully made pillowcases out of worn-out bed sheets, creating a linen closet stocked with at least fifteen pillowcases for every one set of sheets. Depression survivors didn't throw anything away. Long after the Depression ended, she washed aluminum foil, plastic bags, and pie tins for reuse. She saved bacon grease, not just for seasoning but as the foundation of her homemade lye soap. She and her friends believed themselves the original "recyclers"—long before it became chic.

She also made root beer from scratch—as well as homemade beer, a concoction referred to as Choc.[1] So penny-conscious were they both that Ernie reminded her in a letter that "it only takes 6c to send letters air mail now. I see you still put 8 cents on your letters."

Thrift became a cruel lesson of Bernice's young adulthood, learned when her oil wildcatter father, Isaac Columbus Copeland, went broke. Before then, she and her six siblings enjoyed a rather middle-class lifestyle. Their family left the agrarian life in Taft, Oklahoma, when Isaac Copeland struck oil. He built a four-bedroom house in Okmulgee, at 1002 E. Third Street, in 1925. A stone mercantile building that he had built in 1920 at 607 E. Fifth Street has an engraved nameplate with the name of Robert B. Copeland, Bernice's only brother, in an upper wall. Both structures still stand and are in use. The mercantile building is now House of Winn Funeral Home, open each month from the first to the fifteenth only.

When times were good, Bernice remembered, her father drove a Winton Super Six, considered the finest-engineered American gasoline car of its time and reportedly the first American "horseless carriage in the early twentieth century." Legend has it, he would speed down the main street in Okmulgee, and one time he was promptly stopped by police and issued a fifty-dollar ticket. Copeland reportedly handed the officer a hundred-dollar bill, and said, "Because I'm coming back the same way!"

Copeland went broke while Bernice was in college at Tuskegee Institute. When she started her studies in 1925, she went in style, by train, with trunks of clothing. It was unclear exactly how or why the family fortune was lost—trickery, naiveté, mismanagement, or all three. The Rockefeller family was sometimes blamed, as the oil-rich property ended up in the hands of Standard Oil, at one point the world's largest oil refiner. After the Copeland family's financial catastrophe, when Bernice returned to Tuskegee she had to work in the school's laundry, ironing sheets, she said, to earn her way. After graduation it was her duty to help a sibling with her college education— her sister Mae Doris, fifth of the seven Copeland children, who enrolled at Langston University and graduated in May 1938.

After dating Ernie for about five years, Bernice began to inquire about her musician boyfriend's intentions. Ernie reasoned that he wanted to "have something" before marrying. Bernice suggested that they could work together to make a life. They were married in Snake Creek, Oklahoma, on February 25, 1933. Ernie would later insist they did not "elope"—he felt the term had a negative connotation. He told me they simply "slipped off and got married." "There was no reception or no nothin'," he said. "But when we came back I remember Mama throwed rice on us when we walked in the door. She was wishing luck."[2] They moved into the house at 530 E. Marshall Place, Tulsa, the home of Ernie's mother, Mary Jane (Garrett) Fields, and her mother, the formerly enslaved Amelia Garrett, and started the journey of building a life together.

In 1939, the couple bought their own home. Family had warned them against the five-thousand-dollar investment, saying, "Your grandchildren will be paying for it," according to Bernice. It was a two-bedroom brick bungalow with a brick carport and a rock fence along the front of the property. Census records indicate they sometimes had a boarder. Bernice recalled their dining room was used as a bedroom for the boarders.

The house purchase elicited an undated item in a newspaper—probably the *Oklahoma Eagle*, Tulsa's Black weekly. It read:

> And . . . speaking of summer plans . . . beautiful Bernice (Mrs. Ernie
> Fields) is radiant these days because (1) she is having her first real fling
> at housekeeping . . . moved into the former residence of the late Escoe

Jackson on North Peoria on Sat'day.... (2) Ernie and his band have just been signed by the William Morris ... and so ... will have a fling at big-time ... in New York about mid-June.... (3) Bernice will bring back that coveted M.A. from Colorado State College of Education [in Greeley] when she returns in August. Recipe for radiance! Yes Siree!

Next door, to the south, was a garage apartment where, a few years later, Bernice's mother, Mattie (Hollis) Copeland, moved in. At one point, she rented her back bedroom to Ernie's guitarist Jack Scott—and mentioned that she noticed he seldom bathed. When Mattie took ill and moved in with Bernice's sister Lydia, the entire apartment was let out to some of Ernie's musicians, who rented rooms there. The front room with fireplace and porch was one bedroom, another was in back of the kitchen. There was one bathroom, with a wringer washing machine in it. Downstairs, on the north side of the garage, there was another small apartment, also sometimes rented by musicians, other times somebody else. It was home for a few years for singer "Little" Clifford Watson. Behind the garage apartment was a two-strand clothesline. Between the garage apartment, which sat back from the street, and the house there was a six-foot-high chain-link fence around a dog pen, about ten feet square, for Ernie's prized hunting dogs: a pointer named Count and another named Duke. Ernie was a sportsman and relished hunting anything that was in season, mostly quail, dove, and occasionally pheasant, and from time to time, wild turkey or rabbits. Next to the dog pen was a small brick incinerator (trash was burned back in those days) and next to it, the Fieldses' garage. Next to the garage, behind the Fieldses' home, Bernice kept her garden—tomatoes, collard greens, okra, lettuce. She took great pride in saying, when complimented on vegetables at a meal, "Thank you, it came from my garden."

Bernice was quiet and soft-spoken. The Bible verse she usually recited after daily grace at meals was Proverbs 15:1, "A soft answer turneth away wrath." The verse continues, "but grievous words stir up anger." Proverbs 15:2 notes, "The tongue of the wise useth knowledge aright; but the mouth of fools poureth out foolishness."[3] Perhaps that biblical lesson was on her mind one day during "girl talk" among her, Ernie Jr.'s second wife, Sandra, me, and one or two other relatives and friends. Sandra was sharing her hopes and fears for her young son, Rodney, then around seven years old. Chatty

Sandra promised not to meddle in her son's affairs—that is, unless he chose a "hussy or a whore" for a mate. Bernice matter-of-factly replied, "You can't say anything then either," because, she calmly explained, "she just might be the hussy he needs." It was like that brokerage firm television commercial: "When E. F. Hutton talks, people listen." Silence fell upon the gathering. Then we all burst out laughing.

Bernice was not one to nag her husband or her children. When general reminders to her son about his responsibility to feed his pet dog Zip were ignored, there was a more direct approach. Little Ernie returned home late one night after carousing with friends to find, when he turned back the covers on his bed, a pan filled with food for his dog on the pillow.

Steady and confident, Bernice seemed if not indifferent, certainly not jealous of her husband's life away from her and its potential for dalliances. From time to time, she would tell a story that drove home her point.

On days of housekeeping, it was her habit to dust or scrub with a pair of her panties on her head, to keep her hairdo in place. One particular day, she put on her husband's overcoat when she took a load of clothes out to hang on the clothesline. As she was coming back inside, the doorbell rang, and as she went to answer, she removed the panties from her head and stuffed them in the coat pocket. Hours later, when her husband prepared to go out on errands, she noticed the look of dismay on his face when he reached in the pocket and pulled out the unexpected piece of underwear. Looking around, not realizing he was being observed, he quickly put them back in his pocket and scampered out the door into the car and away. Bernice would later say that she looked at what happened and said, "I started to make something out of it," but then thought about and decided, "It wasn't worth it."

The couple had been married for sixty-seven years when Ernie died in May 1997. Of the many qualities Ernie admired about his wife (her beauty and work ethic among them), he would say often that most of all he appreciated her accepting, without complaint, his career on the road as he was mostly away from home pursuing his dream of a world-famous orchestra.

"Never did grumble," her husband said. "Never did grumble at all!"[4]

❮ 13 ❯

GOOD WHITE FOLK

Bob Wills (1905–75) was a country and western star who befriended Ernie and helped him secure dates at formerly or usually all-white venues. Not only was his western-style band (Bob Wills and the Texas Playboys) famous, but Wills was also a regular presence on a powerful high-wattage radio station in Tulsa, KVOO. He hosted a half-hour show four or five days a week. That meant nearly "every date he played was a success in the area of Oklahoma and North Texas," Ernie said. "He always had a good band, and he also had a nice gift of gab and personality." Everybody, according to Ernie, seemed to go for Bob Wills. Wills taught Ernie some important booking strategies that would result in better wages. Wills would stress in their conversations, "Don't play yourself cheap. You are an artist." Ernie said, "I wouldn't try to play no western. But I would play enough of the pops, as they called it, and enough of that sweet soul that the ofays was going for it." That way, he remembered, "I could play the same spots that he [Wills] played."

Shidler, Oklahoma,[1] was a little town where an appearance was proposed, for 60 percent or some such percentage of the door. Ernie declined. "You have to give me a guarantee *and* a percentage of the gate," he insisted. "I got to talking to Bob about it and pointed out the difference." Ernie reasoned that Wills could make money in little towns like Shidler because he was broadcast on the radio and had radio advertising every day. Wills counseled that Ernie might not pull as many people in the door as he did, but added, "[You] don't know how they think of you in the area. You can make some money." Wills advised him to insist on 70 percent of the gate *plus* the guarantee, which was usually a flat $125. "He really woke me up. He was nice," Ernie recalled. Wills told him, "Don't be giving yourself away for no $125. You're an artist, get a piece of the gate," Ernie recalled. Wills went even further, insisting that management of Tulsa's Cain's Ballroom book Ernie (the first Black person to perform there) or face Wills using his power to steer other white acts away from the venue.[2]

Bob Wills "opened my eyes to a lot of things as far as business-wise," Ernie said. He also opened venues to Ernie. He recalled,

> I don't know whether just by accident, or that I knew what I was doing or what, but when I started out with the band, I put my mind on music and entertaining the people. I didn't have any western band, but I could play in any place and get a job where Bob Wills or Johnny Lee, Leon McAuliffe or anybody else played. Wills, at the time was one of the—if not the—highest paid bandleaders in America, and often if somebody would ask him for a band, well he would turn them on to me, and they would say, "Bob Wills told us to call you, guaranteed we'd be satisfied."[3]

But often on the road, the musicians had to depend on the kindness of strangers. In an era of rigid segregation and significant racial hostility, encounters with certain whites were a game of chance. Should one smile or not? Speak up or not? Stand firm or run?

If it wasn't dumb luck, Ernie credited safe outcomes to brushes with danger as "the good Lord" looking out for him. Such was the case in a little town in Lee County, Florida. ("You couldn't hardly call it a town," Ernie said, "maybe four or five stores.") The band members were on their way to a gig in Miami when Ernie discovered that the bus had a radiator or water pump leak. He found out later that Lee County (in southwest Florida on the Gulf Coast and named for confederate general Robert E. Lee) was considered one of "those bad counties" in Florida. He drove to a service station and was directed to a one-stop garage by the white attendant, who promised to give him a tow. The attendant had to wait for his partner to return before he could tow them.

They waited and waited—the guys on the bus played cards "and so forth," Ernie recalled. To their relief, a little café next door let them purchase food and eat it on the premises, something that was not often allowed. Soon, a white man Ernie described as "so dirty he was nearly black as me" came along and insisted, "Niggers aren't allowed in his town. You better move this tang [the bus]." The town, he said, "ain't big," and he pointed to a telephone pole a little farther up the road that was the town line. Sometimes, he said, "I work with niggers on the railroad, but we just don't allow them in our town." The bumpkin then insisted the disabled vehicle be moved—and moved quickly.

On most other occasions when there was a need for repairs, the bus driver was able to handle it—and looked for someone's assistance handing him requested tools. Sometimes that someone was Melvin Moore, who besides being a great singer, was known for his jocular inclination. When the driver asked him to hand over a lug wrench when they had a flat or something, Moore's usual retort was, "What do you think we paying you for? I'm the vocalist—and a featured vocalist," he would kid.

After the interaction with the dirty man in Lee County, Moore proclaimed, "You heard what the honky said. We don't want to be in this town if he don't want us in his town!" He reminded his colleagues, "Twelve men can move a house. Let's move out of this town." All the band members scampered out to help push. Observing Melvin huffing and puffing as he pushed, the driver piped up, "I thought you were a vocalist. I didn't know you were going to push a bus!"[4] The guys laughed, Ernie said. They pushed the bus down the road past the telephone pole that marked the town line.

Soon, some Blacks in a truck came along, slowed to a stop, and heard their story. They declined to help, saying, "If we help you, they'll get back at us," and drove away.

Still no tow truck driver arrived. Ernie wondered, "What's going to happen next?" He then recalled the motto of Tulsa-based evangelist Oral Roberts: "Expect a miracle." About that time a white man in a truck came by, going in the opposite direction. He had a little boy with him. Ernie waved him down. He had a tow chain on his truck and agreed to tow the bus the ten or twelve miles to the next town, where a garage would make the necessary repair. To Ernie's amazement, the good Samaritan refused to charge anything for the deed. "I'll tow you there," said the white man, "but you can't pay me." Ernie rode to the garage in the truck with him and there was little conversation except when the driver said, "I wonder when my friends around here will ever wake up. Wake up and be civilized." He must have surmised what had happened.

On top of that, when Ernie asked where the colored hotel was, the driver told them and allowed everyone to put their luggage in the truck, and he carried it and them there. The garage promised to have the repair completed the next day. Ernie said he implored the driver over and over to let him give his rescuer something and was repeatedly met with "no charge." Finally, looking at the man's young son, who was maybe eight or nine years old, Ernie asked, "What about me giving your son something?" The gentleman turned to his son and said quite deliberately, "Dad didn't charge him anything for bringing them up here, he's just tipping, and he's giving it to you." Ernie said he pulled out a roll of bills, and he had a lot of ones on top, and began counting them out. When he got to five, the father said, "That's enough." Ernie handed the youngster the "tip."[5]

Back at the hotel, the staff stressed how lucky the musicians were to have gotten out of the town, saying the area was "one of the worst in the state." The whole incident so rattled Ernie, he considered going back to electric work.

The annals of good white people would not be complete without the name of Robert "Corky" Duffield (born June 3, 1928, died November 24, 1990), the ninth of eleven Duffield children—and the only one without a middle name. He was born in Pawhuska, Oklahoma, which was once Osage Nation.

Duffield heard Ernie play a dance and went backstage during the first break. The men became instant friends. Duffield was what today might be considered a "groupie," but he became much more. He had a love for music and had sisters who were singers; he helped book their engagements from time to time. He soon leveraged that experience and those connections with his friend Ernie Fields. Duffield's wife, Helen, whom he married in 1951, was a nurse, and she joined the mutual admiration society that the families formed, with other Duffield siblings as part of the clique.

But Corky was at the center.

He had been kicked out of high school and subsequently out of the house—something about hitting the principal, his wife, Helen, had heard. He went to Dallas for a bit and stayed with a sister, but later returned to Pawhuska and graduated in 1946. For a while he drove Bob Wills's Cadillac and delivered moonshine at one time. Eventually, he made a living as a self-taught real estate and cattle investor, but he had been known to dabble in politics, running once for water commissioner of Tulsa. He lost in the primary, but on election night his opponent came to the Camelot Hotel on 51st and Peoria, where the Duffield supporters had gathered. He asked if he could join their party, Helen recounted, "as there were so few people at his party—and he had won!" She added, "Of course, we welcomed him in." Though victorious that night, the opponent lost in the final election.

As a couple, Corky and Helen often could be found hearing music at Love's Lounge, a popular spot at 604 East Archer Street, near Greenwood Avenue across from the Small Hotel that was frequented by popular jazz figures of the day. The lounge was run by another big-band leader, Clarence Love, who operated the establishment from 1948 to 1957. "If you could have seen him dance," Helen said of her husband. They took little note of the fact that many times they were the only white people in the room. Sometimes they brought their daughters to performances at the Blue Moon, an open-air dance venue—where one of their three daughters, Cynthia, recalled playing with abandon under the tables. Like Corky, Helen loved the music, she said. Any blowback from relatives or friends about the company they kept—and she stressed there was little—came because they were around liquor. "My mother would have killed me," she said, explaining, "My people were teetotalers."[6]

Ernie Jr. remembers coming home from school one day to be greeted by a "white man sitting on the couch." "Hi, I'm Corky," the man said. Bernice explained to her son, "He helps Daddy. It's OK." Duffield had an open, friendly manner and was well connected. He knew people—like the Lears (of Lear Jet fame) and the Colemans (as in camping gear). Of Duffield, Ernie said, "We got acquainted and he was just a straightforward young man" who loved all musicians, white or Black, "and I just loved him."[7]

Ernie with longtime friends musician Lionel Hampton (*center*) and Robert "Corky" Duffield of Tulsa (*right*). Author collection.

Ernie also spoke highly of Robert Cooksey, manager of Leon McAuliffe's western swing band, whom he called "another fine American as far as I'm concerned." White men like Cooksey and L. E. Buttrick managed the Ritz Ballroom, located at 15½ South Walker Avenue in Oklahoma City. It was "one of the leading ballrooms," Ernie said, and would sometime try to keep Black bands out. But Buttrick "always welcomed you," he explained, "if you could produce and had the right kind of organization."

Ernie prided himself on his relationships with white people. But he did have a few pet peeves. "One thing that got me so much, I met some of what you might call—to tell you the truth—the die-hard rednecks. But I would soon get out of their way when they began to tell me with their deceitful talk that 'I like colored people because I been 'round them all my life.' And one would go so far [to say] that 'colored men raised me' or 'helped raise me' or something. Well, I'm through," Ernie declared. "But when I was fortunate enough to be around whites that said nothing about the past or no connection with any racial conversation but treated me and acted with other people like they would like to be treated, I loved them," Ernie explained. "In other words, they showed me how they felt by their actions and their dealings with me, not by talk."

Ernie explained, "As I said, I just met so many nice people, just plain people, that, I mean, when you'd run into something, you would think about the people that were not right, you just learned to forget and forgive."[8]

⚔ 14 ⚔

LITTLE ERNIE

JoAnn still remembers the bloodcurdling scream that came from her always quiet, always poised mother-in-law, Bernice. The sound came when they walked into a room in Wichita's Saint Francis Hospital and Bernice saw her twenty-seven-year-old first-born child and only son, Ernie Orlando Fields, lying there with tubes and wires everywhere. She screamed and sobbed.

Bernice had driven the nearly two hundred miles from Tulsa to Wichita in silence, with her daughter-in-law JoAnn (Goodwin) Fields in tow. It was a Sunday in June 1962 when Bernice came into First Baptist Church North Tulsa on Greenwood Avenue during the morning service and said firmly to JoAnn something like, "Come on, let's go. We have to go now." She explained, "Ernie is in critical condition. He's been stabbed." She didn't know the who, what, or why of what had happened. All Bernice knew was they had to get there. JoAnn remembered there was no time to pack so much as a change of clothes or toothbrush. Not a word was said during the journey, JoAnn recalled.[1]

Perhaps Bernice was remembering when her son was born. Traveling on the East Coast, her husband had been in Albany, New York, when he got a Western Union telegram announcing their son was born, on July 29, 1934. Shortly before that, Ernie wrote a letter from Caroga Lake, New York, dated July 20.

Hello Sweetheart,

How is my darling this afternoon? Just ate dinner. So full I can't hardly sit up. Excuse pencil lost my pen somehow. . . . Glad you are still feeling fine. Well don't give up you will pull through alright. I have all the confidence in the world that you will and I am praying for you. Really hate I won't be with you. But it may be better that I am not because I couldn't hardly stand to see you shed a tear. But be sure to have them keep in touch with me. . . .

In one of your other letters you were asking what Ora Lee's ex friend was doing. He has a real nice car business. About the best he could have in a town like that [Albany] Because you can eat anywhere anyplace that you choose to so that makes it just a little hard on colored business.

Little Ernie would grow to be a musical prodigy, mastering with ease the piano, clarinet, and violin as a child.

As they rode in silence to the hospital almost twenty-eight years later, perhaps Bernice was recalling the piano lessons with her good friend Carrie Persons Neely, who also directed choirs at Booker T. Washington High School and First Baptist Church North Tulsa. (The "North Tulsa" in the title of the church was significant so that—in rigidly segregated Tulsa—it would not be confused with the other First Baptist Church, which was white.) Or perhaps Bernice recalled the loving tutelage her son received on other instruments from "Uncle Clarence," the elder Ernie's brother who was band instructor first at Booker T. Washington High School in Sand Springs and then the school by the same name in Tulsa. We don't know what she was thinking—but her daughter-in-law remembered that she didn't say anything the whole trip. "Nothing," she said.

Once they arrived in Wichita, the two women never left Ernie Jr.'s side. Bernice sat in the lone chair in the room, and JoAnn slept on the floor at the foot of the bed. At some point, surgery was recommended to repair Ernie's injured lung. Newspapers reported he'd been stabbed in the chest and arm outside a Wichita nightclub. The hospital reportedly did not have sufficiently skilled surgeons, so a family friend—physician and songwriter Dr. David Shapiro—insisted Ernie be moved to Hillcrest Medical Center in Tulsa, where he assured the family there were expert surgeons.

Blessedly, Ernie Jr. recovered.

The family's good white friend Corky Duffield helped organize a 1962 benefit in Wichita—returning to the scene of the crime. Earl Bostic was one

Ernie Fields Jr.'s favorite
photo of himself with his
mother, 1940s. Author
collection.

of the headliners, along with songstress Marilyn Maxwell, a friend of the
Duffield family, who was often a Bob Hope United Service Organizations
(USO) troupe member, as well as several other musicians of note. Ernie Jr.
had his eye on a "sharp" three-piece suit with a long-sleeved vest and short-
sleeved outer jacket. Of course, his father made sure the suit was purchased
and tailored in time for Junior to be wheeled into the benefit wearing it.

Meanwhile, defendant Coy R. Kelley, who was Black, pleaded guilty to
felonious maiming after an August 1962 preliminary hearing that included
testimony by band members Theodore "Rudy" Scott and Elbert "Slim"
Malone, who had been in the car with Ernie Jr. when he was accosted.
According to the testimony, Kelley's wife accompanied Fields and the
musicians to a nightclub, where she was to be given an audition. Kelley met
them at the parking lot and assaulted Fields, who had performed at another

venue earlier, with a knife, puncturing a lung. In November that year, he was
sentenced to one to five years in a Kansas penitentiary. According to published reports, Kelley would receive probation on the condition he served six
months in the county jail.

Ernie Jr. had been playing with his dad for barely a year before the near
tragedy. He went on the road with his father shortly after graduating from
Howard University in 1960. By that time the elder Fields had changed his
promotional strategy, crafting materials that heralded "Ernie Fields and
Son." The son became known professionally as Ernie Fields Jr.—although
his given name was Ernie Orlando Fields and his father's legal name was
Ernest Lawrence Fields.

During the late 1950s, even as the orchestra's singular hit recording of
"In the Mood" was rising on the charts, it was more or less understood that
Little Ernie would join his father's organization. It was something the sax
section would rib David Sherr about, saying they hoped he wouldn't get too
comfortable in his job on tenor, as the spot was not secure. "You know, Little
Ernie will take over your slot soon."[2]

Ernie Jr. didn't start out wanting to become a professional musician, and his
father didn't want that for his son. He thought the medical profession was
likely a better fit. It was the same wish as many fathers in many ethnic groups
had, dreaming of the day he would say "my son, the doctor." He kept the
wish alive, even as his son took to music with ease, becoming agile enough
on the piano at the tender age of seven or eight to be "employed" by First
Baptist Church North Tulsa to play for the Sunday school at a princely sum
of twenty-five cents per Sunday. His musical skills continued to grow. He
picked up and mastered other instruments: violin, clarinet, flute—some of
his learning under the tutelage of his uncle Clarence Fields. Clarence, along
with his wife, Frankie (Robertson) Fields, Bernice Fields, and a handful of
other Black Tulsa educators, would travel to Colorado State Teachers College
in Greeley for three summers to earn their master's degrees around 1939—
the commute required and paid for by the state of Oklahoma, as its higher
education system was segregated. Clarence's thesis had been an investigation
into the differences in instrumentation of marching bands in Black and white

schools. After Sand Springs, Clarence would move to Tulsa, first as Booker T. Washington's band director and later teaching instruments as he traveled from (Black) school to school at the elementary level. Clarence provided individual music lessons to students, supplementing regular music classes held at the schools. "Little Ernie," as he was called, to distinguish him from his dad, "Big Ernie," continued to gain proficiency in many instruments. It seemed that nearly every instrument he touched, he mastered. Some said it was hereditary—how could he be anything but good at music?

The first stop on Ernie Jr.'s road to becoming a doctor was matriculation at a small, historically Black college, Texas College in Tyler, where he enrolled after graduating from Tulsa's Booker T. Washington High School in 1951. His was the first class to graduate from the "new" Booker T., which was moved from the famed Greenwood area, near the heart of the Black community, farther north on Woodrow, off his home street, North Peoria. Tyler is one hundred miles east of Dallas and about ninety miles west of Shreveport, Louisiana, but as far as Little Ernie was concerned, it was in the middle of nowhere.

Texas College had been established in 1894 by the Christian Episcopal Church (CME) leaders to address Black exclusion from Texas colleges. Probably its best-known alum is antiabortion advocate Dr. Mildred Jefferson, a 1944 graduate who went on to become the first Black woman to graduate from Harvard Medical School.

Ernie Jr. recalls the college's primitive conditions. Men shared a single outdoor fountain for brushing their teeth. Food and lodging were "awful." His dear Uncle Clarence had secured him a scholarship—as he did for many of his prized music students, whether they wanted to continue as musicians or not. They thought about such scholarships the same as some think of those handed out to athletes. It's a foot in an important door, and it's left up to the recipient how to use the gift. Not that he didn't love his Uncle Clarence, Ernie just hated Texas College.

When he got home for Christmas vacation, Ernie told his family he was not going back. His mother told him he *had* to go to college. Howard University, he said, was one of a few schools they found that would admit students midyear. So off to Washington, D.C., he went. Without a scholarship, it meant his parents would have to pay. Pay for tuition, pay for room and board, and pay for the considerably higher transportation costs of train travel to the East Coast. Years later, Little Ernie doesn't remember hearing a single word of complaint from his parents. At Howard, he majored in music education and continued to study clarinet and other reed instruments—obviously not on track to medical school.

The subsequent years would include military service. He was drafted and tooted his horn across Europe in the Thirty-Third Army Band with a musician who became a lifelong friend, drummer Gabriel "Gabe" Villani. Saxophonist Eddie Harris was in a jazz counterpart at the same time, and violinist Bill Henderson was in a classical counterpart. Stationed in Heidelberg, Ernie Jr. was given special permission to work at a University of Heidelberg student club, to help promote German-American relations. His father would later promote that in his booking agency materials, noting, "Every weekend, cats like Eddie Harris, Houston Persons, Don Ellis, Leo Wright, Cedar Walton, "Tex" Humphries, and Sam Fletcher would invade the 'Cave' where Little Ernie played. Sessions would often last three nights."[3]

A special in the *Tulsa Daily World* newspaper with a Heidelberg dateline on March 12, 1958, said Ernie Jr. "blows his 'jazz licks' at Die Falle student club. Die Falle, an atmospheric cave-like place run by a board of three Heidelberg University students, caters to American jazz artists who travel from their Armed Forces duty stations all over Europe to play there." The article additionally mentions Pfc. Don Duncan, Sp3 Mike Lara, Sp3 Chan Johnson, and Pfc. Don Ellis. Persons, it was noted, was an airman stationed at Ramstein Air Base. Sp3 Walton was with the Seventh Army Special Services, and Wright with the Seventh Army Symphony.

Little Ernie observed, "Jazz-wise, German players are really fine on their instrument; they have all the technical advantages and are striving for the feel of jazz." Americans, on the other hand, he said, "have this 'feel' for jazz, this free expression that is the heart of our new music."[4]

After army service, Ernie Jr. returned to Washington, D.C., to complete studies for a bachelor of science degree in music education. On June 9, 1960, he was part of the annual commencement concert at Andrew Rankin Memorial Chapel. He played Sonata for Clarinet and Piano, op. 120, no. 2 by Brahms. He was accompanied by Ronald Tymus on piano. Meanwhile, Big Ernie had loaded up his Cadillac with his wife and daughter, and drove the family to the East Coast for the graduation ceremony. He was bringing his son a brand-new Haynes flute, purchased directly from the Boston manufacturer. When he got there, Ernie Jr. persuaded his father he also needed a baritone sax—and his proud father gladly obliged. While studying, Ernie Jr. worked with the Howard Theatre house band under the leadership of Rick Henderson. He also studied clarinet under Robert Swanson of the National Symphony Orchestra.

Besides his studies, Junior, as he was becoming known, worked in the U.S. Postal Service. The Howard Theatre routine in those days usually included a stage show between movies. Graduation week, the family attended the show, which included the vocal groups the Skyliners (who had a hit, "Since I Don't Have You") and the Shirelles (famous for "Dedicated to the One I Love"), as well as a male comic who was also a female impersonator.

The Howard Theatre at one point was an iconic performing venue, like the Apollo in New York City, the Palace in Memphis, and the Oriental in Chicago. Located at Seventh and "T" in the district's Shaw neighborhood, it was the first legitimate theater in the country open to African Americans and is now listed on the National Register of Historic Places. By the late '50s the lights that had shone on Duke Ellington, Cab Calloway, and Ella Fitzgerald were beginning to dim, but were not out by any means.

Upon Junior's graduation, offers to teach music came from Florida A&M University in Tallahassee and Lincoln University in Jefferson City, Missouri. A $350 monthly salary was offered, with free housing included. When he shared the particulars with his dad, the reply was, "I can pay you that!" That was that. By the end of summer, Ernie Jr., with his wife, JoAnn, and daughter Michelle Fields moved back to Tulsa, where he used his GI Bill benefits to purchase a three-bedroom home in North Tulsa. Little by little he began to integrate himself into his father's organization. Ernie Sr. began to promote his organization, during those early travels, as having a "new" sound: "American Sweet Soul."

On March 18, 1967, *Tulsa World* columnist Chuck Wheat ("Wheat's Field") wrote that "Ernie Fields Jr., son of Tulsa's legendary bandleader, has a new band," which had completed a swing around Texas and Oklahoma, backing the Impressions. The column noted that the group worked only on weekends until the summer, "because two members are back in college."

At the Howard Theatre in Washington, D.C., circa 1960. *From left*, Earl "Bang-Bang" Jackson, Luther "Spurgeon" West, Ernie Fields Jr., and Ernie Fields on trombone.

The writer described Junior as a "promethean musician himself, [who] holds forth on alto, tenor and baritone sax, flute, clarinet and trumpet." The columnist described the group's sound as "modern popular, which means it has the driving rhythms of rock. The difference in groups in this vein comes from the way the sounds are arranged." Junior's father continued to assist with bookings and promotions but no longer performed with the band. After Ernie Jr. began traveling, Ernie Sr. said he was "proud that I had made the reputation that there wasn't anywhere that he [Jr.] went where he was ashamed to say that he was my son, and a lot of those promoters down south, all east and west, [said] your dad played for me."[5]

Around 1968, the band became the group that supported blues legend Bobby "Blue" Bland. He was described in his Rock & Roll Hall of Fame induction as "second in stature only to B. B. King as a product of Memphis's Beale Street blues scene." Like his father, or maybe because of his father, Ernie Jr. insisted the billing be: "star Bobby 'Blue' Bland, featuring Ernie Fields Jr. and Co." He added three musicians to Bland's fractured group: New Orleans trombonist and arranger Alfred Thomas, trumpeter Tommy Punkson, and guitarist Mike "Monk" Bruce, a white musician who sprinkled his blues sound with a dose of rock.[6]

They were booked nearly every night. Meanwhile, according to Eugene Chadbourne in the *AllMusic* guide, Bland was "bogged down in booze and bad musicians." Ernie, in collaboration with producer Steve Garrie, he said, is credited with reenergizing Bland's career.[7] But according to a biography by Charles Farley, Bland claimed that Ernie's sound "was not right for me." Nonetheless, Bland would go on to record the two most highly regarded albums of his career, *His California* in 1973 and *Dreamer* in 1974, both from Dunhill Records.

Things were fine for about four years, until, in Ernie Jr.'s words, Bland "stole my band." It was January of 1972 or 1973, and because that month usually has the least performances scheduled, the tradition for many bands is to be off most or all of January. It was also income tax time, and the men were getting W-2 forms and preparing to file personal income tax returns. When Ernie called the drummer with a question, the man's wife said something like, "He's with the group working in Houston." It turns out there was an engagement in Houston, and the bus and the band, without Ernie, was gone, never to return.

In hindsight, Ernie Jr. said, "It was the best thing that could have happened to me."

After the Bland debacle, Ernie Jr. was at a crossroads. He was definitely through with being a band leader. The debt, coupled with Bland's unceremonious disappearance, left a bitter taste. Plus, he would confess to me, "Daddy didn't mind being a father to a half dozen or so genius malcontents. I do."

He wanted to be a musician. He wanted to toot his horn. Even, he confided, if his name was never up in lights. Where best to carve out a niche? In his mind it was either New York City or Los Angeles. He spent time in both cities—and as is the case for many, the perpetual California sunshine and palm trees won. When jazz or funk saxes were mentioned, his name came up sometimes, alongside Houston Persons, Eddie "Lockjaw" Davis—even jazz-funk crossover artist King Curtis. It was anticipated that Ernie Jr. would be colleague or heir to their traditions.

Part of the California attraction was the chance to work under the tutelage of René Hall, still one of his father's best friends—and by this time a

popular studio arranger, in-demand studio musician—mostly on guitar—
and producer (from Richie Valens to Marvin Gaye). Ernie became a copyist,
preparing the charts for all the instruments scheduled for the numerous
recording sessions that Hall produced. He also became a reliable session
musician in his own right, and is listed on recordings by artists as varied as
Stevie Wonder, Patti LaBelle, and Gladys Knight. He is unlisted on many
more recordings and has been a part of live shows for Aretha Franklin;
FreedomFest (London's concert honoring Nelson Mandela's seventieth
birthday); numerous foreign tours with Fred Wesley and with French
superstar performer Johnny Hallyday (known as the French version of Elvis
Presley); and PBS's "In Performance at the White House" presentations in
2010 and 2012.

Trombonist Wesley met Ernie Jr. when he was contractor and tenor
player for a project. Wesley was arranging horns and strings for an album
for rhythm and blues singer Vernon Burch. Wesley said in his book *Hit Me,
Fred* that Ernie Jr. was the "epitome of what you would expect a Hollywood
musician to look like." He described him as "tall, not too dark, and very
handsome, drove a big Cadillac, had a white secretary and dressed in the
latest clothes." According to Wesley, Ernie Jr. and trumpet player Harry Kim
were the "only ones who understood exactly how to phrase my music." He
had to force everyone else. They became fast friends; Ernie Jr. was Wesley's
go-to person for a music contractor. It was not just about getting the musicians—it was getting the right musicians for the music. The contractor keeps
everything in line and on schedule and makes sure everyone gets paid.[8]

Ernie Jr. formally established his own company, Jade Sound/Fields Musical Services Inc., in the 1980s. The multiservice company provides arranging,
copyist, contracting, and payroll services for recording studios, television
shows, and movies. The first company pamphlet and business cards were
designed by Ernie Jr.'s second wife, Sandra (Kinji), who said she created the
logo, depicting a French horn, and much of the text. It said in part, "Let's
face it; you cannot: produce, arrange, orchestrate music, conduct, contract
quality musicians, evaluate and select engineers, rent studios, schedule sessions, select background singers, pay earnings to musicians, compute and
pay applicable federal and state taxes, pay social security and union fund
requirements, comply with American Federation of Musicians and required

agencies *and be creative.*" Jade Sound, the marketing pamphlet promised, could reduce your costs and leave you "the freedom of creating the sound that today's competitive music demands." Jade offered "confidential assistance in all areas of production and [the promise to] see your name on a hit record." The company set up shop at 6263 Hollywood Boulevard, Suite 1230.

According to a profile in the August 1993 issue of *L.A. Record*, among the albums or singles for which Ernie Jr. was musician/contractor that achieved gold or platinum status were Marvin Gaye's *Let's Get it On* (René Hall was arranger), *Twistin' the Night Away* by Sam Cooke, *Bundle of Joy* by Freddie Hubbard, and "Go Away Little Boy" by Marlena Shaw. Ernie Jr. conducted performance/recording sessions for Roy Clark, Josephine Baker, Lou Rawls, and Telma Hopkins. While in his father's band he backed and toured with the Temptations, Sam Cooke, the Impressions, and Lionel Hampton, and he has gigged with too many to mention. The spring 2013 publication of the Los Angeles Jazz Society noted Ernie's longtime coordination of the monthlong Jazz in Schools program each year during Black History Month, describing how he would get up at an "unearthly hour [to brave] L.A. traffic to excite, educate and entertain." Some 23,000 students were beneficiaries of the program and "laughed, sang, participated, marched and thoroughly enjoyed the performance, while learning about different instruments and the origin of jazz."[9]

When asked what is happening in the music business today that bothers him, Ernie Jr. zeroed in on the musicians' union, echoing his father: "Side deals involving the musicians concern me greatly." According to Ernie Jr., the union "sanctions exclusive arrangements that exclude all but one of its members, essentially precluding the opportunity for other contractors and musicians to compete for jobs on the basis of talent, experience, efficiency etc."[10]

Ernie Jr. not only became a trusted contractor and reliable studio multi-instrumentalist (baritone sax, flute, soprano sax, and bagpipes, among others), but would make appearances on television shows (*Rhoda, Sisters in the Name of Love,* and *Motown 25,* among them) and in movies (*Choose Me* and Sarah Bernhard's *Without You I'm Nothing*). By the time Jade Sound was incorporated in 2003, besides performing with most major artists, Ernie Jr.'s contracting assignments would include *American Idol, The Voice,* Steve

Harvey's *Little Big Shots*, and *Forever Young*, among others. He could also on occasion be seen as a model in print ads and television commercials. One television ad with a speaking role was for Orville Redenbacher's popcorn. Another time he was the father of the bride in a Chrysler New Yorker ad that ran in October 1992 in *Emerge* magazine.

From time to time, Ernie Jr. would book himself as a musician in a show's production. When *American Idol* music director Rickey Minor requested a didgeridoo, Fields decided to book himself. That May 2010 performance on a didgeridoo, accompanying *American Idol* finalist Crystal Bowersox as she belted out the Lennon/McCartney tune "Come Together," drew comment and an on-air identification from the show's judge, Simon Cowell. How did this come to pass, Cowell asked after calling Ernie Jr. back onto the stage. Ernie demurred, saying, "I'm just the contractor." He had hired himself. Earlier in the day, Minor had asked Ernie how he was coming with locating a didgeridoo player. Ernie's response, "Don't worry, there'll be one."

In his '80s, Ernie Jr. continues to contract, practice, and perform. Accolades include induction into the Oklahoma Jazz Hall of Fame, where he and his father are the only father-son members. In October 2019, he coordinated and headlined a tribute to his father's music. Called the Golden Age of Greenwood, it featured reconstruction of his father's recordings from the '30s, '40s, and '50s and was presented by the Tulsa Signature Symphony of Tulsa Community College.

Ernie Jr.'s highest praise to anyone is to say they are "Kool Man Kool." It is the way he signs much of his correspondence and reacts to messages or exchange of information. Closest friends call him "Mr. Kool Man Kool." Sometimes it is shortened after his signature to simply KMK—which is also on his vanity license plate, once gracing his Maserati and now his bright red 2020 Tesla SUV.

He's leveraged his skill and his father's good name and reputation to move in circles the elder Ernie Fields could not imagine, let alone aspire to.

15

WHAT MAN IS THIS?

In the late 1920s, when Ernie Fields Sr. was attempting to establish his name and the orchestra, he visited Sand Springs, Oklahoma, from time to time, and there he made the acquaintance of a certain young lady named Frankie Madison. Ernie's brother Clarence lived in Sand Springs then and taught band, sometimes tipping off his younger brother about music students with potential. Ernie confided years later in a self-recorded audiotape that he, Frankie, and some other fellas often attended Sunday school together, "so I got to dating Frankie," and before he knew it, he had "really fallen in love" and was thinking about marriage. But his mind, he said, told him, "You got no business marrying now." He rationalized, "You got nothin'. She's got nothin'." When he found out Frankie was pregnant, he said, his brother Clarence "didn't think that I should marry." He took his older brother's words to heart, as Clarence was like a father to Ernie after their father died. "Look like he'd say things that a father would be talking," Ernie explained. "I admired him."[1]

Ernie wrestled with his decision and said, "I just don't feel it's right to have a girl pregnant and just leave her. I should have some better excuse than saying 'we just ain't got nothin'." Eventually young Frankie went to Saint Louis to have the baby. She had relatives there. Ernie said he bore "the expense. We didn't fall out, 'cause I didn't [marry her]," Ernie said. She returned to Sand Springs after their son, Charles Lawrence Fields, was born, January 12, 1929. Everybody, Ernie said, "is saying he sure favors you."[2]

As he grew, Frankie's brother, Eddie, who also played in the Ernie Fields Band, would bring the lad to Tulsa to visit with his grandmother, Mary

Fields. "Mama fell in love with him," Ernie said. Charles and Ernie Jr. were also childhood pals, with a close bond that continued until Charles's death on April 28, 2017. Frankie married a preacher, the Reverend Jordan M. Horne, and she worked in various housing positions at Langston University. Charles graduated from Lincoln University in Missouri and became a successful executive in the liquor industry.

At some point, seeing Mother Fields's fondness for Charles, and how well Charles and Ernie Jr. got along, Clarence offered to adopt Charles. Frankie Madison made it clear her son was not up for adoption. "She didn't go for that any kinda way," Ernie said.[3]

Not long after, Ernie and Bernice Copeland met.

Youthful indiscretions aside, Ernie was, by his own description "a square." He smoked cigars occasionally, but never cigarettes. He liked a drink from time to time, but bragged, "I have never been drunk!" He had an erect bearing, sat and walked tall, confident in his five feet, ten inch stature with slightly bowed legs. While the men in the back of the bus regularly played games of chance, such as dice, poker, and tonk, Ernie never participated. While his wife, on the other hand, was an avid bridge player and enjoyed low-stakes blackjack with her teacher colleagues, Ernie claimed he did not even know how to read cards.

Ernie's word was his bond. Many deals were made on a handshake and a promise. He believed in discipline, rehearsing unrelentingly. There was a system of fines for tardiness and other infractions. His son remembers a rehearsal when his dad announced a five-dollar fine to Ernie Jr. for being sloppy on the bandstand. No, his son and namesake insisted. "I was not drunk. I stepped in my saxophone case when I stood to take my solo." His father replied quietly, "Then it's a five-dollar fine for stepping in your saxophone case."

Another rule forbade leaving the bandstand during a performance. The fine was ten dollars. From time to time, companions of vocalist Sticks Bradley would appear in the audience, and Sticks was heard to proclaim, "I'll leave then even if Ernie fires me." Her tenure with the orchestra was indeed brief.

According to Ernie in a 1987 conversation of remembrances in René Hall's Los Angeles office, "Well, to tell you the truth, [I was] pretty fortunate, there was a lot of fooling and acting silly, but I was really lucky with gentlemen in [the band] there." Right, René concurred, "other than the alcohol thing, we didn't have any mess, none." No, Ernie concurred, "no trouble at all. That's the whole thing."[4]

As long as money was being made, the musicians would get paid. The pay scale was confusing, to say the least, according to the young David Sherr. When Sherr was hired in May 1960, he said, Ernie took him aside and said, "There's big gigs and little gigs. Big gig pays twenty-one cent, some of the cats get less; little gigs pay what they pay and Jack Scott's the arranger he gets twenty-two. A week we don't work, I pay you fifty-cent, stay 'round town, maybe rehearse. Next week's Chicago, pays a bill six bits, and of course, I want to get you in on that." He was warned not to disclose the financial agreement (which Sherr said he was not sure he understood himself) and not to ask any of the others theirs. "The guy's got not only his own language, he's got his own—this new math," Sherr surmised.[5]

In the '30s pianist Salva Sanders probably was paid "a couple dollars more, you know, for being Salva," vocalist Melvin Moore recalled. Being Salva probably meant that he was older than most of the other musicians in the group and commanded respect for that, not to mention that he was a pianist par excellence. "Nobody bothered him; everybody respected him," said Moore. "He was the dad of the band."[6]

Sanders was not a square. An avid card player—who always won—he would shoo Moore away. He often said, "Man, you can't play no cards, get away from here." He knew he was taking Moore's money.

Ernie was very particular about appearance on the bandstand, and the musicians, explained Spurgeon West, would balk at Ernie's getting after them "about the socks they had on and this and that." While in Harrisburg, Pennsylvania, they saw a Fletcher Henderson performance and West noted to Ernie, "You should have been out there and heard that band. You raise sand with us about socks, I thought Coleman Hawkins was going to plow somewhere, the way he was looking. And Fletcher ain't said a durn thing." Ernie said to the complaining musician, "They got a reputation otherwise, so we have to have the look." Plus, according to René Hall, "We would have guys that liked to be sharp. We had a different caliber of musicians than them guys in the average traveling band."[7]

Melvin Moore concurred. Many in the band were what he called "snappy dressers." In those days, said Moore, a nice suit of clothes showed you were successful in your work—"when you could change three or four cotton ties, you know. That was it!"[8]

There were a few other rules. One was you couldn't curse in the band. And while Ernie "didn't march the band to church or to Sunday school," he would always ask them to go to church with him when they were in a town and had time. If they didn't have time, "We had Sunday school, a Bible reading on the bus, under a shade tree or anywhere on the highway."[9]

Some musicians would, from time to time, request an advance on their pay. When he could, Ernie would accommodate them, and sometimes make loans. If payment was not forthcoming, there were things to barter. Occasionally musicians could be seen painting his Peoria Avenue residence, inside and out. It was not uncommon to find one of their cars in the yard on cinderblocks—until a debt was satisfied. Ernie took seriously his role as surrogate father for many of the members of the organization.

A lecture about something was never far from his lips. Sometimes others would meet "this Ernie Fields in person, before giving permission for their sons to join the group." Such was the case with Hall, who came aboard fresh out of Xavier—and fresh out of trouble with the law, after a tussle on a streetcar. As he told it, "I hit a white man, which was considered a capital crime." Actually, the man hit him, he explained, "and we fell off the streetcar, and he fell under me." The fact that the white man was down, "and I was up and running, it was a crime in Louisiana." Because police "began hassling me," Hall said, he bought a gun, and planned to "kill a bunch of policemen." His mother said he better get out of town. As fate would have it, Tulsan Earl Bostic was living in Hall's home while studying at Xavier and told him about Ernie Fields. With encouragement from Bostic and Luther West, another Tulsan studying at Xavier, Fields met Hall's mother to assure her of his integrity, and Hall joined the band, around 1934.[10] Hall's mother, according to Ernie, agreed for him to travel with the group because "she was afraid he was going to get killed or kill somebody."[11] Hall told him he was tired of being mistreated by whites. Hall mentioned that the way Ernie talked to white people made him "nervous."[12] Ernie said later, in a self-recorded audiotape, that Hall didn't elaborate, but he just wondered "how I got by with it." Ernie replied that he just tried to be respectful and, in that way, he said, "I could demand it [respect], in one way of speaking."[13]

Tulsa native Leon Rollerson, nearly a generation later, came aboard in the late '50s or early '60s when he was a student at Langston University. Ernie talked to his mother about letting her musician son travel. Rollerson would recall the honor of being allowed to drive Ernie's Cadillac from gig to gig. It was, in part, to help with the driving, but it was also to separate Leon— who was a bit younger and probably less worldly than the others—from riding in the other vehicle, a station wagon that towed a trailer hauling the instruments.

Ernie took seriously his reputation for running an organization of clean-cut, snappy-dressing, decent men. That is why a story in the mainstream *Tulsa World* probably rattled Ernie enough to try to set the record straight. The headline proclaimed, "Negro Arrested Here Not Member of Band." It said a singer arrested in a dope ring roundup and "identified in a *Tulsa World* story as a member of Ernie Fields' dance band is not a member of the band." It went on to say that Fields told them the next day "that Robert Oliver, the singer, has never been a member of his band." Oliver was one of five "young Negros arrested by federal narcotics agents in connection with a marijuana ring," the newspaper reported. Fields further clarified that another defendant, Oscar Estelle, saxophone player, "who also was identified as a member of the band, is not a regular member." Fields said Estelle "was hired to play an engagement last weekend with the band after a regular member was drafted."[14] End of story.

Although raised in a Christian home, Ernie did not talk about religion but was a prayerful man. Former band members recalled that on occasion he'd pull the passenger bus off the road at sunrise to meditate and pray. He seldom used profanity—and on the rare occasions that he tried, he would often draw laughter from the awkward syntax of his curses. He "became a laughingstock" when he cursed, recalled singer Estelle Edson Banks in a taped interview at Ernie's home. She said Ernie once remarked after a brush with brutality in a small Texas town, "Those mama-trotters are trying to kill us," adding "That granny dodger hit me from behind." Everyone cracked up, she said. "That's what he called cursing!"[15] He always said grace before eating, on the road or at home, even if the prayer was a quick bowed head over a McDonald's hamburger.

In a taped interview with me, he confided a fear of going broke. Many musicians, he observed, "I knew were making as much or even more than I was at that time, but they didn't have a damn thing." He said he figured "right then, I'm going to invest, going to have something."[16] Among his investments was a farm, 168 acres of land in Porter, Oklahoma, in Wagoner County. He would eventually add a used trailer home to the property, where he, his wife, and friends would spend weekends fishing on the three ponds, gardening, and relaxing. In the '60s Ernie and Bernice moved two small houses to the land and rented them out to enhance their income. The last tenant was a rodeo man, who liked the property so his horses could be nearby. A farmer, Richard "Bear" Thompson Sr., managed the property and raised crops and animals to feed both families, his and Ernie's. Besides the food production, the land had recreation value. Family would gather there for holidays, especially the Fourth of July, because it was legal to use fireworks there, undisturbed by police.

Always entrepreneurial, Ernie made sure that, besides being a recreation spot for family and friends, the farm property provided a revenue stream. For a fee, one could fish in the ponds. A business card for "Ernie Fields Farm Fed Fish Ponds" indicated permits were available "per day, 6 Mo. Or Yr." While no prices were listed on that card, a different business card listed twenty dollars for a two-month hunting permit in 1990 for dove season. It read, "September and October, no in between," with phone numbers for Ernie and R. "Bear" Thompson.

Ernie also purchased, for $1,500, about "60 or 75 acres of land on the other side of Claremore, where they finally put Grand Lake." Created in 1940, Grand Lake is a reservoir in northeastern Oklahoma that hosts camping, fishing, and all manner of water sports. Its website says it boasts a shoreline longer than the California coast. "I forget what I had in mind on that," Ernie said, recalling that "it was a nice wooded area." At the time, Ernie enlisted a man to cut wood and sell it for him. "A lot of hickories up there for barbecuing and so on. It was a good investment." He turned around and sold the land for around three thousand dollars. He was satisfied, but explained, "If I'd have known who was going to buy it [and create Grand Lake] I could have

From left, Bernice Fields, Ernie Fields, unknown, Count Basie, and Bernice's brother Robert Copeland, 1950s. Photo by Ray's Studio, Muskogee, Okla. Author collection.

gotten well on that." He didn't know about the plan for the lake at the time, but concluded, "Anyway, I didn't lose anything."[17] Grand Lake is now one of the state's biggest outdoor attractions, a man-made lake that touches three counties, is the draw for hunting and fishing lodges, and has 1,300 miles of shoreline.

Ernie considered his best investment a thirteen-acre lot on a corner of Mohawk Boulevard, Lewis Avenue, and East Thirty-Sixth Street North in Tulsa. He had a dream of building a motel there, a plan his wife endorsed. She was teaching nearby at Ralph J. Bunche Elementary School and figured, "I'll run by and check up on them [motel staff] and maybe work a while there in the evening, to give who it is a rest, and then go on home and let somebody else come on duty for the night." The property, Ernie said, already had two or three oil wells and gas wells on it, which he subsequently had removed, so as not to interfere with his vision of an "upper-class motel, not a Holiday Inn. Something where any Black would be tickled to say that he stopped there." He was particularly proud of the "good location, you know, just about a block from the main highway." Blueprints were drawn up, but investors never got the construction money together, so the idea was abandoned. Instead, the small rock house on the property was rented out for additional income. "There's many things that I did right," Ernie said in a self-recorded tape. "One thing I didn't do right was keep an accurate account of what I made or what I lost. I didn't have any actual account on that."[18]

With both Ernie and Bernice pinching pennies, they were able to pay off the thirty-year mortgage on their home without help from their children or grandchildren, as had been predicted when they made the purchase. They educated their children, with both graduating from college debt-free, and they took great pride in that. No, Ernie was not a rich man, but as he hoped, when he died, he had "a little something."

Upon seeing in April 1984 that his longtime pal, the great Count Basie, had passed, Ernie noted, "Well, I outlasted Count." Basie was a week his senior. But, Ernie added wistfully, "I think Count had more fun."

16

THE ROAD TO A HIT RECORD

Ernie Fields's very first recording sessions were in August and September 1939, when he recorded the moderately successful "T-Town Blues" and several other tunes in New York City. There would be sporadic other sessions, in 1949, mostly a remake of some of the previous Vocalion tunes, but with a different vocalist and some changed personnel. Ernie was briefly affiliated with the Quality label, too, where the recording of "Thursday Evening Blues" featuring Melvin Moore drew admiration from Stan Kenton, who was captured in a photo listening to the side with Ernie, Moore, and recording executives Ahmet Ertegun and Herb Abramson. Ernie recorded in 1947 with the label he created, Frisco Records. By the mid-1950s, he had shaved his fourteen pieces to adjust to the diminished interest in jazz and swing and to the evolving rhythm and blues sounds that were becoming more popular, and of course, to chase that new kid on the block, rock 'n' roll. As one reviewer noted, Ernie had not allowed much in the way of bebop or progressive jazz, although his featured sidemen sometimes played in that style.[1]

But 1959 brought a big push for a recording contract and prayers for a big hit. By that time, Ernie's longtime and triple-threat musician René Hall (trombone, guitar, and arranger) was based in Los Angeles. He had become a reliable and respected studio musician and arranger. He would be the key player in reenergizing Fields's career with a longed-for hit record.

From 1960 or so, Ernie Fields became known as "Mr. In the Mood." The title came from what in 1959 became his biggest hit record, "In the Mood," a rock 'n' roll version of the Glenn Miller hit from the '40s. One of the song's writers—Joe Garland (born August 15, 1903, in Norfolk, Virginia, and died April 21, 1977, in Teaneck, New Jersey), a Black tenor saxophone player who often played with Louis Armstrong—was known to boast about "In the Mood." He said his rights to the tune, with its publishing and other royalties, "[kept] him well off."[2] The song is a staple in nearly every high school and college jazz band in the world. According to some accounts, the tune was written by Garland, who also was an arranger, with Edgar Hayes, whose orchestra recorded it for Decca Records in 1938, some eighteen months before Miller. But it was Miller's version that topped the charts for thirteen straight weeks in 1940.[3]

The hit record for Ernie was as unlikely a happenstance as was the accident of his entire musical career. His eye was on that target, all the while downsizing from the forty-three-passenger bus with his name emblazoned on the outside to two automobiles, his Cadillac and a station wagon hitched to a trailer to carry the instruments. The organization went from fourteen, sometimes as many as seventeen, to seven to nine musicians. In the fevered attempt to stay with the times, gone were the exotic dancers and the one-legged acts, replaced by "the Brown Beetles"—a few of the men wearing wigs styled like the famed British group. They dubbed singer Clifford Watson, "Mr. Please, Please, Please," after the popular James Brown recording that Watson belted with fervor.

Ernie kept relationships with various promoters and booking agents, among them Jim Halsey, a Tulsa-based agent who handled Brenda Lee, *Hee Haw's* television star; country singer Roy Clark; the Oak Ridge Boys; and some other quasi-country/rock performers. Ernie met Halsey "around Pawhuska," as he remembered it—when Halsey was barely out of high school but was booking on the college scene. When Ernie learned what Halsey was up to, his reaction was, "You mean a youngster is doing that like that?"[4] He also cultivated the college and university circuit, performing at ROTC and other college dance events on both white and Black campuses.

Ernie kept busy. He kept hustling.

He leveraged his close relationship with his former arranger/guitar player René Hall (an idea Halsey gave him), listing on stationery, envelopes, and promotional materials his "West Coast office" as 6253 Hollywood Boulevard, Suite #1230. That was Hall's office address. Ernie confided to Hall that he was "fixin' to give it up," get out of the business. Hall urged Ernie to come to Los Angeles and record. In an interview with *Tulsa World*'s Dave Averill, published April 17, 1983, Ernie recounted that he asked Hall, "Can you guarantee me a hit?" Hall replied, "I can guarantee you a song, but I can't guarantee a hit."

Ernie was on the West Coast in 1958 or early 1959 when Hall had arranged for a recording session. "We were kind of talking about 'In the Mood,'" he recalled. In that session they had Hunter Gray, and a guitarist Hall had suggested, Oscar Moore, who was with Nat King Cole.[5] They went into the session, played several numbers, and then Hall suggested it would be better to use guitarist Butch Luckett—to get a "different sound." Ernie recounted, "So we said OK. We got set up, and that night when we went to record, Butch didn't come because he was drinking." But as it turned out, Hunter "Shoe Sole" Gray was around the corner; he had worked with the alto sax man in Ernie's band, and Hall knew him. Hall said he'd get some guys over to the session. He got drummer Earl Palmer (1924–2008) and Gray, who Ernie described as a "liquor head." Irving Ashby, who also had a tendency to drink, was the guitar player. On tenor sax was Plas Johnson, a leading session player known for his solo on Henry Mancini's "The Pink Panther Theme." There was Ernie Freeman, pianist and arranger (August 16, 1922–May 16, 1981), Hall on guitar, and Earl Palmer. Hall, Johnson, and Palmer were all originally from Louisiana. The three, who did not have much success as solo artists, pooled their talent in the studio as an ongoing session production team. (They can be heard on countless rhythm and blues and rock 'n' roll recordings. Sometimes augmented by Freeman on piano and Red Callender on bass, Hall's team became the busiest and best session unit on the West Coast, and some believe in the nation.) Black Cat Rockabilly describes the team's work from 1957 to 1960 as "the very essence of rock n roll."[6]

Because of the revolving door of musicians for the session, sober or not, "maybe they don't want to play with you," René surmised. They taped "a number or two" that satisfied none of them. One was called "Strolling after School." But of the several they did, they didn't feel any was "going anywhere." Ernie ended up leaving California, and Hall and Palmer got together later and made another master. Hall paid for it, intending to "peddle the thing and make Ernie Fields the leader."[7]

From left, Ernie Fields, Earl Palmer, René Hall, Ernie Fields Jr., and Plas Johnson, circa 1962. Reproduced by permission of Universal Music Group (formerly Capitol Records), Santa Monica, Calif.

The master included recordings of "In the Mood" and another rearranged '40s staple, "Chattanooga Choo-Choo," with Ernie Fields named the leader, and it became one of their most successful efforts. Besides the session musicians Plas, Earl, Freeman, and Hall, no one on the recording was a member of Ernie's band. Hall told Ernie to figure out when he could return to California so he (Ernie) and the four musicians would overdub additional parts. While getting ready to do that, Hall got in touch with Rod Pierce of Rendezvous Records, who liked the idea. So Ernie went back to Los Angeles, and that's when "In the Mood" and "Christopher Columbus" were finalized, with Ernie committed to travel with his already-established organization—but without the studio musicians. The tunes were released around July 1959.

The publicity department at Rendezvous released the subsequent long-playing album and titled it *In the Mood, Ernie Fields, the Big Young Sound*.

Early reviews in the trade publications were promising. *Cash Box*'s "Best Bets" column on July 4, 1959, gave it a B-plus: "The Glen Miller favorite, excitingly in tune with teen tastes, this instrumental sparkler could come on big. Watch it." The reviewer called "Christopher Columbus" "another revival of an oldie for teen tastes, and results in making the grade too." Ernie remembered, "We got a good review in *Billboard* also and so they made 'Christopher' No. 1—I mean A (side)."[9]

The push was on for "Christopher Columbus." Ernie remembered, "We were playing it, and a DJ in Oklahoma City who used to be in Tulsa, and he knew me personally," played the record. "He plays around with 'Christopher' for a week or two, and then he played 'In the Mood' [the B side], but he never would play it on the air." The record company had designated the A and B sides. "So, he called me up and finally got a hold of me and said, 'Ernie, I have your new record. I think both of them are real nice, but I would like to flip and make 'In the Mood' the A side.'"

"I don't know why, but I just think it has a jump on 'Christopher,'" the disc jockey said. He explained, "'Christopher' is a good number," but then he reminded Ernie, "but it never was as big as 'In the Mood'" had been back in the day. Ernie recalled, "He believed 'that new version of "In the Mood" you have, has to make it. With the name, I think it will make it.'" Ernie immediately called Rendezvous Records president Rod Pierce, who told Ernie, "Anything you think, if it will help, go ahead."

"By then, I think it had been out about three months and hadn't done anything. The guy over at WKY in Oklahoma City flipped that side and the first round he made, the green light came on, and think I called Rod and told him, and Rod then called everywhere and told them to flip it, play 'In the Mood.' And from then on there was no turning back." It was listed as one of ten "Hot Prospects" in a Mike Stephens column in the *Gazette* of Montreal on Saturday, October 24, 1959.

"In the Mood" would remain on the *Billboard* chart for twenty-three weeks, and led to appearances on Dick Clark's *American Bandstand*. "Then I did another session for Rod," Ernie said.

Before *Soul Train*, the dance show featuring Black teenagers and popular performers, and long before *Dancing with the Stars*, Dick Clark's *American Bandstand* television show was it. It came on weekday afternoons, after school, and youngsters watched and imitated the dance steps of the participants. It should be noted that the camera operators, very much on purpose, avoided showing the few Black dancers in the studio—and there were never more than four or so, always in the background.

There were actually two appearances on Dick Clark's *American Bandstand*—in November 1959 (with Bobby Rydell and the Skyliners) and again in February 1960. The second was on a theater-style weekly stage show, different from the daily afternoon dance program. When he introduced the group, Clark was in the audience and handed out toy instruments to audience members seated near him—seven in all—and made the point that these instruments re-created what used to be the "big band" sound—for a new audience. On that segment, the cameras seemed to like saxophonist Earl "Bang-Bang" Jackson, a Tulsa musician, who later played steadily in a house group at a Tulsa club called Trade Winds West. That night, he played his tenor solo in part on his knees, and wide-eyed, with head-swinging gyrations. Other guests included Paul Anka and Annette Funicello, singing a medley of songs from their new album, *Annette Sings Paul Anka* (Anka also sang his hit, "Puppy Love"); the Crew Cuts, singing "No, No, Never More"; and Brenda Lee, singing "Sweet Nuthin's." Ernie Fields and his Orchestra performed "In the Mood" and "Chattanooga Choo-Choo."

British rock 'n' roll historian and record producer Stuart Colman said in the liner notes for an Ernie Fields album compilation reissue, "It's hard to imagine but in 1959, amidst an ever-growing sea of teenage rock 'n' roll stars, along came a middle-aged trombone player who proceeded to scoop some of the most prestigious musical awards of the year." The Colman notes continued, "He was placed high in *Cash Box* as leader of 'The Best Pop Orchestra' of that year, he was rated runner-up in the annual nationwide DJ's poll and, in short, was generally accepted as one of the hottest newcomers of the season." Nobody, Colman added, "could have been more amused than the recipient Ernie Fields, who had just celebrated his 54th birthday when he hit with 'In the Mood' and the 'newcomer' tag would only have been appropriate when he first started recording some 29 years earlier."[10]

At the record's height, Ernie continued to perform and enjoyed hearing "In the Mood" on the car radio as the group traveled from gig to gig. Rock 'n' roll disc jockey Wolfman Jack (1939–95) hosted a popular nationally syndicated radio show. While Ernie was particularly happy when Jack played his hit, he complained bitterly when the radio personality sounded his trademark raspy wolf howls in the midst of Ernie's record. "Why does he have to do that now?" he fumed.

Ernie said he made good money with the recording, but "I didn't get as much as promised me because it had to be split so many ways" among the studio musicians who were his "partners."[11] About twenty years later, without Ernie's knowledge, Hall would sell those masters, the process making way for subsequent release and presumably for Hall's financial benefit. Ernie Jr. remembers the negotiation, as by this time he was an apprentice in Hall's office, doing copying and learning music contracting before he established his own flourishing business. Little did he know that the snatches of conversations he overheard were not to his dad's advantage. When both men, Ernie Sr. and Jr., figured out what had happened, there was perhaps a shrug and an "I'll be doggone," but never a cross word and never any damage to the longtime Fields-Hall friendship.

The *American Bandstand* appearances were probably the high point of what was already a fading career. There would be more recordings under contract with Capitol Records, but none "did anything," in Ernie's words. But Ernie promoted the *American Bandstand* appearances in his literature and dubbed himself "Mr. In the Mood." "In the Mood" would earn Fields a gold record, meaning it reached one million record sales. It was a big deal then—not so much now, with "platinum" records more commonplace, indicating multimillion sales. It was still a big deal for Ernie. The gold record, loaned for display, currently resides at the Oklahoma Jazz Hall of Fame in Tulsa.

"Mr. In the Mood" became a part of all Ernie's promotional materials, and was displayed on a vanity plate he purchased for the Cadillac that by now was his preferred vehicle, and later on a Mercedes-Benz that Ernie Jr. purchased for his parents.

Ernie Fields never expressed regret about his life or his circumstances. He maintained his humor and enthusiasm about life. He was always optimistic and persistently "hustling" for another opportunity—whether for a gig, a booking date for a client, or the opening of game hunting season. Speaking of hunting, in a letter to me dated "Sun a.m. 3-5-72," he wistfully mentioned, "If I could take a vacation anywhere that I wished, I would like for it to be a safari hunting trip and fishing if not both, hunting. Canada, Old Mexico, or Africa. Where what was game that you are hunting is in abundance."

Through ups and downs, sweet and challenging financial times, and in the trying late '40s, Ernie "doggedly kept his [group] together."[12] There were other solid, maybe even better, music organizations, but the ones that didn't record for the most part were left in obscurity. After his big hit "In the Mood," my father continued to record. Some of the Capitol Records sessions attempted still to put a rock stamp on '40s standards like "Chattanooga Choo-Choo," "The Charleston," and others. None of them caught on.

But Ernie can lay this specific claim: Having started in the late 1920s and continued into the mid-1960s, he maintained his highly regarded territory band, the Ernie Fields Orchestra, longer than most others. "Of the earlier territory bands," jazz historian Albert McCarthy wrote, the Ernie Fields Orchestra "was the last to give in and the final survivor of a once flourishing tradition, [and] it deserves its honorable niche in big band jazz history."[13]

ROLL CALL

When work on this memoir first began in the early 1980s, my dad embraced the idea wholeheartedly. He began in earnest trying to remember names, conversations, and incidents. He also began the important task of identifying the names of musicians in the huge trove of photographs illustrating his career over the years. Many years later, after his death, I was going through the materials as I began to write. I found a note with a list of musicians' names. The note said that, as many as were listed, he probably "was leaving out some." He urged me to please "mention as many as you can." They may not have become famous, he continued, but he must have seen something in them, "or I would not have had them in the band." The following "roll call" is my effort to honor that request. Some I was able to trace and locate through newspaper or magazine mentions, or they were listed as personnel on recordings. Sometimes I relied on obituaries, or the memories of other musicians or their family members. I found information about many of the musicians, but many others seem simply to have vanished.

Hortense Aikens. Featured vocalist in the late 1930s, her name is seen in an Ernie Fields newspaper ad in the *Kalispell (Mont.) Daily Inter Lake*, on August 13, 1937, for a dance at Island Park's the Old Stomping Grounds, and in another ad in the *Logan (Utah) Herald-Journal*, on September 24, 1937, for a performance at the Dansante Ballroom. The ballroom, according to the Bear River Heritage Area website, was built in 1900. Playing a central role in the social life of the Cache Valley community, it is the area's premier dance hall, with space for some three thousand guests at events. Later, it was used as a clothing factory and is now renovated and houses offices, recital and rehearsal halls, and practice room for the Utah Festival Opera Company.

Curby Joseph "C. J." Alexander Jr. (born October 25, 1920; died March 1956). Alto sax and clarinet. Alexander grew up on Latimer Street in Tulsa, near Hal Singer's family, and graduated from the city's Booker T. Washington High School in 1937. He attended Prairie View College in Texas, because he heard it had a good band, and then Langston University in Oklahoma. He was a member of the house band at the Apollo Theater in New York City for years, and he performed with the USO in Germany before playing with Lucky Millinder and Clarence Love. When he died, of pancreatic cancer, recounted his sister, Juanita Hopkins, the entire Ernie Fields orchestra played at his funeral. Al Harrison sang before the eulogy. The minister of Morning Star Baptist Church in Tulsa cleared the whole front of the altar to accommodate the musicians. "It was beautiful," Hopkins said. She described Ernie Fields as a mix of father figure and employer. "He tried to keep the fellas straight."[1]

Eugene "Gene" Ammons (born April 14, 1925, in Chicago; died August 6, 1974, in Chicago). Tenor sax. Ammons worked the Apollo circuit with Ernie Fields in the '40s. He was known alternately as "Jug" and "the Boss." Ammons replaced Stan Getz as a member of Woody Herman's Second Herd (Herman dubbed his bands "herds").

Benjamin Franklin "Chops" Arradondo Jr. (born January 1914 in Dallas; died October 1986 in Dallas). Trumpet player. "Chops" was in the band in the early '40s along with vocalist Melvin Moore. A January 29, 1943, article in the *Omaha Star* about an upcoming Fields performance at the Dreamland on Monday night, February 1, referred to Arradondo as "the singing trumpeter." The last ten years of his life were spent volunteering at a Dallas community center. A room and an event there are named in his honor. Bob Wills reportedly once told him in New Orleans that it was "too bad" that his boss would not let Bennie come and play with him and the Texas Playboys.

Leroy "Pete" Bailey. Tenor sax. Bailey was with one of earliest Fields groups of 1927 or 1928 and early '30s. His father, Peter Bailey, ran a pool hall at 210 East Archer Street in Tulsa and the family lived at 1323 North Greenwood Avenue. His father had a brand-new Studebaker that he let him use when group made its first "away" trip to Longview and Gladewater, Texas, big oil boomtowns at the time.

Hobart Banks (born August 17, 1907, in Rentiesville, Oklahoma; died in 1957). Piano and fiddle. Banks was considered a child prodigy. He grew up in Muskogee, Oklahoma, and graduated from the public schools there. In addition to playing with the Fields organization, Banks played with Don Byas, Aaron Bell, and Clarence Love.

Albert Bartee (born in Kansas City, Kansas; date of death unknown). Drums. Bartee is believed to be among the 1949 Ernie Fields personnel and may have recorded in a New Jersey session, per a Walter Miller interview in Paris in 1967. Later he was affiliated with Tulsa native Earl Bostic, vocalist Linda Hopkins, Nellie Lutcher (according to a *Jet* magazine article from June 19, 1952, p. 40), and pianist Dorothy Donegan (according to *Jet* magazine's November 5, 1964, issue, which includes his picture on p. 64).

John William Baul (born 1880 in Kentucky; died 1961 in Tulsa). Violin and other instruments. Baul was one of the first to invite Fields to gig, when Ernie saw Baul and others rehearsing in the Royal Annex apartments. Baul

John William Baul, circa 1905.
Photo courtesy of Orville Baul.

lived at 1142½ North Greenwood Avenue in Tulsa, according to the 1935 city directory. Later, he was in the charter group of the Black musicians' union local in Tulsa, living at that time near Ernie's mother on East Marshall Place. He served as secretary for Local 808 of the American Federation of Musicians and was the local's first convention delegate. He is believed to be one of few Black musicians ever to perform with the Tulsa Symphony. He worked for Sun Oil Company as a maintenance supervisor for thirty-seven years.

Fred Lee Beckett (born January 23, 1917, in Nettleton, Mississippi; died January 30, 1946). Trombone. Beckett also played with the Andy Kirk organization and was featured in Nat Towles's orchestra. He died of tuberculosis.

Parker Thomas Berry (born November 24, 1899 or 1900; died July 1975 in Los Angeles). Trombonist and arranger. Berry was from Hamilton, Ohio, near Cincinnati. He played with Curtis Mosby, who owned the Club Alabam in Los Angeles, in the '20s, and with Speed Webb in Los Angeles and arranged for Les Hite. Berry was in the Ernie Fields orchestra from the early '40s to the '50s, including when drummer Al Duncan joined. His favorite exclamation was "Jeeeeezus!" He used to tease trombonist Russell "Big Chief" Moore after he came in the band, "Chief, ain't you glad Ernie came down [Route] 66 and saw you with that blanket on your back out there hitchhiking? You finally found out the Indian was free, too." Chief would reply, "Aw hell, shut up, P. B." After Ernie Fields, Berry played with Lionel Hampton. He is on the November 1949 Regal Records sessions in New York and Kansas City. Parker's wife, "Dimples," was a dancer in the band. In a January 3, 1942, *Pittsburgh Courier* "All-American Band" poll, Parker Berry was one of ten arrangers listed. Other Fields personnel in the poll included drummer Clarence Dixon and guitarist René Hall. In another *Courier* article, from January 5, 1940, southwestern music maestro Don Parcells noted that Berry "worked extensively in and out of Hollywood" and credited Berry's arrangements for his success in a Dallas Battle of the Bands sponsored by American Federation of Musicians Local 186. Later on, Berry worked for the post office in Los Angeles, according to Melvin Moore.

Earl Bostic (born April 25, 1913, in Tulsa; died October 28, 1965). Alto sax. Bostic was inducted into the Oklahoma Jazz Hall of Fame in 1993. He started his music career at age eighteen with Tee Holder's Dark Clouds of Joy, out of Muskogee, Oklahoma. He was a top soloist with the organization of Charlie Barnett, a white bandleader out of New York City, who became famous in part for being among the first to feature Black soloists. Bostic played with many, many other jazz luminaries, as well as forming his own band at one point. The great tenor sax man Buddy Tate, who boasted of hiring Bostic for Tee Holder's group, said, "He could do anything on alto, and he could write like crazy."[2] Bostic played with Ernie Fields while he was in high school and sometimes between college studies.

Sticks Bradley, a.k.a. **Sticks Lee**. Vocalist in the early '50s. Ernie described Bradley as "tall, brown skin." He said she called herself "a peach from Georgia." Ernie said she "handled herself well" and was just as good as Leora Davis. He said she lasted with his organization about a year. She was also featured as a drummer and dancer, as indicated in newspaper ads in 1952 in Greeley, Colorado, and in 1953 in Carlsbad, New Mexico. On April 16, 1954, she was mentioned in an item in a Hedda Hopper column promoting a holdover appearance at Miami's Black Orchid Lounge with the Jimmy Wiley Trio. She performed there regularly through July that year.

Billy Brooks (born August 16, 1926 in Mobile, Alabama; died December 24, 2002, in Amsterdam). Trumpet player and composer. Brooks was in the band when drummer Al Duncan joined in the '40s. He also played with the Lionel Hampton Orchestra for eighteen years.

Harold "Al" Bruce (born September 26, 1919, in Tulsa; died March 20, 1993). Trumpet. Bruce was described as an "undisciplined lead player and fond of the upper register."[3] Before he was with Fields, he was with Omaha's Nat Towles and Benny Carter. While with Jay McShann, he was Charlie Parker's roommate. Bruce is on the November 1949 Regal label Ernie Fields recordings made in New York City and Kansas City, Missouri.

Mike Wray "Monk" Bruce (born September 10, 1946, in Bartlesville, Oklahoma; died August 24, 2005, in Bentonville, Arkansas). Blues guitar. Bruce graduated from Nathan Hale High School in Tulsa and grew up playing music in Tulsa. He was white. He was with Ernie Fields as the group transitioned to Ernie Fields and Son. That group then backed Bobby "Blue" Bland from 1969 to 1971. Monk Bruce hooked up with Tulsa musician David Teegarden Sr. and recorded several albums, and performed with scores of bands in styles ranging from country to jazz. (He is not to be confused with the original Alice Cooper Band guitarist by the same name.) Bruce contracted hepatitis, he believed, during a Far East tour with Rebbie Jackson (Michael Jackson's sister) and died awaiting a liver transplant.

O. Z. Burley (born January 24, 1911, in Tulsa; died November 1, 1979, in Contra Costa, California). Violin. According to the 1930 census, home for the nineteen-year-old Burley was Holdenville, Oklahoma; he was "not attending school" and his occupation was musician, in the "orchestra" industry. In the 1940 census, he was listed as single and twenty-nine years old, residing in the California State Prison in San Rafael, more commonly known as San Quentin. For education level, the census showed he had completed two years of high school. Prison records say he was incarcerated for manslaughter and his occupation at the time was porter. In July 1941 he was transferred to the state prison in Chino, California. He registered for the draft at age thirty-one, on January 16, 1942, listing his employer as the Idyllwild Café; the draft registration lists his complexion as light brown and his eye color as brown. At the time he lived in Los Angeles, in the same household as his mother, Edna Walls. Dope, Ernie believed, "was his ruination."

Don Byas (born October 21, 1912, in Muskogee, Oklahoma; died August 24, 1972, in Amsterdam). Tenor sax. Byas was briefly with Ernie Fields in the 1930s. It was bad how "whiskey messed up so many," Ernie said. According to Wikipedia, Benny Carter, who played many instruments, was Byas's idol. Byas started playing in local orchestras at age seventeen, and played with Bennie Moten, Terrence "Tee" Holder, and Walter Page. He founded and led his own college band, Don Carlos and His Collegiate Ramblers, in 1931–32 at Langston University in Oklahoma. Byas lived in Europe the last twenty-six years of his life.

Jefferson "Jeff" Edgar Carrington (born February 10, 1909, in Galveston, Texas; died January 4, 2004, in Detroit). Trumpet. For a long time Carrington was a confirmed bachelor, but then he and wife Mildred settled in the Detroit area. Jeff Carrington was with the Fields band from about 1937 to around 1945. He played Ernie Fields's first Vocalion recordings, in 1939. He kept his room "in order," said vocalist Melvin Moore. "Everything was always in place." Moore described his buddy as "a gambler—but a good gambler." Carrington came from Tee Holder's band after matriculating at Texas Southern University. Ernie switched Carrington's chair with trumpeter Edwin Middleton. Carrington, who was on the first and second eastern tours with the organization, was considered a peacemaker of the group. He'd been in the Tee Holder band and was used to good gates and used to bad ones. "In that way, if somebody was grumbling or sticking their mouth out, Jeff would be the one to first tell them that some would be good, some would be bad," Ernie said. An obituary notice in the *Detroit News* said he was remembered "for his adventuresome spirit and good humor."

Oliver Carwell. Vocals. Carwell was with the orchestra from approximately 1938 to at least 1941. He was mentioned in newspapers as being a featured soloist (along with Leora Davis and Melvin Moore) in the Ernie Fields floor show that included a full male chorus.[4] An article in the *Grand Junction (Colo.) Daily Sentinel*, on September 13, 1938, noted the fifteen-voice male chorus was "made up from the 17-piece band personnel" and was a "highly remarkable feature of the band." On August 7, 1941, the *Salt Lake Tribune* called Carwell a featured soloist along with "Melvy Moore." It is unclear to me why he is not mentioned in any of Dad's notes about the big 1939 trip, nor is there a mention of where he came from or what became of him.

Gus Chappel (or Chappelle). Trombone and vocals. From Chicago, Chappel was with Ernie Fields around 1942. Songs he recorded with Earl Hines and René Hall in 1945 were "Nonchalant Man," "At the El Grotto," and "Spooks Ball." He also recorded with Dinah Washington.

Rozelle Claxton (born February 5, 1913, in Bartlett, Tennessee [near Memphis]; died March 30, 1995, in Lake Forest, Illinois). Pianist-arranger. Claxton grew up in Memphis and after graduating from Manasses High School, later settled in Kansas City. That was where he was recruited to join Fields for his 1939 East Coast tour and recording debut. He was on the 1939 Ernie Fields recordings on Vocalion Records. A prolific arranger, he provided scores for Count Basie, Jimmie Lunceford, and Andy Kirk, among many others. He also worked as an accompanist for Pearl Bailey. He spent the last fifty years of his life living and working in the Chicago area.

Teddy Cole. Vocals. Cole sang on the 1949 reissue of "T-Town Blues" on the Regal Records label and "Long Last Love" in 1952 on the Gotham Records label. Before he worked with the Fields organization, he was with Count Basie. "Teddy fits the band and the band fits him," said a September 23, 1950, *Pittsburgh Courier* article about a Memphis performance. The writer described Cole's style as "the greatest combination I've seen since the days of Earl Hines, Billy Eckstine, Andy Kirk and the late Pha Terrell." The article continued, "He opened his spot with the popular 'Mona Lisa' and came back with an original, 'Traveling Blues.' It was blues then on until he finally went off stage."

Leroy "Tex" Cooper (born August 31, 1928, in Dallas; died January 15, 2009). Baritone sax. Cooper was a Ray Charles orchestra mainstay and sometimes director. He was with Ernie Fields from 1948 to 1951 until he was inducted into the armed services. At the time, the early 1940s, drummer Al Duncan was also in orchestra. Leroy Cooper was no relation to jazz trombonist George "Buster" Cooper (born April 4, 1929; died May 13, 2016), contrary to liner notes on the recording *Big Band Jazz*. Ernie described Tex as a "big, light, heavy-set guy."

Billy Davenport (born April 23, 1931, in Chicago; died December 24, 1999, in Chicago). Drums. Davenport was with Ernie Fields in the early '60s. Later he played with the early Paul Butterfield Blues Band. He was posthumously inducted into the Rock & Roll Hall of Fame in 2015.

LEROY(Big Tex)COOPER Featured with   GENERAL ARTISTS CORPORATION
ERNIE FIELDS And His Orchestra   NEW YORK CHICAGO HOLLYWOOD CINCINNATI LONDON

Leroy Cooper, when he was with Ernie Fields and His Orchestra, 1948–51. After leaving Fields's organization, Cooper became a mainstay with the Ray Charles Orchestra. Author collection.

Leora Davis. Vocals. Davis was the band's first female vocalist. She was featured on Ernie Fields's 1939 Vocalion recordings "You Gave Me Everything but Love," "I'm Living in a Great Big Way," and "Blues at Midnight." Fields described her as the first vocalist who "meant anything." She could do a fast tune and scat if necessary, or a slow tune, he said. René Hall thought a lot of her, so she was hired for five dollars a night. She lasted about three years with the band, Ernie said. But, he said, she "wasn't as exciting as Sticks [Bradley]." Davis sang like Ella Fitzgerald, he observed, but "I wasn't big enough to know Ella at the time." According to Ernie, Davis fell in love with the band's bus driver, Thomas Hamilton "Zack" Zackery, who wasn't ready to marry. So, she disappeared, leaving no contact information. Ernie and Hall tried fruitlessly for years to find her, hearing at one point that she was in the Los Angeles area. The only photograph I found of Davis was with an article in the *Grand Junction (Colo.) Daily Sentinel* from September 13, 1938. The story called her a "singing entertainer of considerable talent."

Miles Davis (born May 26, 1926; died September 28, 1991). Trumpet. Davis was with the Ernie Fields band for a few dates in the Saint Louis area. Melvin Moore claimed, "In fact, I found Miles."[5] Moore insisted he was the first one in the organization to meet and advocate for Davis. A two-week tryout ended with Fields passing up the chance to keep Davis. The monumental miscalculation would be a joke between the friends thereafter.

Clarence "Dick" Dixon (born August 20, 1911, in Rosebud, Texas; date of death unknown). Drums. Dixon's family moved from Texas to Tulsa when he was a youth, and his drumming in marching band earned him a scholarship to Xavier University in New Orleans. He married Laura Ann Zackery (sister of the Fields orchestra's bus driver, Thomas Hamilton "Zack" Zackery) on May 2, 1935. They had a son named Clarence del, born in July 1935, who died in 2005. Dixon's military draft card in 1940 listed him as five feet, seven inches tall and weighing 138 pounds. He joined Ernie Fields in 1931 and remained until 1947. Dixon and his family lived in South Haven, a Black enclave west of Tulsa. Many Blacks fled there after the 1921 race massacre in Tulsa. Dixon was on the 1939 Vocalion recordings. In a 1940 *Downbeat* magazine poll, Dixon was voted No. 2 drummer. This recognition of his talent made him much sought-after for his artistry, but he remained with the Ernie Fields Orchestra, traveling all over the country. Gunther Schuller, in *The Swing Era: The Development of Jazz, 1930–1945*, referred to Dixon as a "fine, clean drummer, one of the most experienced of the territory band percussionists." Los Angeles–based drummer Washington Rucker, a Tulsa native, credits Dixon (who lived across the street from him in South Haven) with teaching Rucker the concept of "melody drums," which he says is an asset to his career.

Roy "Buck" Douglas (born March 26, 1913, in Eskridge, Kansas; died February 1974 in Chicago). Tenor sax. Douglas became a leading player around Kansas City, sometimes referred to as "sin and saxophone country." He was on the Ernie Fields 1939 Vocalion recordings. Gunther Schuller said that on those recordings Douglas "crossed his style with Herschel Evans [his sound] and Lester Young [his notes]." He is listed in some sources as being on the November 1949 Fields recordings on the Regal label in New York and

Kansas City. Douglas was part of the musical family that included brothers Gil, a.k.a. Bill, on trumpet and Tommy on alto sax. The Tommy Douglas Band, along with leaders Chauncy Downs, Jay McShann, Harlen Leonard, and Oliver Todd, were reliable purveyors of the Kansas City style.

Chauncy Downs (born in 1904; died in 1966). Violin. Downs, who was from Kansas City, Missouri, was considered a close second to Count Basie among Kansas City jazz figures of the 1940s. Downs led the first African American band, the Rinkey Dinks, to play the newly opened white venue Pla-Mor Ballroom in Kansas City, in May 1928. He later operated the popular Casa Loma Ballroom at Eighteenth Street and Prospect Avenue in Kansas City.

Cliff Dudley (born July 28, 1917, in Springfield, Ohio; died December 7, 1983, in Omaha, of a heart attack). Trombone player and arranger. Dudley moved to Omaha in 1945 to join the Nat Towles Orchestra. He later moved to Oklahoma to play with Ernie Fields, then went back to Omaha to lead his own quartet. In 1956 he became Omaha's first Black city building inspector. "Very nice trombone player," said Ernie Fields.

Alrock "Al" Clifford Duncan Jr. (born October 8, 1927, in Corsicana, Texas; died January 2, 1995, in Las Vegas). Drums. Al Duncan recorded with a wide array of artists, including Ernie Fields (1949 Regal Records sessions in New York and Kansas City), B. B. King, Jay McShann, Curtis Mayfield, Willie Dixon, Muddy Waters, and Phil Upchurch, to name a few. Duncan was a longtime session drummer for Chicago labels Chess, Vee-Jay, and others in blues, jazz, and gospel. He was integral to the development of postwar rhythm and blues in Chicago. After a stint with the Ringling Brothers circus, he joined Ernie Fields in the late 1940s, staying, he said, for about two years. "I can tell you who was in the band," he told Bill Greensmith in an interview published in the magazine *Blues and Rhythm*. "Leroy Cooper, baritone; Harold Minerva[e], and Luther West, altos; Eli Watkins, tenor; Parker Berry, trombone. The other trombone player when I first got in the band was Benny Powell. The trumpet section was Billy Brooks, Walter Miller and Robert Moss. His guitar player was Ernest Luckett, they called him 'Butch.'"[6] Duncan was one of the few studio legends—fewer than half a dozen—sometimes called "the Grandfathers of Groove," as he was comfortable playing jazz with Willie Dixon, Basie, and Duke Ellington, as well as rock 'n' roll soul with the Temptations or Marvin Gaye.

Dave Duncan (born December 29, 1905; died April 4, 1975). Piano, trombone, and arrangements. From Ponca City, Oklahoma, Duncan was with the group in early 1928 and rented a room in Ernie's mother's home. It was considered revolutionary in the day to have a white musician in a Black band. Ernie told Duncan he could tell people he was the manager if he needed to. Duncan said, "I understand." The 1938 Ponca City directory lists Duncan at 310 West Central Street, the same address as the Kola Tepee Music Store, where he was a music teacher, and the Kola Tepee Beauty Shop, likely run by his wife, Ruth. Duncan's 1940 draft card gives an address of 409 No. Fifth Street, Ponca City. Explained Ernie in an interview in Boston with arts reporter Kay Bourne, "I saw talent and didn't see any color."[7]

Mack Easton (born April 6, 1914, in Mississippi; died May 1, 1986, in Chicago). Alto sax. Easton was a well-regarded session musician, especially in the blues genre.

Estelle Edson Banks, a.k.a. **Stella Edmerson** (born January 25, 1920, in Manor, Texas; died December 5, 2006, in Austin, Texas). Vocals. In the early 1940s, Estelle Edson was billed as "dynamic songtress" on a promotional placard featuring Ernie Fields. Top billing went to Bill "Bojangles" Robinson, "heading his Own All Colored Revue." Edson was with Ernie Fields approximately six and a half years, touring the United States three times by her own account. She described the organization as "all talent." She joined in 1942, after she finished Sam Houston College, and Ernie raved, "She could really sing the blues." He said, "She was best at everything she did. She was also a 'good mixer,'" he said. She could talk to "college people or ignorant people." In school she was going with a tenor sax player, Earl Warren, and Ernie hired him later. "I was always glad if I could get a college [trained musician]." A review of a 1941 Denver Rainbow Ballroom performance said Edson was a "good seller," doing the "jive work while Melvin Moore works the ballads." A record shop ad on March 30, 1946, in the *Jackson (Miss.) Enterprise* listed

Vocalists Helen Humes (*left*) and Estelle Edson with Ernie Fields, early 1940s. Author collection.

Edson's "Don't Drive This Jive Away" for sale (Edson had recorded the song on the Black & White label with Oscar Pettiford, who coauthored the tune with her). The previous week, an ad in the *Baltimore Afro American* listed Edson's "Be-Baba-Le-Ba/Rhythm in a Riff" in stock at Good Time Records on Fremont Avenue.

Theodore Marcus "Teddy" Edwards (born April 6, 1924, in Jackson, Mississippi; died April 20, 2003, in Los Angeles). Tenor sax. Fields said he suggested Edwards switch from alto sax to tenor. He hired him and guitarist/arranger Jack "Earlie" Scott as a pair, reportedly in Tampa, Florida, where a teenage Edwards hoped to get to New York. Instead, Edwards "hopped off the band bus in Los Angeles in 1945 and started working with Roy Milton's combo."[8] Some reviewers suggested Edwards was the first to play bebop on the tenor, possessing a unique sound—not like that of Coleman Hawkins or Lester Young, from whom most drew inspiration. Edwards claimed in an interview with me at his home in Los Angeles that he and Melvin Moore often found themselves in competition for the attention of the same woman. He said he found out the hard way that "Melvin always won." Edwards was considered the star of the Los Angeles jazz scene. He performed with, and in some cases recorded with, many premier musicians and orchestras of his day.

Rick Eilerts. Bass. In his words, the Shadow Lake Eight founder/leader "toured as a fill-in" with Fields. "I was the only white guy in the band." That's where he met arranger Jack Scott (who called him Ricky) and persuaded him to do arrangements for his fledging integrated touring group in order to give it a "Black" sound, and met "Little" Clifford Watson, an Ernie Fields alum who became a vocalist in Eilerts's group. Eilerts called Watson "a dynamic showman." The Shadow Lake Eight, started around 1958, disbanded in 1967.

Russell Embray (born February 5, 1922, in Wichita, Kansas; died November 7, 1962, in Wichita). Trumpet. Before he played with Fields, Embray played with the Nat Towles Orchestra. The February 3, 1955, issue of *Jet* magazine, in a column called "Talking About . . . ," mentioned "the divorce pending between globetrotting June Embray and her estranged husband, trumpet playing bandleader Russell Embray of Wichita." Ernie called Embray a "fine lead trumpet player."

Booker T. Ervin Jr. (born October 30, 1930, in Denison, Texas; died August 31, 1970, in New York City). Tenor sax. Ervin taught himself the instrument while in the air force; he had enlisted after high school graduation. On his way home after a year of study at what became known as Berklee School of Music in Boston, he went on the road with Fields. It was 1954, and the group was then a ten-piece rhythm and blues outfit, described later in liner notes as playing the "ultra-rhythmic aggregation so popular in the dance halls of the South and Southwest." Ervin learned a lot about swinging, from "playing the band's 'back-beat' rhythm section." He left the band around 1958, going to Dallas for gigs with James Clay, then Portland, Oregon, and subsequently New York City, where he joined Charles Mingus's Jazz Workshop.[9] Fields would later describe him as one of the greatest instrumentalists in his band's career.[10]

Oscar Estelle (born August 18, 1929; died March 1968 in Tulsa). Baritone sax. He was taken from Ernie Fields in 1953 by Lionel Hampton, along with Elon Watkins. Recorded with Fields, Hampton, and Art Farmer.

Jo Jo Evans (born Josie Mae Evans on February 10, 1921, in Hazelhurst, Mississippi; died October 27, 1986, in Milwaukee). Vocals. Fields says he hired Evans away from Billy Eckstine at René Hall's suggestion. He said he hadn't heard her before he hired her. He said Eckstine wanted to hold on to her but she didn't want a contract because her mother would get on her about college. Evans attended Christ Missionary and Industrial College, a boarding school in Jackson, Mississippi, founded in 1897—likely because of segregated schools in her home community. There, she was part of a traveling sextet who were tutored on the road as they raised money for the school. "I was an alto," she said, "if you want to call me that. I had a heavy voice." She graduated at fifteen, then went to Los Angeles, deciding to go single. She was hired by Clarence Muse to sing background for Warner Bros. Pictures. She never got any on-camera film roles, she said, "because I photographed too light." Her recordings on Black & White Records included "Goody Goody, Baby" and "Root of All My Evil." On September 23, 1950, a *Pittsburgh Courier* review of a Memphis performance said, "Jo Evans came on with blues which is always big in Memphis. With a lovely voice and gorgeous gown, she's a natural." One discography includes an Evans recording with the Ernie Fields orchestra in 1951 called "Frustrated Woman" (Gotham 281, Krazy Kat LP 814).

Clarise/Clarice Ford. Exotic dancer. Singer Jo Jo Evans described Ford as a "shake dancer." A *Pittsburgh Courier* review on September 23, 1950, described her moves as "contortions." Ernie said she was "a very, very important single with the group." Ford died in Kansas City. Another exotic dancer with the orchestra was Pat McMillan, who was mentioned during a half-hour radio broadcast of a Fields Orchestra performance from the Jacob Brown Auditorium in Brownsville, Texas, in the 1950s. (Back then, the Jacob Brown Auditorium was the largest venue in town, with a capacity of 1,300. Today, it is used for everything from athletic events to banquets. It is on the campus of Texas Southmost College.)

Ernie Freeman (born August 16, 1922, in Cleveland; died May 16, 1981, in Los Angeles). Pianist/arranger. Freeman was one of the studio musicians on "In the Mood" and other, later Ernie Fields recordings. In 1958, he was part of the house band for the newly formed Rendezvous Records label, where Fields's hit version of "In the Mood" was recorded. Freeman remained a successful session musician, arranging and appearing on material of Frank Sinatra, Connie Francis, Johnny Mathis, and others. He also played on many early rock and R&B sessions in the '50s with many white artists. He played piano on the Platters' "The Great Pretender" in 1955. In 1956, the Ernie Freeman Combo and the Platters appeared in the movie *Rock Around the Clock*, introduced by Alan Freed.

A. G. Godley (born October 17, 1903, in Fort Smith, Arkansas; died in February 1973 in Seattle). Drums. Godley was briefly with Fields in the 1930s. Previously he was with Alphonso Trent's orchestra in Muskogee, Oklahoma; he had joined that group in 1924, replacing Trent's cousin on drums. Godley, according to jazz trombonist Leo "Snub" Mosley, was "one of the greatest drummers I ever listened to." Mosley also claimed the skillful drummer drank heavily. He added he believes Godley may have started "that bit where everybody jumps off the bandstand and leaves the drummer to work out by himself up there."[11] Godley's nickname in Trent's group was "Ananias Garibaldi." The initials A. G. did not stand for anything, Godley said; they were his first name.

Hunter "Shoe Sole" Gray. Alto sax. Believed to be a Tulsa native, Gray played on the 1939 Vocalion recording "Lard Stomp." His brother Henry Gray was a Los Angeles trumpet player. Hunter Gray also worked for Jay McShann and Count Basie and later headed his own trio in California featuring Fields alum Estelle Edson. The *Sacramento Bee* on September 14, 1946, advertised his Jam Session at Zanzibar, at Sixth Street and Capitol Avenue. On October 26 that year, *Billboard* reported that Gray was "held over for another four weeks at Zanzibar."

Freddie Green (born March 31, 1911, in Charleston, South Carolina; died March 1, 1987, in Las Vegas, of a heart attack). Rhythm guitar. Green left Fields to join Count Basie around 1937 and was a mainstay for almost fifty years. "He undoubtedly was worth something, else I wouldn't have had him in the band," said Fields.[12]

Teddy Hale (born in 1926 in Philadelphia; died in May 1959 in Washington, D.C.). Tap dancer. Hale was with the Ernie Fields Orchestra briefly in the 1940s. He was a child prodigy, and at the height of his career Hale was considered "the Art Tatum of tap." Milton Berle introduced Hale on his television variety program in 1949 for three minutes of national fame. "Teddy Hale was everyone's idol," said hoofer Gregory Hines, who with his brother Maurice was on the same bill with Hale at the Apollo Theater in the 1950s. Some sources say Hale died of a brain hemorrhage; others say it was a narcotics overdose.

René Joseph Hall (born September 28, 1912, in Morgan City, Louisiana; died February 11, 1988, in Los Angeles). Trombone, guitar, and arranger. Hall married Octavia Renfro and later Gertrude "Sugar" Hall. Melvin Moore described Hall as Ernie's "ace boon coon." He wrote arrangements—and was another one who "didn't spend no money" (gambling). He was also considered the "straw boss." According to Moore, "He was what you called the 'Music Man,' whom Ernie had to pay more money." Hall and Moore were perhaps Ernie's closest friends, remaining so for life. Hall was with the Fields organization from 1935 to 1942, and when he left, he went with Earl "Fatha" Hines, playing second trombone. Hines and later Basie "did not go for all that guitar" that Hall was playing. Hall wrote a book, *Rock 'n' Roll Guitar*, in 1965, a beginning guitar method covering tuning and general positioning and illustrating various techniques of guitar stylings. Hall was arranger on Ray Charles's 1966 album *I Choose to Sing the Blues*. One of Ernie Fields Jr.'s daughters and the author's daughter have the middle name René, in Hall's honor.

Jim Halsey (born October 7, 1930, in Independence, Kansas). Promoter and booking agent. Halsey, who is white, is credited with guiding the careers of Roy Clark, the Oak Ridge Boys, Reba McIntire, and others, He now resides in Tulsa. While a student at Independence Junior College, he began organizing dances, big band shows, and other entertainment. He met Fields around 1949 or '50 while still a student, and started booking him then, first at the colleges and other schools in the area, then at other performance venues, mostly in Missouri and Kansas. Many years later he would say he always respected Ernie Fields because "he had so much integrity." Fields said Halsey "went on and got big, and never did give up on me." In a six-page handwritten letter to Fields dated January 19, 1993, Halsey said, "I always enjoyed working with you and you always had a great band." He added, "More than anything, however, was your knowledge of the business and the integrity with which you conducted your life."

Other booking agents Fields enlisted after Willard Alexander's interest waned included the Frederick Brothers Agency (L. A. Frederick was president and his brother Bill Frederick was secretary-treasurer) of Chicago and New York City, who booked him into the mid-1940s. Frederick Brothers began around 1932 as a band agency in Oklahoma and Kansas City, and in ten years the agency was handling some one hundred musical outfits as well as theater, nightclub, cocktail, and ice show units.[13] They opened offices in Cleveland (1934), New York City (1938), Chicago (1940), and Hollywood (1942). They had as clients many amusement parks, which all had ballrooms. Fields said he felt close to them in part because of their Oklahoma roots and their aggressive bookings for him during the '30s in Los Angeles, a Black theater in Chicago, up and down the West Coast, Portland, and Seattle. "They were one of the first that got me in some of the big places," he said.[14]

Other agents included Jess Coates of Duncan, Oklahoma, who ran a filling station and an open-air dance hall; Robert Cooksey of Tulsa, who also managed Leon McAuliffe, a country and western star; H. E. Schoonover, who came to Tulsa from Boise, Idaho, to hear the band and book their first Northwest tour; Woodrow "Woody" Winton of Pawhuska, Oklahoma; and Reg D. Marshall Agency of Los Angeles, which signed western band star Bob Wills in 1955. Marshall provided engagements at many military installations, country clubs, colleges, and universities, as well as VFW, American Legion, and Elks Club halls and other such venues. "Doc" Johnson of Dallas, a Black promoter who was photographed by Marion Butts at his desk with an Ernie Fields poster on the wall in the background, also owned the Rose Room in Dallas. An *Amarillo Globe* newspaper item promoting a Fields engagement at the Aviatrix Club on Highway 66 said Earl Hooper was his manager. It notes, "Manager Hooper suggests that anyone planning in attend tonight to make reservations." William P. Falkenberg was the first promoter to encourage Fields to enlarge his small band into a big band. Falkenberg had managed Tee Holder, who had moved his band from

REG. D. MARSHALL AGENCY

Orchestras   *Artists Representatives*   Attractions
∗ ∗
P.O. BOX 4, EAGLE ROCK STATION
LOS ANGELES 41, CALIFORNIA
HOllywood 9-8238

Dear Friend:

We are now booking engagements in your territory on the
finest entertaining show-band in the country...........

ERNIE FIELDS and his World Famous ORCHESTRA and Floor Show.

For years an established "name" in the show business....
Ernie Fields is on his annual coast to coast tour carrying
the same fine group of entertainers, the same great dance
orchestra and presenting the same fine entertainment. The
package includes Lawrence "Pepper" Neely, vocalist and star
of Capitol Records; Thomas Hodge, the famous Internationally
known one leg dancer; Ethel Mooney, vocalist and Clarice Ford
exotic dancer. Company of 13 people.

The name Ernie Fields has been a household word in the traveling dance orchestra business for many years. His hundreds
and hundreds of repeat engagements speak for themselves.
Ninety percent(90%) of all engagements this season are return engagements.

Please let me hear from you immediately as to your interest
in playing one or more engagements with ERNIE FIELDS.

Write..........Wire.......... or phone for dates and terms.

Cordially,

REG. D. MARSHALL AGENCY

RDM/rm
131-55

Letter from Reg. D. Marshall Agency soliciting bookings for Ernie Fields and His World Famous Orchestra, 1955. Marshall's bookings included country clubs and many military related venues. Author collection.

Muskogee to Tulsa in 1927, but got tired of Holder not paying his musicians. In 1930, he managed the Crystal Ballroom in Tulsa, where lots of orchestras performed. Harold Oxley also booked Fields even though Reg Marshall had a formal booking agreement. Oxley also managed Jimmie Lunceford, who Ernie always admired and tried to emulate. "Did I grin," Ernie said in an undated note to me, "when people use to say you sure remind and look like Lunceford on the bandstand." Upon his death in 1952 at age fifty-two, Oxley, a Providence, Rhode Island, native, was described in a *Billboard* magazine obituary as a "leading figure in the management of Negro attractions." He is credited with discovering T-Bone Walker and Joe Liggins. Oxley's father, Benjamin, was one of the founders of the American Federation of Musicians.

But the very first promoter, "as far as I could figure," in Ernie's words, was Earl L. Roberts, a carpenter and building contractor based in Pittsfield, Massachusetts. He was co-owner of the Showboat dance hall, built in 1930 in nearby New Lebanon, New York. He operated the venue with his brother,

Arthur, when his partner and fellow builder Edmond Flynn Sr. died in 1935. The Showboat was not near water, but resembled a ship, complete with portholes, anchors, a ship mast, and a gangplank for entrance. It became a showcase for big bands, locally and nationally. Featured performers included Fletcher Henderson, Paul Whiteman, the Dorsey Brothers (Tommy and Jimmy) among others. Ernie's first trip east, in 1934, included bookings (by Roberts) in Connecticut, Vermont, Maine, and upstate New York.

Opal Harris (Patricia Mae Willis) (born January 16, 1938; died June 24, 2010). Vocals. Harris graduated from Tulsa's Booker T. Washington High School in 1957. Her professional career began with the Ernie Fields Orchestra but was cut short, her obituary said, because her parents felt she was not mature enough to travel on the road. Later, she was the window decorator for Lerner's, a women's apparel store. She was among the first to integrate the American Airlines workforce in Tulsa in the late 1960s, when she was hired as a clerk and subsequently trained as a communications specialist.

Wynonie Harris (born August 24, 1915, in Omaha; died June 14, 1969, in Los Angeles). Vocals. In an ad for an appearance at the Apollo Theater the week of November 22 (year unknown), Harris is called "King of the Blues" and is considered one of the founding fathers of rock 'n' roll. He had several Top 10 hits between 1946 and 1952.

Wendell O. Haynes (born January 1, 1914, in Beggs, Oklahoma; died July 19, 2010, in Durham, North Carolina). Double bass. Haynes grew up in Sand Springs, Oklahoma. He graduated from high school there in 1932 and from Langston University in 1937. He was the older brother of basketball Hall of Famer Marques Haynes. For a while, he taught math and shoe rebuilding in Sand Springs. Haynes told his son of making extra money with big bands who came through Tulsa. He moved to Durham, where he was an insurance executive, retiring in 1974. Haynes would occasionally play a bass horn with his son Wendell Jr. when he was in junior high school. He told his nephew, Boston architect David Lee, that he "sat in on bass with the Ernie Fields orchestra one night, but he realized pretty quickly that he [Fields] was out of his league."[15]

Lawrence Heatley Sr. (born July 19, 1907, in Fort Smith, Arkansas; died September 29, 1951 in Tulsa). Bass and banjo. Heatley was raised in Baton Rouge, Louisiana, and was an only child. The Heatley family moved to Tulsa, where Lawrence went to public schools and graduated from Booker T. Washington High School in 1926. He was in the first group to invite Fields to gig with them and joined his fledging traveling organization, albeit briefly. After his music aspirations ended, Heatley became a city bus driver and sold real estate. Ernie described him as a "clean-cut gentleman" whose hobby was fishing. He taught Ernie how to use a rod and reel.

Lee Hilliard. Trumpet and alto sax. Hilliard was described by Fields as a "terrific musician," though "whiskey finally got the best of him." Fields first saw him in the early days of Hilliard's traveling, in the late 1920s and early '30s, with Tee Holder's group, where he played alto sax. Hilliard is also listed as personnel on Alphonso Trent recordings. He joined Fields in the late '40s or early '50s.

Larry Hollis (born August 9, 1941, in Oklahoma City). Tenor sax. Hollis's father bought him a Selmer Mark VI tenor sax when he graduated from high school in 1959. Sometime in the early '60s, he played a couple of weeks as a fill-in for the reed section in the Ernie Fields organization, placed between Ernie Jr. and Elbert "Slim" Malone. According to a postcard he sent music sleuth Dan Kochakian, Hollis remembers that everyone had a nickname—such as "Buski" for the bus driver and "Boneski" for a trombonist, and, for himself, since he was only there for a while, "Fayski" (probably from an abbreviation of "ofay," a common term for white people). The audiences during his stint were mostly white, "country clubs and the like," Hollis said. He later played with Curtis Mayfield out of Chicago but stuck to mostly jazz and blues organizations in Oklahoma. He is listed as an annotator on the album *Legends of Acid Jazz: Tenor Titans* on the Prestige Records label and on some forty other jazz and blues recordings on different labels. At Central State University in Edmond, Oklahoma, he majored in literature with a minor in journalism. After moving his independent record store operation to his home, Hollis now writes reviews for music publications, most notably the quarterly *Cadence* magazine, based in Portland, Oregon.

Wellington "Frenchie" Hughes (born in May, possibly 1899; died June 18, 1981, in Tulsa). Sax. Hughes was at Tuskegee with Ernie and for years after leaving the band lived a few blocks away from the Fields family, on North Peoria Avenue in Tulsa.

Aaron Izenhall (born April 10, 1924; date of death unknown). Trumpet. Izenhall was with the Fields orchestra around 1942. He also played trumpet with Louis Jordan, Louis Armstrong, and Ella Fitzgerald. Izenhall's military draft card describes him as having a "light brown" complexion, standing five feet, five inches tall, and weighing 140 pounds, with brown eyes and black hair. He had a 1949 film credit in *Lookout Sister* along with another Fields alum, Paul Quinichette. The film is shown periodically on the Turner Classic Movies channel.

Earl "Bang-Bang" Jackson (born in Kansas City; died December 25, 1974, in Tulsa). Tenor sax. Jackson was the first Black person to become a house band performer at Trade Winds West, a club in South Tulsa, which was a white area. During his Ernie Fields tenure in the late '50s, Jackson was featured soloist on "In the Mood" when the band performed its hit version of that popular tune on its second appearance on Dick Clark's *American Bandstand*, on November 7, 1959. Jackson mentored many younger Tulsa musicians, including pianist Pat Moore and bass guitarist Leon Rollerson.

Frank James (born about 1926 in Tulsa). One-legged dancer. "The act that you must watch is Frank James, the one-legged dancer. Seeing only is believing and then you wonder," insisted the *Pittsburgh Courier* on September 23, 1950, in an article about a Memphis performance. James was part of the nightclub act James and Nealy, with California tap dancer Francis E. Nealy (born October 18, 1918; died May 23, 1997). An August 2, 1961, article in the *Regina (SK) Leader-Post* described "The Original Three-leggers" as "two dancers with only three legs." It said the two men in question, James and Chicagoan Carl Wright (1932–2007), "put on a dance routine worthy of any nightclub." Another similarly featured talent was Thomas Hodge, a one-legged dancer with Fields in 1955 described as "not peg-leg, one leg." An ad in a Corpus Christi newspaper for a "One Night Only" Fields performance promoted "his own sensational floor show featuring Thos. Hodge, Latin One leg Dancer and a 'Bevy of Beauties' Admission $1.50."

Floyd "Candy" Johnson (born May 20, 1922, in Madison, Illinois; died June 28, 1981, in Framingham, Massachusetts). Tenor sax. Johnson worked briefly with Ernie Fields, then Basie, and later with Duke Ellington, taking Paul Gonsalves's place when he fell ill. Ernie said he picked Johnson up in Ohio, where he attended Wilberforce University. He got his nickname because he preferred candy to alcohol. After working with Fields, he worked with Tiny Bradshaw and Andy Kirk, recording with Andy Kirk on Decca Records. In the late '50s, Johnson played rhythm and blues with Bill Doggett, who enjoyed hits with "Honky Tonk" and "Night Train." Johnson also recorded as a sideman with Helen Humes in 1973. He retired to Toledo, Ohio, where he taught in local schools.

J. J. Johnson (born January 22, 1924, in Indianapolis; died February 4, 2001, in Indianapolis). Trombone. Johnson was one of the earliest trombonists to embrace bebop. He began his professional career in 1941 with the Clarence Love Orchestra, which was based first in Kansas City, then Tulsa. He was with Ernie Fields for several weeks in the early '40s—"not long," Ernie said. "We got very tight and he gave me some arrangements—they can cost, but J. J. said, 'I'm just glad you're doing them and hope if you can tell somebody about my writing.'" Jimmy Wilkins was in the Fields organization at same time. Some say Johnson did for jazz trombone what Charlie Parker did for jazz saxophone.

Alvin Jones. Trombone. Nicknamed "Boneski," Jones graduated from Tulsa's Booker T. Washington High School in 1954. His last known address, in the '80s, was 811 N. Osage Avenue, Apt. R, Tulsa.

Gay Jones. Keyboardist. In a review of Ernie Fields's weeklong engagement at the Rainbow Ballroom in Denver in the '40s, Jones was referred to as "a paleface." He achieved moderate success in the '50s as a jazz keyboard player in the Seattle area. He was believed to have cut Seattle's first-ever jazz record.[16]

Lee Wesley Jones (born August 18, 1918; died August 20, 1984). Piano. A jazz and rhythm and blues pianist in the 1950s, Jones also worked with Johnny Otis at one point. (He is not to be confused with Lee W. Jones Jr.)

King Kolax (born William Little on November 6, 1912, in Kansas City, Missouri; died December 18, 1991, in Chicago). Trumpet. Kolax's tenure with the Fields band coincided with the tenures of Teddy Edwards and Jack Scott in the '40s. He was with Ernie Fields again in the early '60s. Kolax was an executive with the Chicago local of the American Federation of Musicians and had a large home, which he made available for musicians visiting the city.

Robert B. Lacefield (born in 1925; died in 2009 in Inglewood, California). Baritone/tenor sax. Lacefield is believed to be from Texas. He was with the Fields band in the late '50s.

Yusef Lateef (born William Huddleston [his father later changed the family name to Evans] on October 9, 1920, in Chattanooga, Tennessee; died December 23, 2013, in Amherst, Massachusetts). Tenor sax. Known professionally as Bill Evans at first, he converted to Islam in 1949 and took his Muslim name. He had a routine in the Fields shows along with Leon Wright, and Ernie called him "the Showman." By his own account, Lateef was with Ernie Fields for a few months in 1947 before he decided to go to Chicago. He later earned a master's degree and a doctorate in music education. He was teaching at the University of Massachusetts at Amherst at the time of his death.

Harry Lee Lewis Jr. (born September 15, 1928, in Omaha, Nebraska; died November 2, 1961, in New York City, buried in Omaha). Tenor sax. He was with Fields around 1942 along with King Kolax and Eddie Walter. He was also in the group in the early '60s when David Sherr joined. He was from a musical family in Omaha and played with Count Basie and served as bandleader for Fats Domino and Etta James. In Omaha Lewis played with Preston Love's orchestra. He was father of keyboard player Andre Lewis, who was also in the Fields organization in the '60s.

Helen Lewis (born June 16, 1918; died July 7, 2003). Piano. She was with the band in the early '50s.

Michael Andre Lewis, a.k.a. **Mandré** (born December 7, 1948, in Omaha; died January 31, 2012, in Shreveport, Louisiana). Keyboard. Lewis was in the Ernie Fields organization in the '60s and later toured and traveled with Rufus, Buddy Miles, Labelle, Frank Zappa, and others. Lewis was also band leader for Johnny "Guitar" Watson. Even though he could not read music, he is credited with being an unsung music technology innovator—as one of the first musicians to use multiple signal processors on keyboards and synthesizers on records. Lewis was married to Tulsa vocalist Paulette Parker, known professionally as Maxayn, now residing in Los Angeles.

Milton Lewis. Trumpet. Lewis was in the band around 1942 along with King Kolax and Eddie Walter. Lewis's father was principal of Dunbar High School in Little Rock, Arkansas. He was friends with Indiana swing pianist Lester "Les" Loving, who he met while Loving was a student at Philander Smith College in Little Rock, according to an April 11, 1942, column in the *Evansville (Ind.) Argus*. The item identified him as "the solid cat who knocked those fine notes on his trumpet" with the Ernie Fields Orchestra.

Robert "Baby Boy" Lewis. Double bass. Lewis was on the Ernie Fields 1939 Vocalion recordings. Some sources list him as drummer, but he was listed as bass player in 1942. He was at Tulsa's Booker T. Washington High School at the same time as Earl Bostic and Hal Singer, other Ernie Fields alums. Lewis was entrusted with keeping tabs on fellow musicians and turning in a list of infractions, such as being late, to Ernie, who would impose fines. He was so meticulous, he even fined himself on occasion.

Robert "Brooks" Lewis. Bass. Lewis is on Ernie Fields's 1949 Regal recordings. Drummer Al Duncan called him a "wonderful bass player." He was in the band when Duncan joined in the late '40s.

Charles Fronzelle Littlefield (born June 2, 1930; died November 14, 1965, buried in Oakwood Cemetery in Fort Worth, Texas). Tenor sax. Littlefield weighed over 250 pounds, and David Sherr remembers that the sight of Fronzelle dancing would bring a wave of laughter from a theater's full house.

He was given the solo when the band performed backing up singer Billy Bland's hit "Let the Little Girl Dance."

Hiawatha "Hy" Lockhart (born March 19, 1926, Troy, Alabama; died August 9, 2010, Randolph, Massachusetts). Trumpet. Lockhart told me he was with the orchestra for a brief stint in the '40s mostly in and around Dallas. He also played with Clark Terry, Jimmy Heath, and Sam Rivers. During his navy service, Lockhart played in the U.S. Navy Band, and is described as a skilled composer and arranger of jazz music. An alumnus of both Berklee College of Music and the New England Conservatory of Music, he was active with the Boston Jazz Society. His son, guitarist Jeffrey Lockhart, is an associate professor at Berklee College of Music.

Ernest "Butch" Luckett. Guitar. With Ernie Fields, Luckett wrote "Butch's Blues," recorded on a 78 rpm disc in 1952 on the Frisco label, Ernie Fields's own company. It was later also released on the Gotham label. He was in the

On the bus, early 1960s. *Front row, from left,* Robert Lacefield and Butch Luckett; *second row, from far left,* Ann Walls, Ernie Fields Jr., and unknown person; *third row, on right,* Ernie Fields Sr. in his usual seat. Author collection.

band when drummer Al Duncan joined in the late '40s. He was a combination jazz and blues player. An online biography of King Kolax indicates that Luckett was with King Kolax and His Seventeen Knights for a stand at Detroit's 666 Club in 1943.[17]

Warren Luckey (born March 5, 1920, in Dallas; died July 11, 2005, in Uniondale, New York, on Long Island). Tenor sax. "Not long in the band," said Fields, who described Luckey as "a Texan who married a girl in New York" (vocalist Myrtle Mae Medley). Luckey was described in an obituary written by Todd Jenkins as "a nearly forgotten pioneer of bebop" who worked with Dizzy Gillespie and toured with Louis Armstrong.[18] Luckey "came up in the Ernie Fields territory band in the mid-1940s," according to his biography by Eugene Chadbourne on the website allmusic.com.

Eddie Madison Sr., a.k.a. **Eddie Lawrence** (born January 15, 1907; died June 20, 1997). Trumpet. Madison was part of Fields's earliest organization in the late 1920s, along with Roy Milton, Arnold Booker, Oscar Warner, Lawrence Heatley Sr., and Roy Randall. He later formed his own group, named the Eddie Lawrence Band, which performed for a half hour weekly on Tulsa radio station KVOO. Later, Madison established a shoe repair shop on Greenwood Avenue in Tulsa. He learned shoe repair at Booker T. Washington High School in Tulsa and in Sand Springs, from Clarence Fields, Ernie's brother, who was also the bandmaster.[19] His daughter, Phyllis (Madison) Wilson, was maid of honor at the wedding of Ernie Fields Jr. and JoAnn Goodwin.

Elbert "Slim" Malone Jr. (born September 9, 1937, in Lubbock, Texas; died November 1, 1977, in Lubbock). Tenor sax. The Langston University graduate was recruited in the early '60s to play with Ernie Fields. After that, he played with Bobby "Blue" Bland, then Joe Tex and Ike and Tina Turner. Malone and Ernie Fields Jr. had a number they performed together as the "Siamese Saxes." After music, Malone's last job, according to Ernie Sr., was a salesman at Sears. "He was just as great at that as he was in front of the band, singing and blowing that horn. And he was terrific, one of the most outstanding tenor men that I'd had."[20]

Hosea Lee Martin (born April 30, 1921, in Ardmore, Oklahoma; died July 24, 1992, in Tulsa). Trombone. Martin attended Wiley College in Texas. Besides the Ernie Fields Orchestra, Martin played with Don Albert and Fletcher Henderson. Martin wrote a letter to the editor published in *Ebony* magazine in February 1962 praising a December 1961 article headlined "The Soul of Soul" for its treatment of jazz. Martin was an original member of the Oklahoma Jazz Hall of Fame and played in Tulsa with a group called the Sounds of Music. He became a member of the U.S. Civil Service Board of Examiners. Martin was also a contributing author for *Negro Digest*, publishing the article "Negro Apathy: How to Combat It," in March 1965 (vol. 14, no. 5).

William "Bill" Maxwell (born April 4, 1949, in Oklahoma City). White drummer. Maxwell's mother was a jazz pianist and worked in a piano store, and his father was a electronics engineer at Tinker Air Force Base. He remembers being aware of music early and playing along with Grand Ole Opry on the radio. He saved money from his newspaper route to buy drums and hit the road after graduating from high school—with a band called the Jades, which later became the Third Avenue Blues Band. Maxwell did a short tour with Ernie Fields, mostly in supper clubs in Missouri and Oklahoma, but was treated like family by "your Dad and Ernie Jr. . . . I learned SO much," he said, mostly about pleasing an audience. "Your father was kind," he told me. "He encouraged me." At the time in the late '50s the band stayed in Black motels and restaurants and "went in the back door of the club." Regardless, he added, "I had the time of my life." Now based in Los Angeles, Maxwell arranged the vocals for the 1973 Grammy-winning "Take Me Back" album by Andre Crouch.[21]

Helen Jean McCoy (born in 1926 in Texas; died September 2, 2013, in Tulsa). Piano. McCoy grew up in west Tulsa's South Haven community and graduated from Tulsa's Booker T. Washington High School in 1944. She played with Fields from 1950 to 1956. Band members nicknamed her "Mamacita," and she traveled with the Fields organization all over the United States and Canada. Her obituary in the *Tulsa World* on September 8, 2013, quoted fellow musician Frank Swain as saying, "She could make an organ sound like a [string] bass . . . using her left hand and a foot pedal." After leaving Fields, McCoy continued to play publicly in church and such Greenwood Avenue venues as the Flamingo Club.

Morris McCraven (born April 22, 1941, in Byhalia, Mississippi). Tenor sax. After earning a four-year scholarship to Langston University, he moved to Oklahoma City upon graduation. He fell in love with the saxophone in fifth grade when he heard it being played. In ninth grade, his father bought him a horn. He was with the Ernie Fields organization while Ernie Jr. was taking over (mid-1960s), joining another former Langston student, Elbert "Slim" Malone. After a stint with the Soul Messengers, McCraven would own his own club, the "#1 Club" in Oklahoma City, where the elder Fields would sometimes book acts like Gene Ammons and Sonny Stitt. He currently lives in Oklahoma City, performing locally. He remembers Ernie Sr. as "cordial" and "very direct," he said. Fields, he added, "did not take no stuff."[22]

Edward and Edwin Middleton (identical twins, born July 12, 1913, in Tulsa). Trombone (Edward) and trumpet (Edwin). Their father, Joseph, was a porter, and their mother, Eleanor, was a homemaker, according to the 1920 census. They had an older sister named Ruby. Edwin and his wife, Josephine, lived on East King Street in Tulsa and had a telephone at that time, according to the census. Edwin died December 21, 1971, in Tulsa. On the bandstand, Edwin would be between Jeff Carrington and Amos Woodruff playing second or third trumpet. Edward, who became band director of Deland Euclid High School in Florida in the late '50s; died April 30, 2000, in Florida. He married Armine Matherson, his second wife, in 1973. The twins, both navy veterans, were on the 1939 Vocalion recordings with Ernie Fields.

Walter Miller (born February 7, 1907, or [according to another source] in 1920, in Birmingham, Alabama; died March 28, 2004, in Cambridge, Massachusetts). Trumpet. According to the liner notes for *Big Band Jazz: Tulsa to Harlem*, Miller was a part of the recordings, believed to be made between 1949 and 1953, which included a November 1949 remake of "T-Town Blues." Miller was with the Fields band for about a year and a half; he was with the band when drummer Al Duncan joined in the '40s. He was also a member of an Alabama twelve-piece aggregation led by Sonny Blount (Sun Ra). He toured with Ray Charles in 1967 and later with Sun Ra's Arkestra.

Roy Milton (born July 31, 1907, in Wynnewood, Oklahoma, part of the Chickasaw Nation; died September 18, 1983, in Los Angeles). Vocals and drums. Milton's maternal grandmother was a Chickasaw. His father was a gospel singer. Milton graduated from Tulsa's Booker T. Washington High School in 1928, then attended Sam Houston College in Austin, Texas, and Langston University in Oklahoma. He was with the Fields group in its earliest days, in the late '20s and early '30s, before he went to Los Angeles, where he enjoyed moderate success.

Harold "Geezil" Minerve/Minerva (born January 3, 1922, in Cuba; died June 4, 1992, in New York City). Alto sax. In his first clarinet lessons while barely a teenager, Ernie Jr. remembers Minerve as his "very patient" teacher. Raised in Florida, Minerve was in the Fields organization in the early '40s before serving in the army 1943–46. Afterward, he returned to Fields for a short stint. Ernie said of him, "He could make the whole band sound like Ellington by himself." Minerve is best known for work with the Ellington orchestra (Duke and Mercer), taking Johnny Hodges's spot after his death.

Ethel Mooney. Vocals. A southerner from Texas or Louisiana or "somewhere," Ernie said, Mooney was with the band in the '50s. Ernie said he promoted her using Sticks Bradley photographs. Mooney couldn't do both styles as well as Leora Davis, and wasn't as exciting as Sticks, he said.

Melvin Moore (born October 31, 1917, in Oklahoma City; died June 27, 2002, in the Bronx, New York). Vocals. Moore was on the Ernie Fields 1939 Vocalion recording sessions—his first ever. The other soloist was Leora Davis, held in high regard by Moore and others at the time. Moore is featured on "T-Town Blues," "Bless Your Heart," and "Just Let Me Alone." According to Moore, the recording was producer Ahmet Ertegun's first record as well. Ertegun would later become CEO of Atlantic Records and help guide Ray Charles's recording career. When Moore left the Fields organization in the late '40s, he went on to Dizzy Gillespie's Big Band, replacing Johnny Hartman. That big band disbanded after less than a year, Moore said, even though personnel included Jimmy Heath, Al McKibbon, and John Coltrane. Moore then joined Fletcher Henderson, and also played with Lucky Millinder and later the Ink Spots. With the Ink Spots, he traveled the globe from 1952 to 1963. In 1964 Moore became national promoter for Decca Records; later, he was with other labels, working with such artists as Jackie Wilson, the Chi-Lites, Tyrone Davis, and Hamilton Bohannon.[24] He remembered a big mural on the wall in the studio at his first recording session, depicting a Native American with an arm outstretched and a tear in his eye. The caption was "Where is the melody?" That was the first thing he noticed when he walked to the microphone. He said he'd never forget it. "You wonder about that nowadays. Where the hell is the melody?"[25] Moore's daughter, Melba (Joyce) Bradford, is a vocalist who traveled with USO shows, and his granddaughter is jazz vocalist Carmen Bradford.

Russell "Big Chief" Moore (born August 13, 1912, in Komatke, Arizona; died December 15, 1983, in Nyack, New York). Trombone. "Chief," a Pima American Indian, was in the band for nearly four years, joining in New York City in 1939 as the band was ending its stand there. His unusual embouchure perplexed many, as he played with the horn on the side of his mouth. Louis Armstrong told Ernie once, "I don't know how a man can play that much horn and look like doing all of it wrong." No teacher or anything would have that, Ernie agreed, and added, "but brother, what was coming out of there!"[26] Ernie and Bernice Fields spent three days visiting with him in 1980 as he was preparing to go to Europe with a Dixieland group the following summer. He had cataracts or something, Ernie observed, "but [was] doing just fine." Melvin Moore and Chief called each other "blood brothers" because they had the same last name, Ernie recalled. "And when it came to drinking that whiskey, Melvin said, "Boy! He could tear up a place." Fellow trombonist Parker Berry teased Chief unmercifully: "You know you didn't know you were really free the same as the white man until we played Pawhuska." (Pawhuska, Oklahoma, according to Fields, was practically an Indian town.) "A lot of them when we play there," Ernie said, "they'd grab Chief and carry him out for a drink and all that and go wild." On the road, they could go everywhere the white people could go, Berry told Chief. "Aw hush, P. B.,"

Chief would retort. But Moore found out "sho nuff that it was a difference in privilege," Ernie noted. "Pima was one of those very poor tribes." He didn't know they could be treated like white people. But Fields also remembered seeing a sign in an Arizona restaurant window that read, "No dogs or Indians allowed."[27] In a long and distinguished career, Moore played with orchestras led by Louis Armstrong, Sidney Bechet, Red Allen, and Noble Sissle, among others. He also performed at a wedding reception for Prince Charles and Lady Diana. Influences included New Orleans and Chicago roots, as well as his native Pima-Maricopa tribe in Arizona. Bemoaning not ever recording Moore while he was in the band, Ernie wrote on the back of an autographed photo from Chief, "How I do regret it so much." Fields's assessment of Moore was that "for outright blowing and sensational Dixieland," Moore was "the greatest all over."[28]

Rudy Morrison. Trombone. Morrison left Fields around 1944 for Billy Eckstine's band. Later he settled in Oklahoma City and started his own band, the Rudy Morrison Band, which became popular on the social club circuit in the city. He's listed among the personnel on some Jay McShann recordings.

Lawrence "Pepper" Neely (born in 1913; died in 1977 in Phoenix). Vocals. Neely became a Capitol Records soloist during performances on "What a Dream," "Come Back, Baby," and others. "Listen to the Mockingbird," not recorded, was one of his signature songs—Neely would "tear the house down," said Ernie. He ended with a whistle that sounded just like a mockingbird. "He was sensational!" He has a credit in the 1943 movie *Moving On*, about an African American soldier.

Eddie Nicholson. Drums. Nicholson was in the earliest Ernie Fields group that traveled in the early '30s, including the 1934–35 trip to the Northeast. He's pictured in the Ernie Fields Christmas photo from the early '30s. At that time, he replaced drummer Roy Milton, who became the featured vocalist. Preston Love dubbed Nicholson "the original hip cat." According to bass player William King Hadnott, who grew up in Tulsa, Nicholson would "smoke anything, he'd drink anything." Hadnott said Nicholson later worked with Billie Holiday and "kept her fixed up, if you know what I mean."[29]

Onis Pankey Sr. (born April 25, 1919, in Sapulpa, Oklahoma; died May 12, 1990, in Sapulpa, buried at Green Hill Memorial Gardens). Trumpet. Pankey graduated from Tulsa's Booker T. Washington High School in 1937 and joined the Fields organization then. He was in the Fields organization throughout the '40s and into the '50s, except during the World War II years, when he served in the army. After his time with Fields, he played locally with different combos. Later Pankey worked for the Frisco Railroad and then he was a custodian for the Liberty Glass Company in Sapulpa. The 1940 census listed him as Chinese and a "new worker," living with his grandparents. The Tulsa city census listed his race as "colored" and ethnicity as African American.

Artis Paul. Trumpet. Paul was from Tyler or Corsicana, Texas. Ernie recalled, "I think he got into whiskey; had a good tone, but sometimes you wouldn't get the best of Artis. He was just awful bad on the whiskey. A moody guy, but a fine note man; he was on the session that impressed Stan Kenton." Paul played the high notes near the end of "Thursday Evening Blues." Paul would switch to the Nat Towles band and come back to Ernie Fields, because "he would always demand that salary." But, Ernie said, "When he was sober, he was worth it!"[30]

Frank Perry. Tenor sax. Perry was with Fields in the '40s. He was also an alum of the Don Redman and Louis Jordan groups, and he recorded with Les Brown and His Band of Renown.

Kenny Pernell. Alto sax and arranger. From Seattle, Pernell began playing in high school with group led by teen multi-instrumentalist Evelyn Bundy and Fields alum Creon Thomas. He joined Fields in the early '40s along with Thomas, who played piano.

Don Peterson. Guitar. Peterson was a soloist on "Empty Bed Blues" during an Ernie Fields Brownsville, Texas, radio broadcast, circa 1945.

Harry David Augustus Pettiford (born November 27, 1911, in Muskogee, Oklahoma; died June 1981 in Minneapolis). Alto and tenor sax. From a musical family with eleven children, Pettiford lived first in Minneapolis, then Okmulgee, Oklahoma. His brother Oscar Pettiford was an internationally acclaimed bassist. A notation in a history of the Minneapolis jazz scene says that Harry was a well-known and in-demand Twin Cities saxophonist who "played a million notes" and likened Harry and his sister Margie to Charlie Parker.[31] Pettiford was with the Fields organization in the '50s. Harry "meant a lot to me," Ernie said, "far as a quick gun, a guy who could 'read' nice." But Pettiford did not like the road life or touring. "It wouldn't be the money," Ernie said. "He was just spoiled that he could get around and gig and be at home. That was the kind of guy that he was."[32]

Benny Powell (born March 1, 1930, in New Orleans; died June 26, 2010). Trombone. After his tenure with the Fields organization, Powell went to Lionel Hampton, then Count Basie. He also spent twenty-five years with pianist Randy Weston. Joining in 1948, he was with Ernie Fields when drummer Al Duncan joined in the '40s. In an interview by Bob Bernotas, Powell, a teenager at the time, told of being stranded in Oklahoma City after a stand with King Kolax's band. He got word about a band in Tulsa led by Ernie Fields. At that time guys lived two, three, or maybe four to a room, waiting for work. After being hired by Fields, Powell said, he went into the hotel lobby "like I was going out shopping or something and I went around behind the building." His roommate, drummer Vernel Fournier, lowered Powell's bag out the window on a rope, "and I grabbed it and ran to the bus station." That, he said, "is how I got out of Oklahoma City to join Ernie Fields' band in Tulsa."[33]

Paul Quinichette (born May 17, 1916, in Denver; died May 25, 1983, in New York City). Tenor sax. Quinichette was with Fields in 1942. Before that he was with Jay McShann and later was featured with Count Basie. He was dubbed "Vice Prez" for his similar style to Lester "Prez" Young. He was also featured on some Dinah Washington recordings from 1952 to 1954.

Alvin "Junior" Raglin (born March 16, 1917, in Nebraska; died November 10, 1955, in Boston). Double bass and guitar. Raglin left Tulsa with Eugene Coy in 1935, according to Fields. Later he was with Duke Ellington, where he was part of the second "Live at Carnegie Hall" recording in 1943.

Roy Randall (born in 1908 in McAlester, Oklahoma; died January 1988 in Tulsa). Piano. Randall was leader of the very first group that recruited Fields to play with them and that then asked him to lead the group, the Royal Entertainers, as Randall was leaving to attend Virginia State University. Back then, Ernie said, Randall "had the nastiest mouth that you could hear." He was a graduate of Booker T. Washington High School in Tulsa. In 1953 he became an ordained minister and served congregations at Pilgrim Baptist Church in Sapulpa, Oklahoma, and later First Baptist Church North Tulsa.

La Lomie Robin, a.k.a. **Lalomie Wasburn** (born August 25, 1941, in Memphis; died December 28, 2004, in Los Angeles). Vocals and songwriting. Robin was with Ernie Fields Jr. and Company in the late '60s and early '70s. Later she did backup vocals with many artists, including Ray Charles and Chaka Khan. In her solo career, she drew a large following in Germany.

La Lomie Robin Featured Vocalist   ERNIE FIELDS JR. and Company

La Lomie Robin was a featured vocalist during Ernie Fields's last days as leader and continued with the band when Ernie Fields Jr. took over. Author collection.

Leon Rollerson (born June 26, 1946, in Tulsa). Bass guitar. A Tulsa native, Rollerson was son of local drugstore owner. The first time he went on the road was with Ernie Fields, while a student at Langston University in the mid 1960s. "He taught me how to tour, how to build a band," Rollerson told the Oklahoma Jazz Hall of Fame. "He took me from Maine to California, from Washington State to Florida and all of the southern states in between." Rollerson teaches in a Tulsa high school and continues to gig regularly.

Thomas "Little Gable" Ross (born about 1919). Trumpet and songwriting. Ross, from Tulsa, was a drinker, according to Ernie. He is on the "Thursday Evening Blues" recording. Ernie says he "let the whiskey get him." The 1940 census listed him as a twenty-one-year-old musician, living with an aunt named Flora Temer.

Salva Sanders (born November 19, 1902, in Louisiana; died February 16, 1939, in Okmulgee, Oklahoma). Piano. Sanders led either the Texas Rangers or the Southern Serenaders in the 1920s. He had attended Langston University. Ernie claimed Sanders was Count Basie's "idol," adding, "I'm telling you the truth." He recalled Basie at one time telling Ernie during a Chicago gig that Basie had stopped in to hear the band's matinee and said, "I wish I could do it like Salva."[34]

Jack "Earlie" Scott (New Orleans native). Guitar, piano, arrangements—and astrology. Very talented and silent, Scott was described by some as "weird." He was in the Fields band in the late '50s, when he rented a room in Ernie's mother-in-law's garage apartment next door to the Fields home in Tulsa. Scott was seen in Los Angeles in the late '70s or so working for a record company called Pzazz—but now seems to have vanished. Teddy Edwards, another Fields alum, was president of Pzazz, a company established by R&B bandleader and former Chess Records talent scout Paul Gayten (January 29, 1920–March 26, 1991). Scott is listed alternately on piano and guitar on some of Gayten's recordings in the late '40s. On a 1949 recording called "Backtrackin'," Scott's performance is described: "Jack Scott's guitar cuts loose with some futuristic boogie-based riffing before calming down some and keeping the whole track from flying off into orbit, a smaller role than he had the first time through this song but far more effective in how he approaches it. Gone are the meditative jazz licks he featured last time out and in their place are sizzling licks that point towards tomorrow in both style and attitude."[35]

Herbert (also **Hubert**) **Scott.** Trumpet. Scott was from Trenton, New Jersey, according to Ernie, and formerly was with Bessie Smith's band. He joined Fields in time for the Battle of the Bands in Denver in 1931 or 1932. He is in the photo on the Ernie Fields Christmas card from the early '30s. Scott served as best man when Ernie married in 1933.

Theodore Roosevelt "Rudy" Scott (born December 19, 1934, in Waco, Texas; died November 27, 2020, in Tulsa). Piano. Rudy Scott was in the band in the late '50s and early '60s, and for a while he was with Ernie Fields Jr. and Company in the mid-1960s.

Leslie Sheffield (born June 11, 1910, in Muskogee, Oklahoma; died October 17, 1979, in Oklahoma City). Piano and arranger. Sheffield was on Ernie's first trip to New York in 1934. He helped set up for the trip by putting Ernie in touch with the promoter Earl Roberts in Pittsfield, Massachusetts. Fields first saw Sheffield while he worked in Terrence "Tee" Holder's organization. Sheffield was also believed to be one of the originals in the Al Trent Orchestra—and eventually took it over when Trent became ill. The Trent Orchestra was said to be the most polished and successful of the Texas bands. In an undated letter, Ernie said the men met "when he came into Tulsa either with the Southern Serenaders band out of Little Rock, or Al Trent's orchestra, the first big band to hail from these parts." He said the Trent organization "was caliber and had the personnel to have been worldwide known as Cab Calloway or Duke Ellington, but seemingly just did not get the breaks and was not at the right place at the right time." Ernie said Trent had his band for ten or twelve years before there was a Count Basie band. Sheffield went east with Trent before joining Ernie Fields. He spent his last years in Oklahoma City, after many years on the road with many groups large and small, and fronting his own bands and combos. "I did not become famous, nor did I get rich," he said in a 1977 career summary that was posted on Facebook in 2016. He claimed authorship of "Flying Home," a tune he taught to Charlie

Christian when the young guitarist was in Sheffield's band, the Rhythmaires. Christian took the tune with him to the Benny Goodman Orchestra, and Goodman subsequently was credited with authorship.

David Sherr (born May 30, 1941, in Culver City, California). Tenor sax. Sherr heard Benny Goodman play clarinet when he was a youngster and decided that was what he wanted to do. His mother opposed the choice. By high school, he had switched to alto saxophone. He attended Los Angeles City College. His first auditions for jazz band and orchestra were unsuccessful, but "people kept dropping out," he said, so he eventually he got in. During a jazz band summer session, a fellow sax player told him about an opening in the Ronnie Bartley Band, a white group, for a tenor sax player. The band was based in Tulsa. In January 1960, upon hearing back from Bartley, he went out and bought a tenor sax. He was with Bartley for three unhappy months before he met Ernie and eventually joined the Fields organization, on May 11, 1960. His first gig with the group was Friday, May 13, that year at Chicago's Regal Theater. Based in the Los Angeles area, Sherr is active with studio work and often performs with classical groups.

Charles Sherrill. Piano and arranger. Called "Jazz Baby," Sherrill was in the Fields band when drummer Al Duncan joined. A 1954 *Billboard* magazine piece noted his participation on instrumental Atlantic Records recordings of Jerome Kern and Rodgers and Hart music. Atlantic also recorded *Charles Sherrill Plays Music from "Pal Joey" and "A Connecticut Yankee."* Sherrill was on piano for a Fields recording titled "88," a Basie boogie-type number from 1949, but it was not issued until a 1988 Delmark album called *Big Band Jazz: From Tulsa to Harlem.*

Theodore "Ted" Shirley. Bass. Shirley started in Clarence Fields's high school "pigeon" band and eventually got to Los Angeles working as a sideman. Fields said Shirley "passed real early without getting to show his ability or talent as a musician." He was with the group in the early '30s and appears on the early Ernie Fields Christmas card.

Billy Gene Silmon (born July 12, 1941; died April 9, 2017). Vocals. Silmon grew up in Eufaula, Oklahoma. He toured with the Fields orchestra in the late '50s. Later he was employed as a paint and body repair man for Tulsa Public Schools' Department of Transportation. He was also a licensed barber.

Harold "Cornbread" Singer (born October 8, 1919, in Tulsa; died August 18, 2020). Tenor sax. Singer, a graduate of Booker T. Washington High School in Tulsa, was with the Fields organization in the early '40s, when he was nineteen, after dropping out of Hampton University. A friend helped him get the job with Fields. "From Ernie," said Singer, "I learned how to be kind to other people and respect them." After leaving the group, for reasons that years later neither Singer nor Fields claimed to remember, he joined Jay McShann. He was later affiliated with Oran "Hot Lips" Page, then Billie Holiday, before moving to Paris. He moved to Paris in the mid '60s and toured there with the Charles Watts and Duke Ellington orchestras. His Savoy Records recording of the instrumental "Cornbread" in 1948 gave him a No. 1 R&B single, and a nickname that stuck. He was inducted into the Oklahoma Jazz Hall of Fame in 1996 during an Ernie Fields tribute, and was honored there again in 2013, receiving a Lifetime Achievement award.

Buster Smith (born August 24, 2904, near Dallas; died August 10, 1991, in Dallas). Saxophone. Smith played with Basie and the Blue Devils, but not with Ernie Fields, who said Smith did arrangements for him. Nicknamed "the Professor," he was known for a big tone like Herschel Evans. He played baritone, but tenor sax was his main instrument (he later excelled on alto), according to Fields. Some claim he is the actual composer of the famed "One O'Clock Jump," which is credited to Basie. He told friends if there was anything he'd change in his career, it would be to copyright his arrangements.

Vernon "Geechie" Smith. Trumpet. A Tulsa native, Geechie Smith worked with the Ernie Fields organization in the late '30s. Ernie explained, "When he began to play, we all predicted he was going to turn out good, and he sure did. Geechie Smith turned out to be a very nice musician and he was one of those high-note trumpet players." Smith later worked with Charlie Barnett. One of his first Capitol recordings was called "T-Town Jump," which he composed. Smith recorded extensively as a sideman with the likes of Earl Hines and Johnny Hartman. He also spent many years living and playing in

Kansas City and worked as a photographer in his seventies and eighties. He retired in the 1990s.

Odell Stokes (born February 17, 1945; died August 14, 2000, in Tulsa). Guitar. A self-taught musician, Stokes was in the Ernie Fields organization sporadically in the early '60s. In the late '60s, he joined Ernie Fields Jr., who by then was directing Bobby "Blue" Bland's band. "Odell didn't like traveling, so when he left, I replaced him with [white guitarist] Mike Bruce," said Ernie Jr.[36] Stokes is credited with being the founding guitarist for the popular GAP Band, which originated in Tulsa. At the time of his death, he was a switchman for the Burlington Northern freight railroad network.

Frank Swain (born March 2, 1938, in Bristow, Oklahoma). Alto/tenor sax. Swain was a graduate of Tulsa's Booker T. Washington High School, class of 1956. He played with Fields for two years, 1962 and 1963. Before that, he worked sporadically with Fields while still a student at Langston University. His mother was a classmate of Ernie Fields in Taft, Oklahoma, and one of Ernie's two sisters was one of her first teachers. Swain played with various groups—mostly in the blues idiom—including with popular Tulsa bluesman Flash Terry.

Robert Lynn Talley (born February 27, 1920; died August 1, 1995, in Memphis). Trumpet. Talley played with various dance bands, including the Ernie Fields Band. He enlisted in the military in 1943 in Pulaski, Arkansas, where he was part of the 768th Army Air Forces Band.

Verbie Gene "Flash" Terry (born June 17, 1934; died March 18, 2004, in Tulsa). Guitar. Terry drove the bus for the Ernie Fields organization in the 1950s and became known as a blues guitarist in his own right, later opening for many popular acts. He also drove a bus for the Tulsa Transit Authority for over thirty years, while continuing his music career.

Creon Thomas (born August 20, 1904, in Portland; died November 12, 1982, in Imperial, California). Piano and electric fiddle. Thomas joined Ernie Fields around 1942 in Portland, Oregon. While in Tulsa, the address he listed on draft registration card was the Small Hotel; he is described as five feet, six inches, 140 pounds, with a light brown complexion. At the time, his mother, Ruth Thomas, lived at 113 Twenty-Second Street, North Seattle. Ernie described Thomas as "Sharp as he could be . . . intelligent and always sharp when he's seen, lot more than me." Ernie also prized his independence: "If he needed anything, [he] wouldn't have to open his mouth to me. Would get it and Creon just meant a lot."[37]

Chester D. "C.T." Thompson (born March 9, 1945, in Oklahoma City), Hammond B3 organ. Thompson has worked extensively in rock, R&B, and jazz. He started playing piano and organ in church. After high school he began performing in bands throughout Oklahoma, including the Ernie Fields organization in the early '60s (along with Morris McCraven) He has toured across the United States with the Rudy Johnson Trio, Tower of Power (composing most of the group's instrumental tunes), and Carlos Santana. He was with Santana for nearly twenty-five years, during which time he cowrote songs and collaborated on several recordings.[23] Thompson lives and works in the Bay Area. He is not to be confused with Chester Thompson, the drummer who was with Frank Zappa and Mothers of Invention.

William Harrison "Harry" Vann (born January 25, 1931; died July 31, 1997, in Tulsa). Tenor sax. Vann was with Ernie Fields in the mid-1950s. He also played with Preston Love's Omaha-based orchestra. He intermittently led his own orchestra, Harry Vann's All Stars or the Harry Vann Combo, which played in the region, with engagements at Okmulgee's Frontier Room in 1951; the county fair in Porter, Oklahoma, in September 1954; a "Tramp Party" for Sigma Chi fraternity at the University of Oklahoma in February 1955; and as a guest artist for a party at Lincoln University in Missouri in March 1957.

"Little" Joe Walker. Saxophone. Walker was with the group in the early '30s and was featured on the Ernie Fields Christmas card. He played with Louis Armstrong briefly before joining Fields.

Roy Walker. Trumpet. Roy Walker was with the earliest Ernie Fields band, in the early 1930s. Before Louis Armstrong hit the big time, Walker played with him. He was also "a kind of arranger, too," Ernie said. "Had a brother

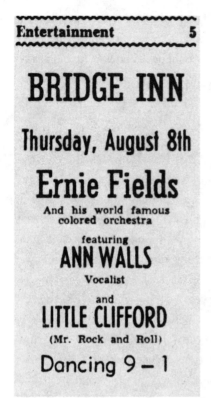

Ad for the Bridge Inn in the *Victoria (Tex.) Advocate*, August 8, 1957. Author collection.

named Joe who played with Louis, too."[38] He was in the group for the ill-fated Battle of the Bands in Denver versus Smiling Billy Stewart and the Sarasota Serenaders in the '30s.

Ann Walls (born in Forth Worth, Texas). Vocals. Walls recorded "Be Anything but Don't Be Sorry" as featured vocalist with the Ernie Fields Orchestra in 1961. Written by Dr. David Shapiro, a Tulsa physician, the song made the charts that May, albeit briefly. The flip side on the Rendezvous label was "Fallin'," written by Walls and Fields. A number called "T-Town Mambo," written by Walls and Fields, went nowhere. "Oh, she was a female who could sing sweet and then could holler and could sing you the blues," said Ernie.

Oscar "Haircut" Warner. Warner was one of the original Royal Entertainers (Ernie's first band) along with Eddie Madison Sr., Lawrence Heatley Sr., Arnold Booker, Roy Milton, and Roy Randall. He was in the group that went

ERNIE FIELDS and his Orchestra
Exclusive
RENDEZVOUS Recording Artist

ERNIE FIELDS ARTIST
1825 N. Peoria Ave. Tulsa 6, Okla.
Ph: CI 7-0421

From left, unknown bass player, vocalist Ann Walls, guitarist Jack "Earlie" Scott, Ernie Fields with trombone, and Earl "Bang-Bang" Jackson on sax, late 1950s. Author collection.

to Denver for the Battle of the Bands against Smiling Billy Stewart. Later he moved to Phoenix and worked at a hotel. He made enough in tips to buy a Cadillac, which he never drove to work. He didn't want the people at work to know he had it. "He'd go to work in an old piece of car and kept the Cadillac in the garage. They wouldn't give no tip if they knew that," Ernie said.

Lafayette Joseph Waters (born February 5, 1926, in Tulsa; died January 19, 2008). Drums. Waters graduated from Booker T. Washington High School in Tulsa in 1943, served in the navy during World War II, and later attended Tuskegee Institute, where he studied applied electricity and played with the marching band. He was with the Ernie Fields band in the late '50s, early '60s. His obituary in the *Oklahoma Eagle* on January 25, 2008, described him as "a very quiet person and an avid reader." When his days with Ernie Fields ended, he worked for many years with the Scroggins Electric Company in Bartlesville, Oklahoma. After retiring, he worked part time at Saint John Hospital until his health failed.

Elon "Knocks" Watkins (born December 4, 1928, in Atoka, Oklahoma; died in November 1990). Tenor sax. Watkins was a graduate of Booker T. Washington High School in Tulsa. He is on the 1949 Regal Records session. He was in the band when drummer Al Duncan joined around 1947 and is mentioned in the liner notes for *Big Band Jazz: Tulsa to Harlem.* "[Lionel] Hamp[ton] raided my band, took Elon and Oscar Estelle," Ernie said. Watkins didn't stay long; it seems he didn't like being away from Tulsa. "Some just don't go for it [traveling]," Ernie said. "He was a good sideman and easy to get along with [and] he was one who could hold his own in any A-class band, as he was with Hamp."[39]

Julius Watkins (born October 10, 1921, in Detroit; died April 4, 1977 in New Jersey). Trumpet and French horn. Watkins joined Ernie Fields at the suggestions of Bill Evans (Yusef Lateef) in 1943. "So as soon as I had a trumpet opening I got Julius." Ernie described Watkins as a "very fine trumpet player," and the fact that he doubled on French horn "attracted my attention." He stayed until 1946. Watkins recorded playing French horn with many jazz musicians, including Thelonious Monk and Sonny Rollins, and he toured with Quincy Jones and his band from 1959 to 1961. There have been several jazz horn festivals held in Watkins's honor—for instance, in New York City (1994–98), Seattle (2009), and Virginia Commonwealth University in Richmond (2012).[40]

"Little" Clifford Watson (born September 24, 1938; died December 1, 2000). Vocals. Watson graduated from Tulsa's Booker T. Washington High School in 1956 and joined the Fields organization shortly thereafter, continuing into the 1960s with Ernie Fields Jr. and Company. Short in stature and dark-skinned, he was sometimes teased about both. Behind his back, some of the musicians nicknamed him "Little Black." But there was no denying he had a way with a song. Promotional material listed Watson "Mr. Please, Please, Please" because of his rendition of the popular James Brown tune. He was sometimes dubbed "Mr. Rock 'n' and Roll." Later, he and his wife, Juanita, ran a Dairy Queen on Lansing Avenue in North Tulsa. He dabbled in drugs (both usage and sales) as well as hot goods. Ernie reportedly once remarked to sax player David Sherr, "If it ain't wrong, he [Clifford] ain't interested in doing it."

Luther "Spurgeon" West (born October 9, 1913, in Redbird, Oklahoma; died January 30, 1977). Alto sax. The Oklahoma native finished Tulsa's Booker T. Washington High School under band director William Jett. He worked for a summer, then went to Xavier University in New Orleans for a semester. West was with the Fields group in its earliest days in the early '30s and was a mainstay into the early '60s. He and another Tulsa native, Earl Bostic, were friends and shared first saxophone duties. He was described by Gunther Schuller as "a first-rate altoist in the [Johnny] Hodges manner," who, as lead alto on the 1939 Vocalion recordings, gave the sax section "its warm vibrant cast."[41] He quit the orchestra in the '50s for a while because of the low salaries and the living conditions on the road, he told David Sherr. During that hiatus, he worked at the Tulsa post office, where he became the first Black to rise to the position of supervisor. He returned to the band in the late '50s or early '60s.

Eugene White. Vocals. White, who was from Tulsa, was known as "Mr. Upside Down" (because he sang standing on his head).

▶ **Upside Down Singer:** Eugene (Upside Down) White of Tulsa, Okla., shouts the blues and keeps time with his feet while singing upside down. White, who was discovered by bandleader Ernie Fields (r.), recently made a successful tour of the West Coast.

Eugene "Upside Down" White, in *Jet* magazine, November 26, 1953, 37. Photo by Eugene Coleman. Reproduced with permission of Eugene Coleman Jr. and Ebony Media Group.

Earl "Pee Wee" Wiley. Vocals. Fields hired Wiley to replace Roy Milton when that singer left for California in 1935. Called Pee Wee likely because of his five-foot stature. He was listed on a Fields poster promoting a performance at the Merry Garden in Modesto, California, sometime in the early 1940s, and some newspaper ads in 1934 and 1935 referred to him as "The Rubber Man" or "the directing rubber man." A review in the *Wilkes-Barre (Pa.) Evening News* on July 3, 1934, described him as the "eccentric dancer." On the Gilt Edge record label, he was on a 78 rpm disc made November 19, 1945, in Los Angeles, with vocals by Wiley and a writing credit for Wiley (presumably the same person) on the song "Jelly Kelly Blues," and on another called "Cherry Red" with Jim Wynn's Bobalibans. "And Now She's Gone/Be Kind to Your Woman" was released in 1945 with his vocals and a Pee Wee Wiley writing credit. He later became a minister, assistant pastor at a church in the Watts neighborhood in Los Angeles. "Back then, he was nothing but devilment," Ernie said, "but he could sing and he could holler."

Jimmy Wilkins (born in 1921 in Saint Louis; died August 24, 2018). Trombone. Wilkins graduated from Sumner High School in Saint Louis and returned to the city after being discharged from the navy at the end of World War II. In a *JazzWax* interview published online on February 29, 2012, he said there wasn't much work in the area when he joined the Ernie Fields territory band, which was playing club dates in Saint Louis and needed a trombone player. First stop was Toledo, Ohio. "After I joined Fields, we headed to New York to play the Apollo Theater," he said. "On our way, we played the Howard Theatre [one week] in Washington, D.C., and the Royal in Baltimore [one week]." The band, he recalled, was still short a trombonist, so "we picked up another one—J. J. Johnson." He laughed. It was just the two of them in the section. "Funny thing about it—I had a featured solo on the show." Johnson complimented him, saying, "You have a nice, clear tone." Johnson, he said, had a shorter solo in another tune, and "he played more notes in his short solo than all of mine." He laughed again. His brother, tenor sax man Ernie Wilkins, soon persuaded Jimmy to join him in the Eddie Mallory band. Ernie Fields, Wilkins said in a video interview with the Detroit Sound Conservancy, didn't want him to go, and offered to raise his fifty-dollar weekly salary. After about six weeks, the Mallory group folded. In 1946 he went back to Wilberforce College on the GI Bill, having first enrolled there in 1940 upon receiving a music scholarship. He finished college in 1949. In 1951, he and his brother joined the Count Basie Orchestra at trumpet player Clark Terry's urging.

Althea "Tiny" Williams. Vocals. Williams's name was included in a promotion item in the *Indianapolis Recorder* newspaper on November 21, 1953: "Coming Sunday, December 6, Ernie Fields and his famous orchestra in biggest dance and show ever here." The newspaper item named Mable Scott, Clarence Ford (probably meaning the dancer Clarise Ford), Althea Williams, Butter Beans and Susie, as well as "Thos. Hodge, one-legged dancer and 5 champion vocalists." Readers were urged to "Reserve a table now!" at the Sunset Terrace Ballroom. Another item, from the *Portland (Ore.) Challenger* on April 23, 1954, has the headline "Jazzman" over a photograph of Ernie Fields, and a subhead, "Famed musician due here." Near the end of the article about the upcoming Elks dance, it said, "Vocalists will be Eugene

ALTHEA "Tiny" WILLIAMS
Vocalist ERNIE FIELDS Orchestra

ERNIE FIELDS ARTISTS
1852 N.Peoria Ave
Tulsa 10,Okla.

Vocalist Althea Williams, early 1940s. Collection of the Smithsonian National Museum of African American History and Culture, Gift of Ernie Fields Jr. and Carmen Fields; Ernie Fields Sr. Estate.

White and Althea Williams," and said Fields "is expected to have on tap symphonic swing, boogie, blues, sweet ballads and bop." It added that his music affords "easy listening and smooth dancing."

Grant Williams. Guitar. Williams was a white Tulsa native who played in the style of guitarist Floyd Smith. He played with Fields in the '30s. Before that he was with saxophone player Alvin "Fats" Wall's band out of Detroit. He'd joined that band because it didn't travel very much and was more predictable. "There wasn't much money, but they said they'd rather have a little money and know they are going to make it, than be out there and don't know what they're going to make," Ernie explained.

Eli Wolinsky (born March 26, 1928; died March 1974). Alto sax. Wolinsky was from Willimantic, Connecticut, and graduated from the University of Connecticut in 1945. He also studied at City College of New York. He had seen alto sax man Preston Love around 1945 in New London, Connecticut, when Love was with Count Basie. According to Love's memoir, Wolinsky loved all things "soul," especially Betty Love's cooking. His favorite was her chitterlings and cornbread. Wolinsky joined the Ernie Fields group in 1952. Ernie said in a June 23, 1987, conversation with René Hall and Ernie Jr. that Wolinksy was "a fine, fine guy, a fine musician too. A little better musician than [Harold] Eiler [another white musician in the band]."

Michael "Booty" Wood (born December 27, 1919, in Dayton, Ohio; died June 19, 1987, in Dayton). Trombone. Wood is on the Fields 1949 Regal Records session. Later, he was featured with Erskine Hawkins, Lionel Hampton, Duke Ellington, and the Snooky Young Septet.[42]

Amos Woodruff (born August 28, 1914, in Savannah, Tennessee; died in 1944). Trumpet. In September 1932, Woodruff was with Bert Furtell and his Twelve Harmony Kings. Woodruff was from Paducah, Kentucky, as was sax player Harry Garnett, who would also join Ernie Fields. Woodruff was the featured soloist in the 1939 Vocalion recordings. According to music historian Schuller's book, Woodruff "took pleasure in crossing the styles of

Leon Wright (*left*) wearing a dress, with Ernie Fields in the back and "Geezil" Minerve(a), early 1950s. They sang, "Smoke, smoke, smoke that cigarette / Puff, puff, puff, and if you smoke yourself to death." Lyrics by Tex Williams and Marie Travis. Collection of the Smithsonian National Museum of African American History and Culture, Gift of Ernie Fields Jr. and Carmen Fields; Ernie Fields Sr. Estate.

Cootie Williams and Rex Stewart into a personal amalgam. . . . Woodruff [and Roy Douglas] give a good account of their work."[43]

Leon Wright. Tenor/alto sax. He was with Ernie Fields in the late '40s, early '50s.

Thomas Hamilton "Zack" Zackery (born November 27, 1914, in Wewoka, Oklahoma; died June 9, 2007, in Tulsa). Driver. After graduating from Booker T. Washington High School in Tulsa in 1934, Zackery played baseball briefly for a team in the Negro Leagues. From 1935 to 1940, he was the bus driver and valet for the Ernie Fields Orchestra, traveling all over the United States. Zack enjoyed travel, his daughter Claudette Black said, as well as the music performed by the band. After leaving the band, he was employed by American Airlines in Tulsa for twenty-six years.

GONE, NOT FORGOTTEN

The following are names of musicians mentioned by Ernie Fields as being in his organization or noted on some recordings. In spite of arduous efforts, I was unable to get any meaningful information about them—on where they came from or where they went.

(Moses?) George Armstrong. Drums. Armstrong was in Ernie Fields's last organization, known as Ernie Fields and Son, in the 1960s.

"Bosom." Drums.

Eric "The Voice" Boyce. Vocals. Boyce was featured in the late 1940s when New Orleans promoter Harry Berns (possibly spelled "Burns") was booking for Ernie Fields, according to Ernie's notes on a Boyce photo from the National Artists Guild in New Orleans.

Otis Bryant. Bryant was with Fields on the group's first big trip east. In a letter dated July 26, 1934, Ernie told his wife, "Otis has been sick and is sick yet. We will have to send him home."

John Cameron. Saxophone. He was from Chicago. David Sherr remembers that Cameron rose early, always practicing, mostly on the bridge to "Confirmation." He was reportedly a good cook, but Sherr complained, "I can't get used to spicy pork chops for breakfast."[44]

Harold "Sy" Cannon. Saxophone. Cannon was from Oklahoma City and was with the group in the '40s, according to Ernie Fields.

Henderson "Dewey" Chambers (possibly born in 1900 and died in 1982, and buried in McAlester, Oklahoma, according to Ancestry.com; more likely lived May 1, 1908–October 19, 1967). Trombone. Listed in Tom Lord Jazz Discography as personnel on 1947 Ernie Fields recordings and according to some references as performing with Tiny Bradshaw, Louis Armstrong, and Count Basie in the '30s and '40s. Ernie mentions an alum called "Dewey" Chambers, but not Henderson.

John Clarke. Saxophone. Clarke was pictured on an early 1930s Ernie Fields Christmas card.

Paul Dennis. Dennis was from Kansas City but eventually made Tulsa his home. He was in the band in the '50s.

Leon Dillard. Trumpet. Dillard was pictured on an early 1930s Ernie Fields Christmas card.

Harold "Cap" Eiler. Alto/tenor. Eiler was in the orchestra for about a month in the '40s, replacing Spurgeon West when he was drafted in the military. Ernie said Eiler had to be called a Creole, or anything but "white," to perform with the band in many areas in the South. Ernie thought he was from Minnesota.

Sammy Edwards. Drums. According to Fields, Edwards was "'always one of the best drummers I had—but didn't go on to be sensational."

C. Wood Evans.

Harry Garnett (born possibly in Paducah, Kentucky). Tenor/alto sax.

Robert Graham. Tenor sax. Graham played in the '30s with Delma/Delmar Willis. He was in the Fields group when the band chartered a union local in Tulsa, American Federation of Musicians No. 808.

Ron Grenell. Organ. Grenell was with the Ernie Fields Jr. group in March 1967.

Wyatt Griffin. Guitar. Griffin was with the group in the early '60s. During the '40s and '50s, he was part of a mostly Kansas City–based group called the Five Scamps, where he alternately played guitar and sang second tenor.

John Hardy. Tenor sax. Hardy was out of Texas and was similar musically to Illinois Jacquet and Arnett Cobb. Ernie Fields described him as having "a big tone, big sound."

Al Harris/Harrison. Vocals. Harris/Harrison was believed to be from either Tacoma, Washington, or Oakland, California, and was with the band circa 1955 or 1956. He may be the vocalist on Ace Records' "Don't Know Where I'm At."

Hensley Hill (born about 1924 in Lexington, Kentucky; died August 1987 in St. Paul, Minnesota). Trumpet. He was a member of Minneapolis Local No. 73 of the American Federation of Musicians. The Minneapolis *Spokesman* of February 13, 1948, identified Hill as a former Ernie Fields trumpet man now leading King Jordan's Cats-N-Jammers. Calling Hill a "young Gabriel," the article noted his "aggregation are sure to thrill you as they have countless others with their sensational renditions." He also worked as a clerk for the state motor vehicle division.

Jimmy Hill. Drums. Hill was with the Ernie Fields Jr. group in March 1967.

Harold Jones. Vocals. Jones was with Ernie Fields Jr. in March 1967.

Elon Knox. Alto sax. Knox was "very talented," according to Ernie Fields Jr. He might have been a Kansas City native.

Paul Loki.

Joe Marshall. Drums. Marshall was with the group around 1942.

George Moreland (born in Oklahoma City). Drums. Moreland worked briefly with Fields in the early to mid-1960s (along with Morris McCraven). Moreland later performed with Gladys Knight and the Pips, the Isley Brothers, and Millie Jackson. A review in the Louisville, Kentucky, *Courier-Journal* (October 8, 1994, p. 63) called the band he led with Jackson "superlative."

Robert Moss. Trumpet. Moss was in the Ernie Fields organization when Al Duncan joined in the 1940s.

Hubert Perry. Tenor sax. Perry was with the group around 1942.

Johnny Rogers. Rogers was about sixteen when Ernie recruited him from Tulsa. Ernie "got his father's permission," he told Roy Milton in a 1980 interview. In fact, "I used to work with his father." Milton described Rogers as way ahead of his time and a "great musical mind."[45]

Wallace Silks. Trumpet.

Cecil Smith. Guitar. Smith was with the earliest Ernie Fields band, in the early '30s.

Henry Smith. Drums. Smith was son of "Geechie" Smith, the high-note trumpet player. Ernie described him as "a very fine drummer."

Lawrence Stone. Vocalist. Stone was mentioned prominently in an article about the orchestra's upcoming show at the Oklahoma City Trianon, Sunday, December 23, 1951. The story in the December 22 edition of the *Black Dispatch* newspaper said Stone was "a little fellow with a big voice. 'Stony,' as he is often called by his friends, has won many fans with his lilting tenor and soft melodic tones." His small stature had advantages, the story went on to say, for "there is always the element of surprise when he opens up and croons one of those velvet ballads." He is listed as vocalist with the Ernie Freeman Orchestra in a 1955 Los Angeles recording of "Without a Word of Goodbye" and "Dark of Night" on the Vita label. The recording was remastered and released in 2014.

T. D. Thomas. Piano. Thomas and J. William Baul were the first to include Ernie Fields in gigs around Tulsa in the late 1920s.

Robert Villan. Trumpet. Villan was with the Ernie Fields Jr. group in 1967.

Eddie Walker. Trumpet. Walker was in the Fields organization around 1942 along with King Kolax and Milton Lewis.

Earl Warren. Tenor sax. Ernie hired Warren in part because he was a college classmate and was going with singer Estelle Edson.

Sam Waters. Saxophone. Waters is believed to have been in the Fields organization in the late '50s.

Carl White. Bass.

John White. Sax. White was in the band in the '40s with white musician Harold Eiler.

Delma/Delmar Willis. Tenor sax. Willis was from Wichita, Kansas. He was in the band in the early '30s.

Thomas "Deek" Wilson. Trumpet. Wilson was with the Fields organization in the mid- to late '50s, after a stint with Nat Towles. He went with B. B. King after leaving Fields.

Wallace Wilson. Guitar. Wilson is believed to have worked as a session musician. He is not to be confused with a musician by the same name known professionally as Red Rat.

Carl Wright. Tap dance. Wright was with the band in 1950 and was mentioned in a *Pittsburgh Courier* article that September as part of the "Three-leggers" act with one-legged dancer Frank James.

Lammar Wright Sr. (born June 20, 1907, in Texarkana, Texas; died April 13, 1973, in New York City). Trumpet. The region and time frame and connection to Cab Calloway's Missourians, Sy Oliver, and Louis Armstrong make Wright a likely alum. However, he is not mentioned in any Ernie Fields notes or remembrances, and, by Ernie's own admission, he may have "left out some." However, the Tom Lord Jazz Discography lists Wright on Fields's 1947 recordings.

TEACHERS

Ernie often counted on schoolteachers to be talent scouts, alerting him to young musicians with promise and steering them his way. The teachers he mentioned most often were the following:

Zelia Page Breaux (1880–1956), who played trumpet, violin, and piano, and was music supervisor for segregated Oklahoma City's Black public schools. Her father, Inman E. Page, was the first president of Langston University, which was also fertile ground for Fields to provide real road experience. Breaux established and directed an orchestra, bands, and choirs at Frederick Douglass High School—many of them well known outside Oklahoma, even during the Great Depression. In 1933 her band performed at the Chicago World's Fair and caught the attention of Duke Ellington. She earned a bachelor's degree in music from Lincoln Institute (later Lincoln University), where her father was principal, and a master's degree from Northwestern University in Evanston, Illinois.[46]

Clarence Fields (1892–1990), Ernie's brother, who taught music at Booker T. Washington High Schools in Sand Springs, Oklahoma, and later in Tulsa. He was trained at Tuskegee Institute, where he graduated in 1920, and later earned a master's degree from Colorado State Teachers College in Greeley (along with his wife [Frankie Robertson] and Ernie's wife). When he was hired for the Sand Springs school, the only funds available were for a shoemaking instructor, so he taught that until 1932. The area Knights of Pythian Lodge paid for a full set of band instruments for the school so that he could teach band exclusively until 1942.[47] In addition to teaching, he directed a group of mostly students called the Music Makers that played dances in Tulsa. Artist Oscar Estelle was once a member. A sergeant-bugler during World War I, Clarence performed taps at various veterans events well into his nineties and recorded himself playing the song for his own funeral. His motto, according to Ernie Fields Jr., was "He who practices the most, plays the best."

William Jett, born in 1902, a Hampton Institute graduate who taught music at Tulsa's Booker T. Washington High School. Census records from 1930 and 1940 describe the Virginia-born teacher as a "bandmaster," who owned his home and owned a radio. Earl Bostic was one of his most accomplished students.

DISCOGRAPHY

NEW YORK, AUGUST 1939
Ernie Fields & His Orchestra

W 24960. "You Gave Me Everything but Love" (vocals, Leora Davis). Vocalion 5240.

24962A. "T-Town Blues" (vocals, Melvin Moore). Vocalion 5073.

24961A. "Lard Stomp." Vocalion 5073.

"Claxton Stomp." Not released.

W 24964. "I'm Living in a Great Big Way" (vocals, Leora Davis). Vocalion 5240.

NEW YORK, SEPTEMBER 1939
Ernie Fields & His Orchestra

W 26070. "Just Leave Me Alone" (vocals, Melvin Moore). Vocalion 5157.

W 26071. "Blues at Midnight" (arrangement, René Hall; vocals, Leora Davis). Vocalion 5344.

W 26072. "Hi Jivin'." Vocalion 5157.

W 26073. "Bless Your Heart" (vocals, Melvin Moore). Vocalion 5344.

NEW YORK, MARCH 1946
Ernie Fields & His Orchestra (all vocals, Melvin Moore)
(produced by Herb Abramson and Max Silverman)

A-33. "This Will Make You Laugh." Quality unissued.

A-34. "Sentimental and Melancholy." Quality unissued.

A-35. "Don't Blame Me." Quality 6061.

A-36. "Thursday Evening Blues." Quality 6051.

NEW YORK, 1947
Ernie Fields & His Orchestra

F-103. "I Can't Give You Anything but Love" (vocals, Melvin Moore). Frisco 2.

F-107. "Thursday Evening Blues" (vocals, Melvin Moore). Frisco 3.

F-109. "E. F. Boogie." Frisco 3.

F-111. "Jazz Axe." Frisco 2.

F-110. "Christopher Goes Bebop" (arrangement, René Hall). Frisco 101.

F-112. "Mouthful of Lies" (vocals, Harold Bruce). Frisco 101.

F-121. "Big Lou" (vocals, Teddy Cole). Frisco 102.

F-122. "Travelin' Blues" (vocals, Teddy Cole). Frisco 102.

TULSA, OKLAHOMA, 1949
Ernie Fields & His Orchestra

F-123. "Long Lost Love" (vocals, Teddy Cole). Frisco 103, Gotham 273.

F-124. "Butch's Blues" (1). Frisco 103, Gotham 273, Krazy Kat (UK) LP814.

"Butch's Blues" (alt). Gotham 281, Krazy Kat LP KK 814.

"Frustrated Woman" (vocals, Jo Evans). Gotham 281, Krazy Kat LP KK 814.

"My Prince." Gotham 281, Krazy Kat LP KK 814.

Untitled (blues). Gotham 281, Krazy Kat LP KK 814.

"Butch's Blues" (previously unreleased take). Krazy Kat LP KK 814.

PROBABLY TULSA, (JANUARY?) 1949
Ernie Fields & His Orchestra

"T-Town Blues." Bullet 302.

"E. F. Boogie." Bullet 302.

LINDEN, NEW JERSEY (OR MAYBE KANSAS CITY, MISSOURI), NOVEMBER 29, 1949
ERNIE FIELDS & HIS ORCHESTRA

R-1123. "Baritone Shuffle" (Leroy "Super" Cooper). Regal 3249, Delmark LP DL-439.

R-1124. "88." Delmark LP DL-439.

R-1125. "T-Town Blues" (vocals, Teddy Cole). Regal 3249, Delmark LP DL-439.

R-1126. "Big Lou" (vocals, Teddy Cole). Delmark LP DL-439.

R-1127. "Ride Mr. Trombone" (vocals, Teddy Cole). Delmark LP DL-439.

R-1128. "Baby—Who's [sic] Baby Are You." Delmark LP DL-439.

LOS ANGELES, 1955
Ernie Fields Orchestra

JP-77-AA. "Long, Long Highway" (vocals, Ann Walls). Combo 77.

JP-77-A. "Skyway." Combo 77.

"Daddy How Long" (vocals, Ann Walls). Ace (UK) LP84.

"T-Town Mambo" (vocals, Ann Walls). Ace (UK) LP 84.

PHILADELPHIA(?), 1957
Ernie Fields Orchestra

EF-2. "Annie's Rock." Jamie 1102.

EF-1. "Strollin' after School" (background vocals, Darlene Love and Fonita James). Jamie 1102.

LOS ANGELES, 1959
Ernie Field's [sic] Orchestra

R110B. "Christopher Columbus." Rendezvous 110, LP1309.

R110A. "In the Mood." Rendezvous 110, LP1309 (July 6, 1959) (also issued on Hi-Oldies 403 and Highland 2000).

LOS ANGELES, 1959
Ernie Fields & His Orchestra, "In the Mood" LP

"Honky Tonk." Rendezvous 142, LP 1309.

"Knocked Out." Rendezvous 142, LP 1309.

R110A. "In the Mood." Rendezvous 110, Rendezvous LP 1309.

R110B. "Christopher Columbus." Rendezvous 110, Rendezvous LP 1309 (this and
     previous track also issued on Hi-Oldies 403 and Highland 2000).

"The Boot." Rendezvous 142, LP 1309.

"Tuxedo Junction." Rendezvous 142, LP 1309.

"Volare Cha-Cha." Rendezvous 142, LP 1309.

"My Prayer." Rendezvous 142, LP 1309.

"Dipsy Doodle." Rendezvous 142, LP 1309.

"Raunchy." Rendezvous 142, LP 1309.

"Tea for Two Cha-Cha." Rendezvous 142, LP 1309.

"It's All in the Game." Rendezvous 142, LP 1309.

LOS ANGELES, JANUARY 1960
Ernie Fields & Orchestra

R-117-A. "Chattanooga Choo Choo." Rendezvous 117.

R-117-B. "Working Out" (February 6, 1960). Rendezvous 117.

LOS ANGELES, MAY 1960

R-122-B. "Begin the Beguine." Rendezvous 122.

R-122-A. "Things Ain't What They Used to Be." Rendezvous 122.

R-129-B. "Sweet Slumber." Rendezvous 129.

R-129-A. "Teen Flip." Rendezvous 129.

R-138-A. "The Honeydripper." Rendezvous 138.

R-138-B. "Tuxedo Junction." Rendezvous 138.

LOS ANGELES, 1961
Ernie Fields

R-142-A. "Happy Whistler." Rendezvous 142.

R-142-B. "Monkey (Honky Tonk)." Rendezvous 142.

LOS ANGELES, 1961
Ernie Fields Orchestra, featuring Ann Walls (vocals)

R-148-1. "Be Anything but Don't Be Sorry." Rendezvous 148.

R-148-2. "Fallin'." Rendezvous 148.

Ernie Fields

R-150-1. "Charleston." Rendezvous 150.

R-150-2. "12th Street Rag." Rendezvous 150.

R-161-B. "Castle Rock." Rendezvous 161.

R-161-1. "String of Pearls." Rendezvous 161.

> **"THE CHARLESTON"** (2:10) [Harms ASCAP—Mack, Johnson]
> **"12TH STREET RAG"** (2:20) [Shapiro Bernstein, Jerry Vogel ASCAP—
> Bowman, Razas]
> **ERNIE FIELDS (Rendezvous 150)**
> The Ernie Fields instrumentalists bring back "The Charleston" in a man-
> ner the teeners should go wild for. This time around it's put in a driving,
> rock-beat showcase that'll have the kids dancin' 'round the jukes day and
> night. Coupler's a similar sock-rock refitting of "12th Street Rag."

"The Charleston" and "12th Street Rag" listings in *Cashbox*, May 20, 1961.

> **ERNIE FIELDS (Rendezvous 161)**
> **(B+) "CASTLE ROCK"** (2:32)
> [Arc BMI—Sears] Fields can
> step back into chartsville with his
> swinging rock-a-teen instrumental re-
> wrapping of the evergreen. Hotstuff
> that oughta keep the hoffers moving
> day and night.
> **(B+) "STRING OF PEARLS"**
> (2:17) [Mutual Music Society
> ASCAP—Gray, Delange] Here the
> Fields crew tastefully shuffle-rocks
> thru the Glenn Miller classic. Great
> two-sided juke material.

"Castle Rock" and "String of Pearls" listings *in Cashbox*, October 14, 1961

R-168-1. "Like a Now" (vocals, Ann Walls). Rendezvous 168.

R-168-2. "Time to Dream" (vocals, Ann Walls). Rendezvous 168.

R-170-1. "Ernie's Tune." Rendezvous 170 (also issued on Pickwick LP-Golden Oldies, vol. 2).

R-170-2. "Hucklebuck (Twist)." Rendezvous 170.

R-181-2. "Me and My Shadow." Rendezvous 181.

R-181-1. "Theme from Perry Mason." Rendezvous 181.

LOS ANGELES, 1964
Ernie Fields & Orchestra

45-51295. "St. Louis Blues." Capitol 5161.

45-51296. "(Theme from) Lilies of the Field." Capitol 5161.

45-52615. "Swanee River." Capitol 5326.

45-52618. "Chloe." Capitol 5326.

PROBABLY LOS ANGELES, 1965
Ernie Fields and Cockroach (likely Ernie Fields Jr.)

C. "Cockroach Walk." BB 4010.

T. "Ten Little Bottles." BB 4010.

NOTES

PROLOGUE

1. Wishart, *Encyclopedia of the Great Plains*, 548.

CHAPTER 1. THE DISCOVERY, A FIVE-DOLLAR TIP, AND A CHANCE AT THE BIG TIME

1. Ernie Fields, interview by Love, 121–22.
2. Ernie Fields, interview by Love; Butler, *Cleora's Kitchens*, 46.
3. Pomerance, *Repeal of the Blues*, 19–21.
4. Victor Davis, "Alexander's Agency Switch Is Big Band News," *Dallas Morning News*, April 16, 1939, 4.
5. Hammond, *John Hammond on Record*, 222.
6. Ernie Fields, interview by Preston Love, 126.
7. The Count Basie mainstay "Papa" Jones is not be confused with Philly Joe Jones, known as the drummer of the first "great" Miles Davis Quintet.
8. Hammond, *John Hammond on Record*, 222.
9. Crouch, *Kansas City Lightning*, 307.
10. Ernie Fields, interview by Love, 134.
11. Ernie Fields, interview by Swindell. Warren C. Swindell headed the Center for Afro-American Studies at Indiana State University in Terre Haute from 1980 to 1999 and now lives in Baton Rouge.
12. Ernie Fields, interview by Swindell.
13. Driggs and Haddix, *Kansas City Jazz*, 178.
14. Moore, interview by author.
15. Schuller, *Swing Era*, 804.
16. Moore, interview by author.
17. Ernie Fields, interview by Love, 7.

CHAPTER 2. TO GO OR TO STAY?

1. Ernie Fields, interview by Love, 114.
2. Claxton recording.
3. Ernie Fields, interview by Love, 118.

CHAPTER 3. PREQUEL

1. Ernie Fields, interview by Love.
2. Claude Jones (born February 11, 1901, and died January 17, 1962) was a trombone player from Boley, Oklahoma. He played with Fletcher Henderson, the Duke Ellington Orchestra, and others. Schuller, *Swing Era*, 7.

3. Teddy Hill (born Dec. 7, 1909, in Birmingham, Alabama, and died May 19, 1978, in Cleveland) was a big band leader who formed his own band in 1934. He also managed Minton's Playhouse, a seminal jazz club in Harlem. McCarthy, *Big Band Jazz*, 286.

4. Shapiro and Hentoff, *Hear Me Talkin' to Ya*, 218.

5. Considered the "dean of Black female musicians," internationally acclaimed Eva Jessye (born January 20, 1895, in Coffeyville, Kansas; died February 21, 1992 in Ann Arbor, Michigan) was one of the first Black women to direct a professional choral group, starting during Harlem Renaissance. Her choral group, the Dixie Jubilee Choir, which later became the Eva Jessye Choir, performed throughout the United States—in Broadway shows and movies and on the radio. She directed the chorus in the original Broadway production of *Porgy and Bess* (where she was cast as "Strawberry Woman" in the show), and hers was the official choir of the 1963 civil rights March on Washington. "Eva Jessye, 97, Dies; Choral Group Director."

6. Clarence Fields, Ernie's older brother who was a public school music teacher and high school band director in Sand Springs, Oklahoma. Lydia Copeland was Bernice's older sister and an elementary school teacher.

7. Ernie Fields, interview by Love, 52.

8. Ernie Fields, interview by Widner.

9. Ernie Fields, interview by Widner.

10. Ayer, "Segregated Musician Locals, 1941–1974." During World War II, James Petrillo led a bitter strike against record companies, protesting a lack of royalties to musicians, according to his *New York Times* obituary. Serrin, "James Petrillo Dead; Led Musicians."

11. Ernie Fields, interview by Widner.

12. Rogers and Taylor, "My Heart Sings." Coauthor Billy Taylor (not the famous jazz pianist) was a tap artist and dance instructor from Oklahoma City.

13. Shirk, phone conversation and emails with author and others, September 18 and 19, 2018. Ken Shirk was assistant to the president of the American Federation of Musicians.

14. Young, "Amalgamation of Local 47 and 767."

15. Banks, "Tribute to Rene J. Hall."

16. Moore, interview by author.

17. Greensmith, "Al Duncan," 328.

18. Ernie Fields, interview by Widner.

CHAPTER 4. FROM NACOGDOCHES TO TAFT TO TUSKEGEE

1. Franklin, *Journey toward Hope*.

2. Ernie Fields, interview by Love, 3.

3. "Eva Jessye, 97, Dies; Choral Group Director."

4. Ernie Fields, interview by Love, 17-A.

5. Capt. Frank L. Drye became bandmaster in 1915. When the School of Music was established in 1931, noted choral composer and choir director William L. Dawson

became director. The band became part of the music school, which in the 1940s became the Department of Music, still headed by Dawson. Captain Drye's title was head of band instruments and director of bands. The seventy-five-piece band included drum majors, juvenile drum majors, majorettes, and herald trumpeters. "The Marching Crimson Piper Band," https://www.tuskegee.edu/student-life /student-organizations/band.

6. Butler, *Cleora's Kitchens*, 26.
7. Ernie Fields, interview by Love, 45–46.

CHAPTER 5. ON THE ROAD, FOR BETTER OR WORSE

1. Gibson, "The Negro Holocaust."
2. Ernie Fields, interview by Love, 96–97.
3. Betts, "Eddie and Sugar Lou's Hotel Tyler Orchestra." Vocalion recording artists Eddie Fennell and Charles "Sugar Lou" Morgan formed their jazz band around 1926 and enjoyed modest fame, thanks in part to radio broadcasts by KWKH in Shreveport, Louisiana, and long stands at the Hotel Tyler. Fennell, the leader, played the banjo and sang. Morgan (1903–69), the pianist, claimed to have written and sold rights to "There'll Be Some Changes Made" for fifteen dollars. Both men spent their last days working as bellboys in hotels.
4. Hennessey, *From Jazz to Swing*, 109.
5. Ernie Fields, interview by Love, 77.
6. Milton and Ernie Fields, recorded conversation.
7. Milton and Ernie Fields, recorded conversation.

CHAPTER 6. MANY LESSONS LEARNED

1. Hentoff, liner notes for *Giant Steps*.
2. Hall, Ernie Fields, and Ernie Fields Jr., recorded conversation with author.
3. Ernie Fields, interview by Love, 145.
4. Hennessey, *From Jazz to Swing*, 129.
5. Hall, Ernie Fields, and Ernie Fields Jr., recorded conversation with author.
6. "Ex-Hotel Owner's Services Friday," *Tulsa World*, October 26, 1972, B3. Wellington H. Small was born May 2, 1893, in Kopperl, Texas, and died October 24, 1972, in Tulsa.
7. Faye (Small) Fields, telephone interviews by author. Faye is the widow of Frank Ronald Fields, son of Ernie Fields's brother Clarence Fields. She resides in Bartlett, Illinois, with her daughter.
8. Ernie Fields, interview by Love, 145.
9. Ernie Fields, self-recorded tape no. 1.
10. Hall, Ernie Fields, and Ernie Fields Jr., recorded conversation with author.
11. Belcher, "Once Upon a Time: The Genial Gentleman of Swing," 30.
12. Ernie Fields, interview by Love, 169.
13. Ernie Fields, interview by Love, 173.
14. "Dunbar Hotel and Club Alabam."

15. Ernie Fields, interview by Love, 51.

16. Heichelbech, "Forgotten Dance Hall Taxi Dancers."

17. Driggs and Lewine, *Black Beauty, White Heat*, 44.

18. Theatre Owners Booking Association (TOBA) was a group of mostly white-owned theaters that booked vaudeville shows in the 1920s, including comedians, jazz and blues singers/musicians, and other performers, including opera singers—for Black audiences. TOBA was also referred to by Black performers as "Tough on Black Asses," as the theaters generally offered low pay coupled with demanding touring arrangements.

19. Ernie Fields, interview by Love.

20. Ernie Fields, interview by Love, 38–39.

21. Evans, interview by Kochakian, 16.

22. "Memphis Palace Acclaims Fine Ernie Fields' Ork Show" *Pittsburgh Courier*, September 23, 1950, 14.

23. Evans, interview by Kochakian, 16.

CHAPTER 7. MUSICIANS COME, MUSICIANS GO

1. Ernie Fields, interview by Love, 97.

2. Russell, *Jazz Style in Kansas City*, 70.

3. Ernie Fields, interview by Love, 97.

4. Ernie Fields, interview by Love, 97.

5. Moore, interview by author.

6. Milton and Ernie Fields, recorded conversation.

7. Milton and Ernie Fields, recorded conversation.

8. Lateef and Boyd, *Gentle Giant*, chap. 5.

9. Lateef, interview by Rusch.

10. Lateef and Boyd, *Gentle Giant*.

11. Moore, interview by author.

12. Heath and McLaren, *I Walked with Giants*, 17.

13. Ernie Fields, interview by Love, 227.

14. Lateef and Boyd, *Gentle Giant*, chap. 5.

15. Dance, *World of Count Basie*, 343–44.

16. Moore, interview by author.

17. Ernie Fields, interview by Love, 156.

18. Ernie Fields, interview by Love, 155.

19. Moore, interview by author.

20. Joyce, interview by author.

21. Ernie Fields, interview by Love, 107.

22. *Tulsa, the Visitor's Guide*.

23. Ernie Fields, interview by Swindell.

24. Moore, interview by author.

25. Moore, interview by author.

26. Ernie Fields, interview by Swindell.

27. Hall, Ernie Fields, and Ernie Fields Jr., recorded conversation with author.

CHAPTER 8. SOMETHING A LITTLE DIFFERENT

1. "Ernie Fields Big Dance, Show Comes to American Legion Hall," *Kansas City (Kans.) Plaindealer*, December 22, 1950.
2. "Fair Dancing Pair Popular," *Regina (Saskatchewan) Leader & Post*, August 2, 1961, 3.
3. *Oklahoma City Black Dispatch*, December 22, 1951.
4. Advertisement, *North Adams (Mass.) Transcript*, July 6, 1934, 11.
5. Advertisement, *Pittsfield (Mass.) Berkshire Eagle*, June 26, 1934, 4.
6. Ernie Fields, self-recorded tape no. 1.

CHAPTER 9. KEEPING HIS NAME FRONT AND CENTER

1. Hall, Ernie Fields, and Ernie Fields Jr., recorded conversation with author.
2. Victor Davis, "Krupa Still Hits and Misses; Randolph Makes Bow Tuesday," *Dallas Morning News*, December 20, 1938, 19.
3. A. S. Kany, from *Dayton (Ohio) Journal Herald*.
4. Diana Nelson Jones, "And All That Jazz," *Tulsa Tribune*, January 7, 1987, 5B.
5. Ernie Fields, self-recorded tape no. 1.
6. Ernie Fields, interview by Love, 271.
7. Ernie Fields, interview by Love, 272.
8. Fields, "Ernie Fields and His Sweet Swing Music."

CHAPTER 10. OLD HABITS DIE HARD

1. "Alphonso's Gold" film proposal description, Fort Smith Historical Society, John McIntosh, producer, Red Cat Productions, 2016.
2. Ernie Fields, interview by Love, 62.
3. Ernie Fields, interview by Swindell.
4. Driggs and Haddix, *Kansas City Jazz*, 66.
5. Ernie Fields, interview by Love, 63.
6. Ernie Fields, interview by Swindell.
7. Ernie Fields, interview by Swindell.
8. Schuller, *Swing Era*, 351.
9. Ernie Fields, interview by Swindell.
10. Ernie Fields, interview by Swindell.
11. Ernie Fields, interview by Love, 234.
12. Ernie Fields, interview by Swindell.

CHAPTER 11. OFAY CATS

About the chapter title: "ofay" is musician slang for a white person. Its origins are unknown; according to *Merriam-Webster's*, it was first used around 1899 and is sometimes considered derogatory, though the author doesn't recall it being used in that way.

1. Belcher, "Once Upon a Time," 29.
2. Maxwell, "Story of 'Ella and Louis.'" The *Memphis Commercial Appeal*, October 7 and 8, 1931, noted that a judge dismissed the case.
3. Ernie Fields, interview by Swindell.

4. Ernie Fields, interview by Love, 69.

5. Ernie Fields, interview by Swindell.

6. Faye (Small) Fields, telephone interviews by author.

7. Ernie Fields, interview by Swindell.

8. Ernie Fields, interview by Swindell.

9. Ernie Fields, interview by Swindell.

10. Sherr, interview by author.

11. Sherr, *Bel Air Jazz.*

12. Sherr, interview by author.

CHAPTER 12. BEHIND THAT PREPOSITION

1. Choc is a home brew believed to have originated in the Choctaw Nation of Indian Territory. The brew was a fermented mixture of barley, hops, sugar, yeast, and other ingredients.

2. Ernie Fields, self-recorded tape no. 2.

3. Prov. 15:1–2 (King James Version).

4. Ernie Fields, self-recorded tape no. 2.

CHAPTER 13. GOOD WHITE FOLK

1. Founded in 1921 and named for Pawhuska, Oklahoma, banker and rancher Eugene S. Shidler, the town grew to about five thousand because of the discovery of oil and the arrival of the Osage Railway in 1922. It is said that robberies were common, giving the town a reputation for violence. By 2010, the population had dwindled to about four hundred. Wikipedia, s.v. "Shidler, Oklahoma," accessed July 21, 2022, https://en.wikipedia.org/wiki/Shidler,_Oklahoma.

2. Ernie Fields, interview by Swindell.

3. Ernie Fields, interview by Widner.

4. Ernie Fields, interview by Swindell.

5. Ernie Fields, interview by Love, 166.

6. Duffield, telephone interview by author.

7. Ernie Fields, interview by Widner.

8. Ernie Fields, self-recorded tape no. 1.

CHAPTER 14. LITTLE ERNIE

1. Gilford, interview by author.

2. Sherr, interview by author.

3. "Ernie Fields Jr., the New American Sweet Soul Sound," undated flier, promotional materials from Ernie Fields Artist, Inc.

4. "Tulsan Plays Hot, Sweet in Germany," *Tulsa World*, March 12, 1958.

5. Ernie Fields, interview by Love, 345.

6. Farley, *Soul of the Man*, 152.

7. Chadbourne, "Ernie Fields Jr."

8. Wesley, *Hit Me, Fred*, 241–42.

9. Los Angeles Jazz Society, *Quarter Notes*, spring 2013.

10. "Chapter Profiles: Ernie Fields Jr.," 3.

CHAPTER 15. WHAT MAN IS THIS?

1. Ernie Fields, self-recorded tape no. 2; Ernie Fields, interview by Swindell.

2. Ernie Fields, self-recorded tape no. 2.

3. Ernie Fields, self-recorded tape no. 2.

4. Hall, Ernie Fields, and Ernie Fields Jr., recorded conversation with author.

5. Sherr, *Bel Air Jazz*.

6. Moore, interview by author.

7. Hall, Ernie Fields, and Ernie Fields Jr., recorded conversation with author.

8. Moore, interview by author.

9. Milton and Ernie Fields, recorded conversation.

10. Hall, Ernie Fields, and Ernie Fields Jr., recorded conversation with author.

11. Ernie Fields, interview by Love, 86.

12. Ernie Fields, interview by Love, 88.

13. Ernie Fields, self-recorded tape no. 2.

14. *Tulsa World*, December 2, 1950, 9.

15. Banks and Ernie Fields, recorded conversation.

16. Ernie Fields, interview by author.

17. Ernie Fields, self-recorded tape no. 3.

18. Ernie Fields, self-recorded tape no. 3.

CHAPTER 16. THE ROAD TO A HIT RECORD

1. Driggs, liner notes for *Big Band Jazz*.

2. According to Preston Love. Ernie Fields, interview by Love, 279.

3. There are two editions of the sheet music for "In the Mood." The 1939 publication credited to Joe Garland and lyricist Andy Razaf (yes, there are words) is in A-flat, while the 1960 reprint credited only to Garland, with piano arrangement by Robert C. Haring, is in the key of G. A dispute over authorship arose when the main theme, a riff from a song named "Tar Paper Stomp," was recorded by trumpet player and band leader Wingy Manone. Manone recorded a version that did not become popular. Band leaders Charlie Barnett and Artie Shaw performed Garland's original, deemed too long to fit on one side of a 78 rpm record, so it fell out of favor. Garland took it to Miller, who created a shorter version, according to Wikipedia. Wikipedia, s.v. "Tar Paper Stomp," https://en.wikipedia.org/wiki/Tar_Paper_Stomp.

4. Halsey, interview by author.

5. Ernie Fields, interview by Love, 273.

6. "René Hall."

7. Ernie Fields, interview by Love, 276.

8. Ernie Fields, interview by Love, 277.

9. Ernie Fields, interview by Love, 280.

10. Colman, liner notes for *In the Mood.*

11. Ernie Fields, interview by Love, 282.

12. McCarthy, *Big Band Jazz*, 112.

13. McCarthy, *Big Band Jazz*, 112.

ROLL CALL

1. Hopkins, telephone interview by author.

2. Dance, *World of Count Basie*, 119.

3. Driggs and Haddix, *Kansas City Jazz*, 190.

4. *Idaho Daily Statesman*, July 15, 1938, 9; *Amarillo Globe*, October 9, 1939.

5. Moore, interview by author.

6. Greensmith, "Al Duncan."

7. Kay Bourne, "The Callboard," *Boston Bay State Banner*, July 3, 1980.

8. Peter Vacher, "Teddy Edwards: Innovative Saxophonist with the Max Roach-Clifford Brown Quintet," *Guardian*, April 29, 2003.

9. Wilson, liner notes for *Cookin'.*

10. Ernie Fields, interview by Love, 271.

11. Dance, *World of Count Basie*, 332.

12. Ernie Fields, interview by Widner.

13. *Billboard* 54, no. 34 (August 22, 1942), 4.

14. Ernie Fields, interview by author.

15. Lee, telephone conversation with author.

16. "Seattle Live Music: A Music Legacy Guide," www.seattle.gov/filmmusic.

17. Campbell, Buttner, and Pruter, "King Kolax Discography."

18. Jenkins, "Early Bebop Tenorman."

19. *Heritage*, supplement to *Tulsa Oklahoma Eagle,* February 24, 2000, 7.

20. Ernie Fields, self-recorded tape no. 3.

21. Maxwell, interview by author.

22. Telephone interview with author, August 13, 2022.

23. *San Francisco Chronicle*, February 3, 2013.

24. "Third Annual Living Legends" program.

25. Moore, interview by author.

26. Ernie Fields, interview by Swindell.

27. Belcher, "Once Upon a Time: The Genial Gentleman of Swing."

28. Ernie Fields, interview by Love, 365.

29. Peter Vacher, *Swingin' on Central Avenue*, 190.

30. Ernie Fields, interview by Love, 222.

31. Goetting, *Joined at the Hip.*

32. Ernie Fields, self-recorded tape no. 1.

33. Powell, interview by Bernotas.

34. Ernie Fields, interview by Love, 97.

35. "Paul Gayten: 'Dr. Daddy-O (Backtrackin').'"

36. Ernie Fields Jr., interview by author.

37. Ernie Fields, self-recorded tape no. 1.

38. Ernie Fields, interview by Love, 54.

39. Ernie Fields, interview by Love, 389 (first and second quotes); Ernie Fields, self-recorded tape no. 1 (third quote).

40. Ernie Fields, interview by Love, 205.

41. Schuller, *Swing Era*, 804.

42. Driggs, liner notes for *Big Band Jazz*.

43. Schuller, *Swing Era*, 804.

44. Sherr, *Bel Air Jazz*.

45. Milton and Ernie Fields, recorded conversation.

46. Arnold, *Oklahoma City Music*, 41.

47. "Clarence Fields, Former Band Director, Dies."

BIBLIOGRAPHY

Arnold, Anita G. *Oklahoma City Music: Deep Deuce and Beyond*. Mount Pleasant, S.C.: Arcadia Publishing 2010.

Averill, David. "Tulsa's Unsung Musicians." *OK Magazine, Tulsa World*, April 17, 1983.

Ayer, Julie. "Segregated Musician Union Locals, 1941–1974." *Polyphonic Archive*. Institute for Music Leadership. Eastman School of Music, University of Rochester. February 12, 2007. https://iml.esm.rochester.edu/polyphonic-archive/article/segregated-musician-union-locals-1941-1974/.

Banks, Estelle Edson. "Tribute to René J. Hall." *Overture* 68, no. 1 (May 1988). Los Angeles American Federation of Musicians, Local 47.

Banks, Estelle Edson, and Ernie Fields. Recorded conversation. Tulsa. [N.d.].

Barnett, Deborah, and Ellen Charles (daughters of Leslie Sheffield). Telephone conversations with author. 2019.

Belcher, Dixie. "Once Upon a Time: The Genial Gentleman of Swing." *Tulsa Magazine*, February 3, 1983. Metropolitan Tulsa Chamber of Commerce.

Betts, Vicki. "Eddie and Sugar Lou's Hotel Tyler Orchestra." Presentations and Publications, paper 44, University of Texas, Tyler, February 2, 2016. http://hdl.handle.net/10950/505.

"Big Chief's Soul." *Sunday Journal News*, December 25, 1983.

"Bill 'Bojanges' [*sic*] Robinson and Big Show at Coliseum Tonite." *Evansville Argus*, April 4, 1942.

Butler, Cleora. *Cleora's Kitchens: The Memoir of a Cook and Eight Decades of Great American Food*. Tulsa: Council Oak Books, 1985.

Campbell, Robert L., Armin Buttner, and Robert Pruter. "The King Kolax Discography." http://campber.people.clemson.edu/kolax.html.

Chadbourne, Eugene. "Ernie Fields Jr." *AllMusic Guide*. www.allmusic.com/artist/ernie-fields-jr-mn0000548166/biography.

"Chapter Profiles: Ernie Fields, Jr." *L.A. Record* 13, no. 4 (August/September 1993).

"Clarence Fields, Former Band Director, Dies" (Clarence Fields obituary). *Tulsa World*, February 23, 1990.

Claxton, Rozelle. Recording C234, side 1, n.d. Box 4, item 16. Jazz Institute of Chicago Oral Histories. Hanna Holborn Gray Special Collections Research Center, University of Chicago Library.

Colman, Stuart. Liner notes for *In the Mood* by Ernie Fields. [N.d.].

Crouch, Stanley. *Kansas City Lightning: The Rise and Times of Charlie Parker*. New York: Harper, 2013.

Dance, Stanley. *The World of Count Basie*. New York: Da Capo Press, 1980.

Driggs, Frank. Liner notes for *Big Band Jazz: Tulsa to Harlem* by various artists. Delmark Records DC-439, 1988.

Driggs, Frank, and Chuck Haddix. *Kansas City Jazz: From Ragtime to Bebop—A History.* New York: Oxford University Press, 2005.

Driggs, Frank, and Harris Lewine. *Black Beauty, White Heat: A Pictorial History of Classic Jazz, 1920–1950.* New York: William Morrow, 1982.

Duffield, Helen. Telephone interview by author. 2019.

"The Dunbar Hotel and Club Alabam." *Finding Lost Angeles* (blog), January 30, 2019. https://www.findinglostangeles.com/all-content/2019/1/29/hotel-dunbar-and-club -alabam.

"Eva Jessye, 97, Dies; Choral Group Director" (Eva Jessye obituary). *New York Times,* March 4, 1992.

Evans, Jo. Interview by Dan Kochakian. September 8, 1986. *Whiskey, Women and . . .* 17 (Spring 1988).

Farley, Charles. *Soul of the Man: Bobby "Blue" Bland.* Jackson: University of Mississippi Press, 2011.

Fields, Ernie. "Ernie Fields and His Sweet Swing Music." Interview by Dan Kochakian. *Whiskey, Women and . . .* 18–19 (Fall 1989).

———. Interview by author. Tulsa. [1987?].

———. Interview by Preston Love. Tulsa. October 31, 1981. Transcript. Jazz Oral History Project. Rutgers University Institute of Jazz Studies. https://doi.org/doi:10.7282/t3 -gf2e-tt40.

———. Interview by Warren C. Swindell. Tulsa. December 4, 1987. Center for Afro-American Studies, Indiana State University.

———. Letter to the author. April 4, 1971.

———. Letter to the author. March 5, 1972.

———. Self-recorded tapes nos. 1–3. Late 1980s–early 1990s. Author's collection.

———. Transcript of interview by Ellis Widner of *Tulsa Tribune.* September 1979.

———. Undated letters to the author. Late 1980s.

Fields, Ernie Jr. Interview by author. [N.d.].

Fields, Faye (Small). Telephone interviews by author. 2020 and 2021.

Franklin, Jimmie Lewis. *Journey toward Hope: A History of Blacks in Oklahoma.* Norman: University of Oklahoma Press, 1982.

Gibson, Robert A. "The Negro Holocaust: Lynching and Race Riots in the United States, 1880–1950." Yale University: Yale-New Haven Teachers Institute. Curriculum unit 79.02.04. https://teachersinstitute.yale.edu/curriculum/units/1979/2/79 .02.04.x.html.

Gilford, JoAnn (Goodwin). Interview by author. Atlanta, Ga. February 7, 2019, and previous telephone conversations.

Goetting, Jay. *Joined at the Hip: A History of Jazz in the Twin Cities.* Saint Paul: Minnesota Historical Society Press, 2011.

Greensmith, Bill. "Al Duncan, A Swinging Drummer." *Blues & Rhythm,* April 2018.

Guralnick, Peter. *Lost Highway: Journeys and Arrivals of American Musicians.* New York:

Little, Brown, 1979.

Hall, René, Ernie Fields, and Ernie Fields Jr. Recorded conversation with author. Los Angeles, Calif. June 23, 1987.

Halsey, Jim. Interview by author. Tulsa. October 2019.

Hammond, John, with Irving Townsend. *John Hammond on Record: An Autobiography.* New York: Ridge Press/Summit Books, 1977.

Heath, Jimmy, and Joseph McLaren. *I Walked with Giants: The Autobiography of Jimmy Heath.* Philadelphia: Temple University Press, 2010.

Heichelbech, Rose. "Forgotten Dance Hall Taxi Dancers—A Dime a Dance!" *Dusty Old Thing* (blog). https://dustyoldthing.com/taxi-dancers/.

Hennessey, Thomas J. *From Jazz to Swing: African-American Jazz Musicians and Their Music, 1890–1935.* Detroit: Wayne State University Press, 1994.

Hentoff, Nat. Liner notes for *Giant Steps* by John Coltrane. Atlantic Records SD1311, 1959.

Hopkins, Juanita. Telephone interview by author. September 30, 2013.

Hurwitz, Cynthia Duffield. Telephone interview by author, January 3, 2018.

Jenkins, Todd S. "Early Bebop Tenorman" (Warren Luckey obituary). Posted on "Warren 'Tenor Sax' Luckey: My Grandpa," December 4, 2008, https://silverinjuly.wordpress .com/2008/12/04/warren-tenor-sax-luckey-my-grandpa/.

Joyce, Melba. Telephone interview by author. 2019.

Lateef, Yusef. Interview by Robert D. Rusch. *Cadence Magazine* 15, no. 1 (January 1989).

Lateef, Yusef, and Herb Boyd. *The Gentle Giant: The Autobiography of Yusef Lateef.* Irvington, N.J.: Morton Books, 2006.

Lee, David. Telephone conversation with author. October 10, 2020.

Love, Preston. *A Thousand Honey Creeks Later: My Life in Music from Basie to Motown— and Beyond.* Middletown, Conn.: Wesleyan University Press, 1997.

Malone, Jane. Telephone interview by author. August 2019.

Maxwell, Tom. "The Story of 'Ella and Louis,' 60 Years Later." *Longreads* (November 2016). https://longreads.com/2016/11/07/the-story-of-ella-and-louis-60-years-later/.

Maxwell, William. Telephone interview by author. February 13, 2022.

McCarthy, Albert. *Big Band Jazz.* New York: G. P. Putnam's Sons, 1974.

Milton, Roy, and Ernie Fields. Recorded conversation. Tulsa. September 1980.

Moore, Melvin. Interview by author. New York. [1987?].

"Paul Gayten: 'Dr. Daddy-O (Backtrackin').'" Spontaneous Lunacy: The History of Rock 'n' Roll—Song by Song. June 12, 2017. https://www.spontaneouslunacy.net/paul -gayten-backtrackin-dr-daddy-o-regal-3230/.

Pomerance, Alan. *Repeal of the Blues.* Secaucus, N.J.: Citadel Press, 1988.

Powell, Benny. Interview by Bob Bernotas. *Online Trombone Journal.* September 1, 1999. https://www.trombone.org/articles/view.php?id=2.

"René Hall." BlackCat Rockabilly Europe. https://www.rockabilly.nl/. Discontinued site archived at TIMS This Is My Story (Biographies). https://tims.blackcat.nl/.

Rogers, A. G., and Billy Taylor. "My Heart Sings: A Tribute to Oklahoma's Musicians." *Applause* supplement. *Oklahoma Eagle,* [1943–45?].

Russell, Ross. *Jazz Style in Kansas City and the Southwest.* Oakland: University of

California Press, 1971.

Schuller, Gunther. *The Swing Era: The Development of Jazz, 1930–1945*. New York: Oxford University Press, 1989.

Serrin, William. "James Petrillo Dead; Led Musicians" (James Petrillo obituary). *New York Times*, October 25, 1984. https://www.nytimes.com/1984/10/25/obituaries /james-petrillo-dead-led-musicians.html.

Shapiro, Nat, and Nat Hentoff. *Hear Me Talkin' to Ya: The Story of Jazz as Told by the Men Who Made It*. New York: Dover Publications, 1966.

Sheffield, Leslie. "The Career Summary of Leslie Sheffield." 1977. Sheffield's Piano Lab Facebook page, last modified March 15, 2021. https://www.facebook.com/notes /275266283640290/.

Sherr, David. *Bel Air Jazz* (blog). http://belairjazz.org/stories-from-the-road.html.

———. Interview by author. Los Angeles, Calif. November 23, 2015.

Shirk, Ken. Phone conversations and emails with author and others. September 18 and 19, 2018.

Singer, Hal. Interview by author. Nanterre, France. June 7, 1990.

———. Official website. http://www.halsingergroup.com/.

Swain, Frank. Telephone interview by author. April 12, 2019.

Taylor, John. "Oklahoma Jazz Hall of Fame presents Washington Rucker." *Tulsa Jazz*, July 6, 2013. https://tulsajazz.wordpress.com/2013/07/06/oklahoma-jazz-hall-of-fame -presents-washington-rucker/.

Third Annual Living Legends Luncheon program. Stouffer's Concourse Hotel. Los Angeles. February 7, 1992. Presented by Warner Bros. Records, Reprise Records, and *Urban Network*.

Tulsa, the Visitor's Guide. Vol. 2, no. 18 (June 30–July 6, n.d.). Official publication of the Tulsa Hotel Men's Association.

"Tulsa Guitarist Dies at 58" (Mike Bruce obituary). *Tulsa World*, August 25, 2005.

"Tulsa Musician Quietly Took Music World by Storm" (Helen McCoy obituary). *Tulsa World*, September 9, 2013.

Vacher, Peter. *Swingin' on Central Avenue: African American Jazz in Los Angeles*. Lanham, Md.: Rowman & Littlefield, 2015.

Wesley, Fred. *Hit Me, Fred: Recollections of a Sideman*. Durham, N.C.: Duke University Press, 2002.

Wikipedia, s.v. "Helen Humes." Wikipedia, https://en.wikipedia.org/wiki/Helen_Humes.

Wikipedia, s.v. "Vocalion Records," Wikipedia, https://en.wikipedia.org/wiki/Vocalion _Records.

Williams, Ann (granddaughter of A. G. Rogers). Telephone interview and email exchanges. January and September 2022.

Wilson, Tom. Liner notes for *Cookin'*, by Booker Ervin. Savoy MT 12154, 1960.

Wishart, David J., ed. *Encyclopedia of the Great Plains*. Lincoln: University of Nebraska Press, 2004.

Young, Marl. "Amalgamation of Local 47 and 767." *Overture* (March 1999). Los Angeles American Federation of Musicians, Local 47.

INDEX

References to illustrations appear in italic type.

Booker, Arnold, 28
Bostic, Earl, 48–49, 86, 113–14, 127, 145;
    Bartee and, 143; West and, 185
Bowser, Buddy, 58
Boyce, Eric, 190
Brabec, Erv, 80
Bradford, Melba. *See* Joyce, Melba
Bradley, Lee "Sticks," 125, 145, 149, 170
Breaux, Zelia Page, 194–95
Brooks, Billy, 145
Brown, Ada, 56
Brownsville, Texas, 155
Bruce, Harold "Al," 145
Bruce, Mike "Monk," 120, 146
Bryant, Otis, 190
Bryant, Roscoe, Sr., 23
Bundy, Evelyn: Pernell and, 173
Burch, Vernon, 121
buses and bus touring, 49–51, *50*, 52, 53,
    55, 95, *166*; Lee County, Fla., 106–8
Butler, Cleora, 40
Burley, O. Z., 28, *31*, 73–74, 146
Buttrick, L. E., 110
Byas, Don, 146–47; Banks and, 143

Café Society (New York City), 14, 82
Callender, Red, 134
Calloway, Cab, 40–41, 42, 56, 73, 74, 118;
    "Gab Galloway," 74–75
Cameron, John, 190
Cannon, Harold "Sy," *97*, 190
Capitol Records, 138, 139
Carrington, Jeff, 12, 16, *18*, *31*, 88, 89, 90,
    147
Carter, Benny, 82; Byas and, 146; Harold
    Bruce and, 145
Carwell, Oliver, 147
Chadbourne, Eugene, 120
Chambers, Henderson "Dewy," 190–91
Chappel (Chappelle), Gus, 147
Charles, Ray, 170; Hall and, 157; Robin
    and, 175; Tex Cooper and, 148; Walter
    Miller and, 170

"Chattanooga Choo-Choo," 135, 137,
    139
Chicago, 21, 58, 79–81, 95–96; Claxton,
    148; Coliseum, 79–80; Duncan, 151;
    Harold Fox, 80; Kolax, 164; Lateef,
    66; musicians' union locals, 31, 164;
    Oriental Theatre, 79–80, 81, 118;
    Regal Theatre, 58, 79, 82, 96, 178;
    Sutherland Hotel, 95–96; tailors, 80
Christian, Charlie, 5, 177–78
"Christopher Columbus," 135–36
Clark, Dick, 136–37
Clark, Roy, 122; Halsey and, 133, 157
Clarke, John, *31*
Claxton, Rozelle, 11, 14, 20–21, 71, 148
Coates, Jess, 158
Cole, Nat King, 92, 134
Cole, Teddy, 84, 148
Colman, Stuart, 137–38
Coltrane, John, 48–49, 171
Conley, Edwin Elkins, 84
Cooke, Sam, 122, 132
Cooksey, Robert, 110, 158
Cooper, George "Buster," 148
Cooper, Leroy "Tex," 148, *149*
Copeland, Isaac Columbus, 101–2
Copeland, Jo Ella Fields. *See* Fields,
    Jo Ella
Copeland, Lydia, 27, 103, 202n6
Copeland, Madestella. *See* Holcomb,
    Madestella Copeland
Copeland, Mae Doris, 102
Copeland, Mattie, 103
Copeland, Myrtle Bernice. *See* Fields,
    Bernice (wife)
Copeland, Robert, 130
Copeland family, 35, 37
Crawford, Jack, 49

Dale, Jimmy
Dallas, 29–30, 79; Berry, 144; "Doc" John-
    son, 158; Holder, 85, 88; KFAA, 86
Dameron, Tadd, 71